The Anger Management Workbook
A Program that Changes Lives

Christian Conte, Ph.D.

Steven P. Miller, Ed.D.

DonPaul Press

DonPaul Press Pittsburgh

ISBN 9781982097936

COPYRIGHT
COVER DESIGN TEXT
DESIGN
ILLUSTRATIONS
PRINTED IN USA

Special Thanks

To my dad, Donald Conte:

Thank you for your help in making this book

(and just about everything else I write) better.

Dedication

My work here is dedicated in the remembrance of

Paul W. Miller, Sr. I am fortunate and proud to have had him as a father. His words guided my life and gave me direction. He taught me the importance of working hard, honoring my word and standing up for my beliefs. He exemplified dedication, sacrifice and the unconditional love of family. I aspire to be man like him but can only dream of being the father he was. There are many heroes in this world, but I thank God every day of my life for allowing me to call mine Dad.

About the Authors

Dr. Christian Conte is one of only four, Level V Anger Management specialists in the world. He is also a Licensed Professional Counselor with more than 20,000 hours of clinical experience. **Dr. Conte** is a television personality, podcaster, author and professional speaker. He co-founded A Balanced Life, Inc., a center in South Lake Tahoe, CA dedicated to helping people live less violent lives. **Dr. Conte** is the creator of Yield Theory, a tremendously powerful approach to change rooted in radical compassion and conscious education. He is the author of several books and videos, including *Getting Control of Yourself: Anger Management Tools and Techniques*.

Dr. Steven P. Miller is a Licensed Professional Counselor and is Board Certified as a Master Addictions Counselor and School Counselor. He has over two decades of clinical experience in the public and private sectors. Dr.Miller has taught, influenced, and impacted thousands of people throughout his career in academia, group homes, hospitals, community agencies, business environments and private practice. He continues to supervise counselors and therapists, and perform direct service through clinical counseling. Dr. Miller is the Founder and President of Behavioral Dynamics, Inc., a private behavioral health agency in Southwestern Pennsylvania providing mental health services to people of all ages and paths.

A Note to the Counselor, Psychotherapist, or Group Leader

The Anger Management Workbook is the culmination of counselors' and psychotherapists' work with thousands of people with anger issues, from those who committed horrific violent crimes to the most "in-control" people who were just tired of allowing anger to alter their lives. In short, this program is for everyone who struggles with anger at any degree of intensity.

The information and exercises in this workbook offer a chance for people to change their lives with your professional guidance. Through these exercises, clients who are struggling to control or eliminate their anger will find new ways to take control of their lives. As their counselor or psychotherapist, you will find in this workbook not just a series of exercises, but a sequence that fosters a dramatic change in outlook and behavior.

This workbook has several underlying principles, but one important dictum is that practicing counselors and psychotherapists need to teach many of their clients how to *align their expectations* with reality. This program teaches about the genuine difference between the *cartoon world* versus the *real world* and how to recognize the difference and implement change. The cartoon world is the world that we create. The real world is the-world-as-it-is, or the world of objective verification (Conte, 2009). The cartoon world is the world the way we want it to be. It is filled with "shoulds" and "have-tos." The cartoon world is packed full of rules and regulations that were either passed down through generations or contemporary peers, or that clients create for themselves. These "rules and regulations" dictate a lifestyle that is often inimical to the well-being of clients. They also force the client into enantiodromia and splitting, both of which this workbook addresses from multiple perspectives and through multiple exercises.

Other underlying principles of this workbook include:

- Change can happen, but it takes time; this program operates on the principle that *change is a process*

- With education, people are less likely to repeat ineffective behaviors

- Punishing people without educating them will not produce positive changes

- People do the best they can with what they know in any given situation; thus, counselors and psychotherapists can enhance positive and effective behavior by providing information that changes perspectives and mechanisms that alter behavior

- Counseling and psychotherapy work when they are specific, i.e., of immediate relevance to the needs of a client

Using This Workbook With Groups

Many authority figures want to be able to say that they have helped make people accountable for their actions. Accountability, however, can be a catchword with no force. Popular and historic anger management programs typically force people to take accountability for their actions by requiring them to acknowledge their responsibility. Unfortunately, simple acknowledgement does not equate true accountability. In some instances people have been shamed into admitting that they are sorry for what they have done. Shaming someone into acknowledging accountability is a negative approach that is not an effective long-term solution. With increasing time from the moment of acknowledging accountability, shame becomes less and less of a motivator; just look at what occurs among former prisoners.

Recidivism for parolees and released felons throughout the country is estimated to be around 70%. Even the most marginally reasonable person knows that when 7 out of 10 reoffend and return to prison, the approach to rehabilitation cannot be called successful. Although no program can be perfect, the data indicates that the time is right to rethink current approaches to rehabilitation. Particularly for those whose anger drives them to violent and abusive behavior, anger management is crucial. As violent offenses mount, however, it is time to make the accurate observation that pejorative approaches to anger management simply do not work. The more we shame people, the more people act out of shame. The more people act out of shame, the more they feel free to act out of anger however they see fit in the moment.

We believe therapists will lead their clients to assuming more accountability for their actions, including making and sustaining long term changes, when they can create an atmosphere of compassion and acceptance for their clients, and combine that compassion and acceptance with relevant and interesting education. For therapists, it is extraordinarily important to find a way to engage people, to meet them where they are, and to provide education that is not only interesting to them, but also immediately relevant to their lives. In short, this program gives people something: it gives people the foundation for a psychologically healthy ground from which they can change.

When empathy, acceptance, and compassion comprise the foundation of anger management groups, group members begin to hold themselves and each other accountable for their actions. Empathy without knowledge tends to reinforce ineffective behaviors; empathy combined with knowledge and consistent consequences leads to transformative and lasting change. This program is designed to accept human beings where they are in any given moment and to inculcate in them new attitudes that lead to different behaviors. When the exercises in this workbook are followed with the guidance of a trained, compassionate professional, the life transformations that can be made have the potential to literally change the course of people's lives.

Ready-Made Anger Management Program for Groups

The accompanying video vignettes can be a guide for group leaders to learn how to present the topics in the workbook, or they can serve as points of departure at the beginning of group sessions, allowing the group members to focus their discussions on specific issues. Group leaders can play a video introduction to any particular exercise, then have the group members fill out their responses to the exercise in their own workbooks. We encourage group leaders to be mindful of the following considerations regarding anger management groups.

- Barring explicit language from group can remove the practicality of the lessons; in other words, if people use expletives in their everyday language, consider letting them use that kind of language in groups so that they can actually use the things you are teaching (rather than putting on an "act" in

Yield Theory:
The Foundation for This Workbook

Imagine that you want to connect with and really understand a client you are about to meet. Imagine that this client is driving in a car down a highway, and you, in your own car, are heading onto the same highway. If you really wanted to connect with this client, you could conceivably come speeding straight at him head on, and while contact would be made, there is a very strong likelihood that the contact would not be beneficial (i.e., a crash).

Instead of crashing into the client's car head on, you decide to merge onto the same road with the client and travel in the same direction. As you merge onto the road at the yield sign, you begin to see the same road the client is seeing, though you see things from your own car out of your own windshield. After you drive next to your client for long enough, your client begins to trust that you are headed in the same direction, so he invites you to ride with him. Now, from the perspective of your client's car, you can see things even more similarly to the way your client sees them. But even from the passenger seat, you cannot see quite the same things as your client.

Over the course of this journey in the car, at some point, the client begins to trust you, and as he gets tired, he asks you to drive. Then from the driver's seat, you begin to see what your client was seeing. You begin to get a clearer sense of what your client sees; and it is from this vantage point that you can help steer your client down a different road.

The analogy of yielding with clients on a highway and eventually merging with them to gain a complete understanding of who they are and what experiences have led to their acting the way that they do is a description of the approach of Yield Theory. Yield Theory goes well beyond this basic analogy, and it encapsulates a way of understanding others and motivating them to change, regardless of anything they have ever done in their lives. Yield Theory can be extraordinarily beneficial to apply to anyone you want to make contact with and positively impact; but Yield Theory is perhaps most powerful when applied to those who get marginalized by society (i.e., angry people who act abusively or violently).

No one sets out to be defined by his or her worst moment in life; yet, almost every violent offender is judged, convicted, and defined by his or her worst moment.

Just imagine if everyone in your life defined you by your worst moment, that this moment accompanied you like a badge of shame throughout your life, limiting all future possibilities, including your hopes and dreams. It would seem terribly unjust; and yet this is what we do to people who act out of anger. They carry the burden of our shadow projections and are left believing that they are terrible people because they have done terrible things. And because they lose hope about the possibility of breaking free from these deeply internalized expectations, they live up to their self-fulfilling prophecies by continuing to respond angrily to stressful circumstances.

Yield Theory constitutes the foundation for our approach to anger management. Yield Theory was designed to help therapists approach difficult clients with love, compassion, and understanding (Conte, 2009, 2013). Yield Theory is predicated on one profound underlying assumption:

"If I lived every day as another human being -- not just walked a mile in his or her proverbial shoes -- and I had that person's level of intelligence, affective capabilities, and all of his or her life experiences, I believe I would make every single decision that that person made, including every act of violence or harm to others."

This can be a difficult concept to assimilate because many people assume they would never make the mistakes that others have made. How can we say that we wouldn't have done something, however, that another person has done if we were that person? We can obviously say that with the way our brain experiences intelligence, with the affective or emotional capabilities that we have, and with the life experiences that we have, that we would have done this or that (good, bad or indifferent). How can we claim, "I would have done things differently"? We can only know (or actually even guess) what we would have done, given our own personal history in that same instance.

When we operate from the foundational assumption of Yield Theory, we can significantly reduce, or even eliminate our judgment on others. Without judgment, we can simply focus on assessing people's actions. The theory was developed as a way for professional counselors and psychologists to connect with clients who had such diverse experiences, but Yield Theory is more than a model; it can be a way of life. Now, for us, the keystone to this anger management program is Yield Theory, both for facilitators and for clients.

The goal for people practicing Yield Theory is to accept clients for the essence of who they are. One never has to condone or accept *actions* to accept the *essence* of who other people are. We believe that people are inherently good, and the hurtful things they do to others along the way are things that they learned in response to their experience of life (given their cognitive functioning and affective range). For many, it is much easier to tell others what "we would have done" had we been in that situation. Imagining "what we would have done," however, is as equally hypothetical as accepting the hypothetical assumption that *we would have done the exact same thing as the other person did given the same cognitive functioning, affective range, and life experiences.* So the question boils down to this: What assumption helps us more as human beings? We believe the assumption of Yield Theory helps us connect more with others.

Learning how to accept others with compassion can change how we approach them. Imagine for instance, the rage people tend to feel when others "transgress" against them in traffic. If a driver cuts off another driver, the person driving the car that was cut off tends to get extraordinarily frustrated or even angry, often yelling obscenities at the offending person. But what would happen if that person applied Yield Theory?

To apply Yield Theory, sometimes it's helpful to recall times when we have offended others. Next we can move to visualizing the world from the offender's position. In the example of the person being cut off in traffic, the person could do a couple things. First, the person could recall times when he or she made driving mistakes. Second, the person could consider his or her own motives behind such mistakes. Oftentimes, for instance, when we cut someone off in traffic, we think, "What's the big deal? It was an accident. I didn't mean it!" When someone else cuts us off, however, we tend to assume a certain sense of cruel intent. By applying Yield Theory, we can envision other people's worldviews. It is possible, after all, that the offending driver was distracted by a disturbing personal problem. Attempting to visualize the situation from the driver's worldview can radically change the level of anger we experience.

Applying Yield Theory to road rage is relatively easy, but not all anger stems from traffic problems. Stressful or hurtful relationships, including abusive ones, present a more challenging test for the method. Whereas we rarely (if ever) see ourselves as "evil" or "malicious" for hurting others, we seem quick to deem others "evil" and "malicious" for hurting us. And when we respond to someone we deem evil or malicious, we are much more likely to respond harshly, as opposed to taking a step back and realizing that had we lived every experience of theirs, with their cognitive functioning and affective range, that we would likely treat ourselves the exact same way that he or she is treating us in the present moment. Armed with Yield Theory, we can respond with compassion that does not exacerbate the other person's anger.

People in general have a tough time dealing with the issue of anger. Part of the reason people struggle with working with others who are angry is that anger can lead to violence, and violence threatens our physical existence. It makes sense that fear-based reactions occur around anger. When therapists operate anger management programs out of the assumption of Yield Theory, they can move beyond the reactionary position that seems almost natural to take when people hear about the awful things others do. Yield Theory helps guide therapists and counselors to take compassionate approaches to others; and when people are approached compassionately, they are much less likely to be defensive. Without defenses up, people can more easily open themselves to insight and change.

We encourage anger management facilitators to implement Yield Theory, to teach it to their group members. We encourage individuals who use this workbook on their own to consider implementing Yield Theory in their personal lives. Yield Theory helps us increase our understanding of others. With greater understanding comes greater compassion, and with greater compassion comes the foundation for awareness and change.

This anger management program is predicated on respecting all people--regardless of their actions--and strives to meet every person where he or she actually is. This "conscious education rooted in compassion" approach can transform people's lives. Even the most resistant clients who ardently deny any accountability for significantly harming others are accepted as readily as those who are actively seeking change. Everyone has a story – and people's cognitive functioning, ability to process emotions, and life experiences shape them and continually influence them.

Though many therapists and counselors may claim to "accept all people," in practice, most people struggle in their work with those who have anger issues. It could be that the natural fight-or-flight response triggers survival fears for therapists working with people who have acted out of anger toward others, and causes them to write off angry people as incapable of change, dangerous, and hence deserving of condemnation. It is hard for most people to grasp that fully accepting a person who hurts others out of anger has absolutely nothing to do with condoning that person's actions. Truly understanding this, however, makes all the difference in our work with those who struggle with anger.

Components of Yield Theory

There are seven key components to Yield Theory:

- Acceptance
- Elimination of shame
- Mindfulness
- Creativity
- Conscious education
- Non-attachment
- Authenticity

Though anger management groups are traditionally open groups, participants can and will share as equally as they do in closed groups if group leaders create a safe enough environment, and Yield Theory helps with that. Remember that vulnerability takes courage, especially amongst people who define themselves in many ways in relation to how "tough" they are. Understanding the components helps therapists to create the kind of safe environment that fosters change.

Acceptance

The potential for everything great and everything terrible resides inside all human beings. If a human being has performed an act, then it is accurate to say that it is "human nature." If we can accept the nature of human beings (that we will at times be loving and kind, at other times hurtful and cruel, and everything in between and beyond), then we can evaluate others, as well as ourselves, in terms of trying to simply understand human behavior. Furthermore, if we accept the premise that we cannot do one single thing to change the past, and we merely have the ability to impact the present to shape the future, then we can see that pejorative, judgmental approaches do little to impact the present or future in positive ways. The stage for conscious learning and change can be set when we learn to meet people where they are and fully accept their essence.

Elimination of Shame

Years of studying people who commit violent crimes has led us to the conclusion that *people who live in shame act out of shame.* Eliminating shame, then, is in many ways central to our work. At first glance, it may seem difficult to swallow the idea of not shaming someone who committed a violent act; however, as David Hawkins (2002) suggested in his "map of consciousness," shame is the lowest form of consciousness that human beings experience. What we have learned is that it is difficult for human beings to make highly conscious choices from low levels of consciousness, so helping people expand their consciousness becomes paramount to changing their actions.

Mindfulness

Engaging in the right mindfulness entails expanding the awareness that we have for not only ourselves, but also for the world around us. Every moment something is happening, and the more mindful we can be, the more open we are to experiencing that awareness. With an awareness that something is always happening, the more likely we are to consider alternative ways of interacting with others. Mindfulness begins with self-awareness, but it also extends to an awareness of the societal and physical environment and what is going on inside other people as well. We believe it is important for group leaders to both practice and teach mindfulness. Though it is fairly easy for therapists to learn how to teach a basic mindfulness exercise in a group setting, it is the role modeling of mindfulness that seems to make the biggest impact on clients.

Creativity

Having the ability to genuinely meet a diverse group of clients where they are often separates average therapists from very effective counselors. If we are charged with meeting people where they are, then we must consider that people have varied learning styles, and forcing clients to get information only in the way that we think works is, in our view, irresponsible. To implement creativity in therapy is to constantly evaluate one's own communication style, and to be open to adjusting it accordingly to what people need. We believe the onus of communicating effectively rests with the therapist, so when clients are not getting what we are communicating, we see it as our responsibility to find creative ways to meet them where they are. Creativity can come in the form of analogies, metaphors, techniques, or even in the openness to develop new ways to say things in ways clients can fully hear them.

Conscious Education

It is the responsibility of counselors, therapists, and group leaders to offer something more than just listening to their clients. Teaching emotional management skills is essential to helping people who are struggling with anger. We cannot expect people to respond differently to the world until we teach them different options. For counselors to implement conscious education, they must be willing to teach concepts patiently and compassionately until clients understand the ideas; this is very different from simply relating concepts and just assuming that clients understand them. In conscious education, therapists do not assume their clients should already have specific information; instead, they make the effort to teach in compassionate ways that meet diverse learners where they are.

Non-attachment

Non-attachment to ideas is particularly difficult in light of societal inculcations. As every counselor knows, introjections permeate every culture, from the smallest of social units to the largest, and every introjection enters the psyche through either overtly or subtly. Thus, both client and psychotherapist hold a storehouse of ideas learned either directly or indirectly during developmental years. It could be useful for the counselor to identify introjections as they crop up during sessions and help the client develop a list of introjections to target for non-attachment.

"There was once a man who thought that the higher he went off a cliff, the easier it would be to fly. This was the reason he had told himself that eagles could fly. People attempted to convince him otherwise, but this man remained so attached to what he believed, that he demonstrably pronounced that he would be willing to prove it. Another fellow made a wager with him. It is said that he claimed to be right the entire fall to his death. The people who witnessed it are said to have learned well how attachment to ideas can lead to poor results."

As a caution to those becoming too attached to the idea of non-attachment, the Zen teach about the "soap of the teachings" as a way for understanding how to eventually disavow even the idea of non-attachment itself. Consider that to clean a shirt, it is necessary to use soap. However, if the soapsuds are not rinsed out, the garment will not truly be clean. In this same way, non-attachment to the idea of non-attachment becomes central to practicing the concept.

Authenticity

People can spot disingenuousness easily. Mirror neurons are not only the root of vicarious learning, but they are also a key part of our neural system that helps us identify when people are being authentic with us or not. It is well known in our field that when clients can discredit their therapists, they can use the inauthenticity of their helpers as reasons why they cannot or should not change. It becomes paramount, then, for therapists to practice what they preach.

The most pragmatic way therapists can exude authenticity is to regularly practice the ideas that they are teaching. We do not have all the answers, nor should we purport to have them. We make mistakes as equally as our clients: not better or worse mistakes, just different mistakes, and we are all in this process of experiencing what it is like to be fully human.

To understand and implement the basic components of Yield Theory is to set the foundation for an anger management program that, when combined with the exercises in this workbook, can change people's lives.

The Accompanying Videos

A set of accompanying vignettes on video enhances the exercises in this workbook. One of the major advantages of such technology is that you will have the option to play the video clips at the onset of each group or individual session, have participants then fill out corresponding exercises, and then simply process what occurs. You may also choose to watch the video clips yourself, and then integrate the information into your own personal approach.

Sometimes it is easier for therapists who are learning how to be non-attached to the information they present to do so by showing a video of someone else. That way, the individuals and/or groups can process their reaction to the information honestly, and the therapist does not have to take any of it personally. The design of such an approach is intended to support therapists seeing that when they present information, people (especially in anger management) may be very direct in their distaste for the information, but that distaste has little to nothing to do with the messenger; instead, distaste for information tends to arise when people are being asked to be accountable for behaviors that, until that point, were being justified.

Introduction
What This Book Is and How to Use It

Whether or not you realize it, you have already made some progress just by picking up this workbook. That simple act means you recognize a need and that you are willing to try something new to meet that need. We believe such willingness is essential to the search for a lifestyle change. For taking that first step, we congratulate you.

Of course, we are realistic enough to realize that just picking up this workbook is no guarantee: You have to take the next step in the process. A challenge awaits you, and, as you probably know, many challenges can be hard. Overcoming anger is a process that requires an effort on your part, and the effort can't be a simple short-term try. We like to compare the effort to a journey into a forest. If you walk ten miles into a forest, you will have to walk ten miles back to get out of that forest. Likewise, if we have lived a certain way for a long time, it is going to take some time to learn to live differently. The journey is certainly possible. The goal is attainable. But you have to do the "walking."

Why Should We Manage Anger?

The decisions that people make when they are angry can destroy their lives. We have seen people throw away everything they have because of anger. We have seen people break objects, prized possessions (others' and their own), and we have seen people break their own bones and severely injure themselves or others out of anger. We have seen people break up their families and friendships, lose their jobs, and ruin their careers over anger. We have seen people rob, steal, and kill over anger. We have seen people take their own lives because of anger. Anger can change anything and everything for the worse in an instant. If we do not know how to handle it, if we do not prepare, practice, and work on our anger when we are not angry, we will have little ability to stop anger from deciding our fate when it arises.

The Anger Management Workbook provides a chance for you to change your life. The contents within this workbook have already helped thousands of people take control of their lives; the information and exercises inside are empowering, eye opening, and life transforming. This program is the culmination of working with thousands of people, from those who committed horrific violent crimes to the most "in-control" people who were just tired of allowing anger to eat away at them. In short, this program is for everyone who struggles with anger.

Expectations vs. Reality

In this workbook you will learn to address one of the root causes of anger: The failure to align your expectations with reality. All of us suffer from this failure at one time or another. There is a difference between the way we expect the world to be and the way the world actually is, and this difference can influence us to become angry. Bigger differences between what we expect (the ideal) and what we see or get (the real), can arouse greater anger. The ideal world wears a coat of rules that either our ancestors, our peers, or we have created about *how things should be* or how our lives should run. Many of the rules we operate by in life are artificial rules whose purpose has long since worn out. Still, we allow those rules to dictate how we respond to embarrassing, shameful, and hurtful situations.

When the rules about how the world around us should work don't seem to fit the circumstances of our lives, we become angry. But we really have a choice in life: We can wait and wait for the world to change into what we want it to be, the so-called *ideal world*, or we can take a long, hard look at our own lives and perspectives, and learn to adapt to *the-world-as-it-is*.

This program teaches about the genuine difference between the *cartoon world* versus the *real world* (Conte, 2009). The cartoon world is the ideal world that we create. The real world is *the-world-as-it-is*. The cartoon world is the world the way we want it to be. It is filled with *"shoulds"* and *"have-tos."* The cartoon world is packed full of rules and regulations that were either passed down to us for generations, or that we made up ourselves.

Examples of Cartoon World Rules:

- People should be nice to me
- People should always tell me the truth
- Children should always listen to their parents

Examples From Real World Realities:

- There is no rule or regulation that everyone has to be nice to me
- I don't always make people feel safe enough to tell me the truth
- Children are not obligated to listen to parents who abuse them or make unreasonable demands

When we live in the cartoon world, we "want what we want," and that desire, when unfulfilled, causes us suffering. When we live in the real world, we are able to face the-world-as-it-is. Oftentimes, due to the tendency to move from one extreme to the other, we believe that if we "cannot have exactly what we want," then we "might as well expect everything to be terrible." But the extreme thoughts lead to extreme actions and emotions, including anger. Life does not need to bounce between extremes. There is a balance in learning to see life the way it is.

Be Accurate

The cartoon world and real world are two completely different realms, and we cannot live in both simultaneously. When we align our expectations with the cartoon world, we are frequently let down, because the world simply cannot live up to what we want it to be. But the world does not let us down; we let ourselves down by expecting unreasonable outcomes. The world just is what it is. Therefore, throughout this program, you will learn how to align your expectations with reality. The more you learn to expect reality, the less you will be let down when reality occurs.

An example of aligning your expectations with the cartoon world is:

"When I leave for work today, there will be no traffic to slow me down. When I get to work, management will be thrilled with the work I've done."

Unfortunately, reality can be different than that. Reality is that traffic might occur. It might not, but it might. The reality is that management might not be thrilled with the work you've done. They might be, but they might not.

When we *align our expectations with reality*, we are prepared for multiple outcomes. When we align our expectations with the cartoon world, we prepare ourselves for only one or two outcomes. What we encourage you to learn to do is be as accurate as possible in how you reflect what is going on in the world around you. The more accurate you are in your assessment of past and present situations, the more likely you will be prepared for future situations.

Expectations and Reality As Two Extremes in Our Lives

When people first hear about the cartoon world versus the real world, it is common for them to say, "Well, I should just expect that everything is going to be terrible so that I'm never let down." But expecting that everything in life is going to be terrible is as equally unrealistic as expecting it to be favorable for you. We will invite you throughout this book to move away from extremes, because extreme thoughts lead to extreme emotions, and extreme emotions lead to extreme actions.

The Anger Management Workbook will help you become familiar with the concept of enantiodromia (pronounced "in-anti-o-drōme-ee-a"). Enantiodromia is a word that means "a tendency to go from one extreme to the other" (Jung, 1944). We often engage in enantiodromia when we change our mind about something. Along the lines of enantiodromia, you will learn about a concept called "splitting." Splitting means seeing things in extremes. For example, we may see people as "all good" or "all bad." Splitting and enantiodromia can go hand in hand, and both lead to a disruption of peace in our lives. You will learn how to see beyond splitting and avoid enantiodromia to find peace in the balance that lies in the middle path.

The Ball and the Boat

Figure II.1

Conte (2009) described things "popping back up" at inopportune times and places through a metaphor of standing on a boat. Imagine standing on a boat. Imagine further that you are leaning over one side of the boat and trying to push a beach ball under the boat. Now, you could watch ever so vigilantly that the ball wouldn't come back up in the spot where you are standing, but over time, pushing the ball down again and again can cause it to drift under the boat and pop up on the other side where you least expect it.

In a similar way, that is what we tend to do with whatever causes our emotions to surface, especially the things that can get us angry. We push things down time and again – but eventually, the things we push down will pop back up – and they usually pop back up when and where we least expect them. We often say that the things we pushed down "popped back up at the wrong time," but in retrospect, when things pop back up, they do so because, for whatever reason, we are not able to actively repress them anymore; in so doing, we actually contribute to creating the wrong time and place with our part in the situation.

If we do not learn to deal with our anger effectively, or if we continue to push things down by not dealing with them, our anger can explode to the surface unexpectedly and without our conscious control. As long as we don't actively deal with our anger, we are setting ourselves up to be controlled by it for the rest of our lives. Learning why we get angry is huge; learning how to not let anger control us anymore is like taking the ball out of the water and putting it on dry land, where it is less likely to exert control over us.

The Quick Answer to Getting Rid of Anger Permanently: There's No Quick Answer

One of the first steps anyone can take in anger management is learning how to deal effectively with the issues that lead to anger. People frequently ask us, *"What am I supposed to do with so-and-so who is angry all the time?"* Time and again, people are searching for the quick answer of what to tell people who are struggling with anger. They also ask, "What am I supposed to do with my anger?" There is a quick answer, and we said it already. If you walk 10 miles into the woods, you will have to walk 10 miles if you want to come back out. What that means is this: Perhaps it's time we stopped looking for the fast-food version of anger management. Perhaps it's time to abandon the idea of "walk away and count to ten" as a panacea, particularly considering that approach has been documented to fail so many people. Quick answers and fast solutions do not change people. To make real changes, people must dedicate themselves to getting rid of the anger that has come to overtake their lives.

In a world where people look for faster, more efficient technology, we have all grown accustomed to getting what we want in the moment that we want it. But just as we cannot make our children move from infancy to full physical maturity any faster than they will naturally, we cannot rush profound changes in the human psyche. It takes time to break life patterns. It takes time to change seeing the world and behaving the way we always have. It takes dedication, but it can happen. Change is absolutely possible, and you can also change. In fact, the changes we have observed in even the most extreme cases of people with extraordinarily intense anger have been profound. The point is that although we have seen people make some changes after completing even the first exercise in this workbook, we recommend and encourage people to complete the entire workbook to ensure lasting change in their lives.

People may say, "Well I don't want to take time; I just want it now." And whereas we respect that perspective (especially because so many people have lived their entire lives in a fast-paced society), we also have seen from experience that just as people who have never lifted weights before cannot walk into a gym and expect to turn their bodies into professional bodybuilder physiques in a magical few days, so too, people cannot expect that reading one or two exercises and putting minimal effort into changing their lives will make that change actually happen. It takes hard work to change. When we have seen people work hard, we have watched them make not only enormous changes in their lives, but also acquire a tremendous sense of personal gratification from the work they have done.

You're Not Alone in Wondering How To Handle Anger and Angry People

People have been conflicted for years on how to handle those who struggle with anger and act out of violence. One reason we believe that people do not know how to handle those who struggle with anger is that we have difficulty handling our own emotion of anger. From the anger of convicted violent criminals to the anger that all people experience, *the intensity of the emotion of anger tends to scare people.* When people are pushed to think about the negative things they could potentially do (given hypothetical situations), people are generally afraid to acknowledge what they are capable of doing. Similarly, driven by their own fear, people, institutions, and lawmakers rely on "tough love." We increase jail and prison sentences; we break up with people; we dole out punishments, and do the "best we can to stop people from getting hurt." Yet, at the end of the day, violence and hurtful behavior still exist, and anger is the primary cause.

The Importance of Anger Management

Anger management or—more accurately—managing any thoughts and emotions that lead to angry outbursts comprised of ineffective choices and hurtful behaviors is an essential aspect of an effective, positive lifestyle that enhances both the individual and the people with whom he or she interacts. *The Anger Management Workbook* is designed to educate you about yourself, your family, and about what you can really do to make positive changes in your life. In one sense, this workbook is designed to make you more conscious of your own motivations and the motivations of others.

All behaviors have consequences. Whereas society and environmental factors influence behavior, individual choice always exists. Human beings are fallible, however, and mistakes, ineffective choices, and hurtful behaviors will always exist to some degree. Individuals who do not learn from their pasts are doomed to repeat mistakes and continually make the same ineffective life choices. With a dedication to self-reflection and the adoption of the knowledge and skills offered in this workbook, you can make and sustain long term positive changes.

The exercises in this manual promote self-awareness and education.
Several fundamental assumptions underlie this workbook:

- Change can happen

- With education, people are less likely to repeat ineffective behaviors

- Punishing people without educating them will not produce positive changes

- People do the best they can with what they know in any given situation – so let's give everyone something more

Anger usually causes us to make decisions and act in ways that we ultimately regret. Working through this program can forever change the way you handle situations that in the past would have controlled you. This program helps us move from a place of *"little control"* over our infuriating situations, to one of *"self-control"* – regardless of the situation - over the very natural emotion of anger.

Taking Responsibility: The "Yes – But" Game

There is no doubt that sometimes taking responsibility for our actions, especially when they hurt others, can be an extraordinarily difficult thing to do. Because it can be so difficult for people to assume responsibility for hurting others, a common game people play is what is known as "The Yes-But Game." The "yes-but game" occurs anytime we acknowledge the hurt we caused, only to follow it up quickly with a justification or rationalization as to why we hurt that person, particularly when we hurt another through our anger. The "yes-but game" specifically has to do with hurting someone else. We say something to the effect of, "**Yes**, I did hurt you, but I wouldn't have done it if you didn't . . . " The "yes-but game" places blame in the victim, not in the angry perpetrator.

We invite you to avoid the "yes-but game" as much as possible. We recognize that it is difficult to do so, but to not do so is to prolong the same behavioral patterns that led to the moment where you are in your life right now.

Here's a "yes-but" that does not fall into the category of a game:

"Yes, taking responsibility is difficult, but as long as I continue to focus on others and how or why THEY made me act a certain way, then I am not likely to change."

Challenge yourself as much as possible to eliminate the "yes-but game" from your vocabulary. If you have hurt others, own it and learn from it. Make analyzing your own behaviors a priority, and what will follow will not be an excuse, but choices and new behaviors that lead to life-transformations that will bring the peace we are all seeking.

How to Use This Workbook

The exercises in this book require you to write down "answers." There's no grade; you cannot be wrong for anything you write down or even how you write it down. You are, in fact, a self-teacher who can work alone or with a counselor or psychotherapist to explore the answers. Writing has long been thought of as a therapeutic activity and a path to self-knowledge and insight. The writing you do here can help you achieve such knowledge and insight.

Writing down answers is empowering because it is in the writing down of answers that we "crystallize" our thoughts. Sometimes thoughts can grow to astronomical sizes (the proverbial mountain from a mole hill), but the moment you see your thoughts written down, you realize how manageable those thoughts really are. Writing down answers, then, is an important part of the process of change. Personal growth is exactly that – personal – so with that in mind, we encourage you to find a secure place to keep this workbook. Our hope is that people feel comfortable being honest with themselves with the answers they provide to the exercises. Keeping this workbook in a secure place helps you avoid trying to answer "the correct way," or how others might want you to answer. We are aware that sometimes people answer questions according to what they might like others to think about them—and you might do the same. Therefore, we do not advocate giving these exercises to someone to "grade" or judge, but you can certainly share your answers with your counselor or psychotherapist, or in a safe group setting.

Remember, you are not looking for a "quick fix." Change requires patience because it is a process. That is also why we recommend that you do all the exercises in the book. It's easy to say, after just one or two exercises, *"Oh! I think I see how I needed to change. I've got it now."* The problem then lies in the lack of reinforcement of the change to make it permanent. The book has more than one exercise for that very reason. We want you to sustain the positive changes you make.

How to Use The Videos

The set of accompanying videos includes vignettes that will introduce you to every exercise. We invite you to watch the vignette that goes along with the particular exercise you are working on. Then, after you watch the introductory vignette that corresponds with the exercise in the workbook, we invite you to complete the exercise. The videos are not meant to be watched from beginning to end; instead, they are designed to be watched on an exercise to exercise basis.

Foundation Keys

When you are well informed and aware, you make better decisions and you understand *how* to make changes. With the importance of information in mind, you are going to read about some of the methodologies that counselors, psychotherapists, and psychologists use to encourage people to make whatever changes are necessary in their lives. One of these is called Transactional Analysis, and it is the first one we explain. Another is Cognitive Behavioral Therapy, and then we take some time to explain the continuum of violence along with some basic information about how the human brain works. Knowledge is power, and the more you understand, the more empowered you become to take control of your life.

Reading through the explanations of these methodologies is part of the process, and what you gain in the following pages will enhance your experience when you do the exercises. We are not trying to make you a practicing psychotherapist, psychologist, or counselor; rather, we are establishing a common ground on which you can build your new life. We have found that the more people can talk a common language, the more quickly personal growth can happen.

Transactional Analysis (TA):

HC

Figure III.1.1 Transactional Analysis of a Healthy State

We talk a lot about something called "Transactional Analysis" in this book. Probably one of the most pragmatic tools counselors can have in their toolkit (and you can have in your knowledge bank) is at least a simplified version of Eric Berne's theoretical approach, *Transactional Analysis.*

Transactional Analysis (TA) is certainly a technical name; however, breaking down the terms helps us understand what it's all about. *Trans* means "across," and *actions* are "behaviors," so transactional means, "across behaviors." In other words, transactions are the interactions between people. *Analysis* means "understanding," so put together, transactional analysis means "understanding the interactions between people."

The Core of TA:

Every person lives out of one of three ego states or "states of mind" all the time (Berne, 1967). The ego states are **Parent**, **Adult**, and **Child** – but, and this is important, a person does not have to be a parent, adult, or child to operate out of any of the three states. The person who created this idea, Eric Berne, just used those names to describe the states that we go in and out of all day long.

I. The **Parent** ego state is divided up into two parts:

   A. The Critical Parent (CP) – the very demanding, critical part of ourselves

   1. A person in the critical parent state is not fun to be around
   2. A person in the critical parent state tends to nag others

   B. The Nurturing Parent (NP) – the loving, caring part of ourselves

   1. A person in the Nurturing Parent (NP) state is comfortable to be around
   2. A person in the Nurturing Parent (NP) state who has no "regulator" (the Adult state) can become an enabler

II. The **Child** ego state is divided up into two parts:

   A. The Hurt Child (HC) – the part of us that feels sorry for ourselves

   1. A person in the Hurt Child (HC) state is in a "poor me" state

2. A person in the Hurt Child (HC) state tends to only see the negative in things

  B. The **Fun Child (FC)** – the part of us that just wants to have fun

   1. A person in the Fun child (FC) state can be great to be around

   2. Too much of our Fun Child (FC) state without a "regulator" (the Adult state) turns us into irresponsible people who cannot keep a job, do well in school, or be a productive team (or family) member

III. The **Adult** (A) ego state is the rational, reasonable, thinking part of us (i.e., the "regulator")

  A. A person in the Adult (A) ego state is calm and reasonable

  B. A person in the Adult (A) ego state is able to see several sides to an issue

   The goal of TA is not to get rid of certain ego states, it is to come to understand them.

Once we understand our own ego states, we can begin to understand how ego states play off each other when we interact with others. In other words, we can start to learn that if we are going to be in our Hurt Child (HC), we will likely bring the Critical Parent (CP) state out of someone else. Or, if we act from our Critical Parent (CP), then we are likely to elicit another person's Hurt Child (HC). Sometimes it's helpful to visually see how transactions take place both inside us and between others and us. There are ways to diagram ego states that can help us see the danger in letting one ego state dominate over the others.

Let's look at the relative perceived size of the three ego states and see their relationship to one another under an "ideal" balanced psychological condition. In such a condition, a person would be considered psychologically "healthy" because the adult state is the overriding control that keeps the other two states in check. Basically, the adult state helps us to avoid extremes that are harmful to us or to others.

Figure III.1.2 A Healthy State of Balance

Notice in Figure III.1.2, whereas the Adult (A) state is the largest, even the healthiest of people still has both Critical Parent (CP) and Hurt Child (HC) ego states; the difference is in a healthy individual, those negative states play a much smaller role and only emerge sometimes as opposed to being prevalent more often.

Now what would happen if one of the other two states became the dominant state?

Figure III.1.3 The Critical Parent

A person who has a "big" Critical Parent (CP) and a smaller "Adult" is someone who is likely to be very critical of others, often nagging and "getting on" others incessantly.

This type of person is difficult to be around, and is often angry because others are not doing what this person thinks they should be doing.

A person who is in the Critical Parent (CP) state is demanding of others. The constant CP is tough to be around, because seemingly nothing is ever good enough for that person. Regardless of how hard we try, a CP will always find a way to identify what we are doing wrong. But before we get too excited about analyzing others when they are in their CP – we need to take a hard, fast look at what we do when we are in our own (CP) ego state.

When we are in our Critical Parent (CP) ego state, we are controlling of others – or at least we try to be. By telling others what to do, we are creating a perspective that we seem to know "the right way" to be in the world, and others are wrong. From the perspective of the CP, we believe that we actually have the answers to life, and others "need to just see things the way we do."

Searching for Control

All human beings are constantly searching for control on some level. Control is not wrong in and of itself, but it exists on a continuum that can go from benign to dangerous. For example, we may want to control our body temperature by taking off a coat, but on the same continuum, albeit much farther along, control can morph from self-control to manipulating others. In short, control can get out of hand quickly. When we struggle with self-control, we tend to attempt to control others. When we are in a place of self-control, however, we have no need to control others. The Critical Parent (CP) ego state is the place we live in when we are attempting to control others.

When it comes to control, most people will justify their control by saying things along the line of, "I am only controlling because . . . " and then they will proceed to justify why they are controlling.

Here are just some examples of how people attempt to rationalize why it is "okay" for them to control others:

- She's not good with money
- He's not in his right mind because he uses (drugs/alcohol)
- She doesn't know better, so I have to . . .
- I don't want him to leave me
- She doesn't make good decisions
- He's not good at . . .
- She even knows that I'm better at those kinds of things . . .
- He won't do it unless I . . .

The fact is that when we are attempting to control others, we can always find a "justifiable" reason for why we are doing it. At the end of the day, however, exhibiting controlling behavior is a way for us to be controlling, regardless of the excuses we come up with to justify it. Most of us are uncomfortable being around someone who is controlling. This workbook helps you understand both how you are controlled by others and your own tendencies to be controlling. By understanding your own predisposition toward control, you will have the best opportunity to understand what part you play in attempting to control others.

Control is important to us, but it is also very damaging to relationships. We waste a great deal of energy trying to get others to think, act, and feel the way we want them to – energy that is better spent on gaining the self-control that we need for our own psychological freedom.

A person in the Hurt Child (HC) ego state has learned to view him or herself as the constant victim. A big difference exists between being victimized in a crime and being a victim in life. People who view themselves as victims in life often do not feel empowered to make changes, regardless of how unhappy they say that they are. They can spend their entire lives complaining about how the world is "not fair," rather than acknowledging that regardless of the unfairness in the world, they are still able to make the changes in themselves that they need to make.

Figure III.1.4 The Hurt Child

A person who has a "big" hurt child and a smaller "Adult" is someone who is likely to feel sorry for him or herself. This person may act like the whole world is out to "get" him/her.

The Hurt Child (HC) is difficult to be around, because he/she believes that "nothing is ever fair," and everything always happens to him/ her.

There are reasons people live primarily out of their Hurt Child (HC) ego state. The most typical reason people revert to their HC is that they hope to elicit a Nurturing Parent (NP) out of others. Unfortunately, the parent ego state that people elicit from others when they are in their HC is not the Nurturing Parent (NP), but the critical one (CP). The HC appears to directly elicit the CP of others. When we come across to others as "poor me," helpless, or otherwise incapacitated, then those with whom we are interacting take on the role of telling us what to do. The more helpless we are, the more demanding (CP) they become.

Learning about the different ego states empowers us. Once we are aware of what it is that we are actually eliciting or bringing out of others, we can choose to stop "playing the game" and simply ask for what we want. For example, consider the three ego states of the same interaction:

Situation: *You don't get a job you tried to get*

Critical parent: "They should have hired me!"
Hurt child: "I'll never get a job anywhere."
Adult: "I would have liked to get that job, but it's not the end of the world."

Changing our self-talk around can literally impact both how we *feel* about a situation and what we *do* in response. Evaluating the differences above, we can see that if we tell ourselves that someone *should* have done something that was not done, then we will be extraordinarily frustrated, if not downright angry; our actions then stem from that anger. If we tell ourselves that we will *never* get something, we can begin to feel hopeless; our perspective and actions will follow from that hopelessness.

If, on the other hand, we are able to use more balanced, accurate language when we talk to ourselves, then we are likely to act from the more balanced, Adult (A) ego state. The key is in the language we use. Yes, there are many things we *would have liked* to have happened in our lives, but that is very different from *needing* those things to happen. Changing our self-talk can change the ego state we are in, and that can make all the difference.

Being the Couch

There is a difference between **content** (the words that people say) and **process** (how they say it). The difference can be small or very big in any one given situation, but regardless, understanding the difference between content and process is enormously important. The content is the words that you hear a person say, but the process holds the key to what the person is actually communicating.

"I'm fine."

Perhaps the most classic example to see the difference between content and process is around the response, "I'm fine."

Content = "I'm fine."
Process = "I'm not fine; I'm actually hurting a lot right now."

Learning how to listen to the process can make all the difference.

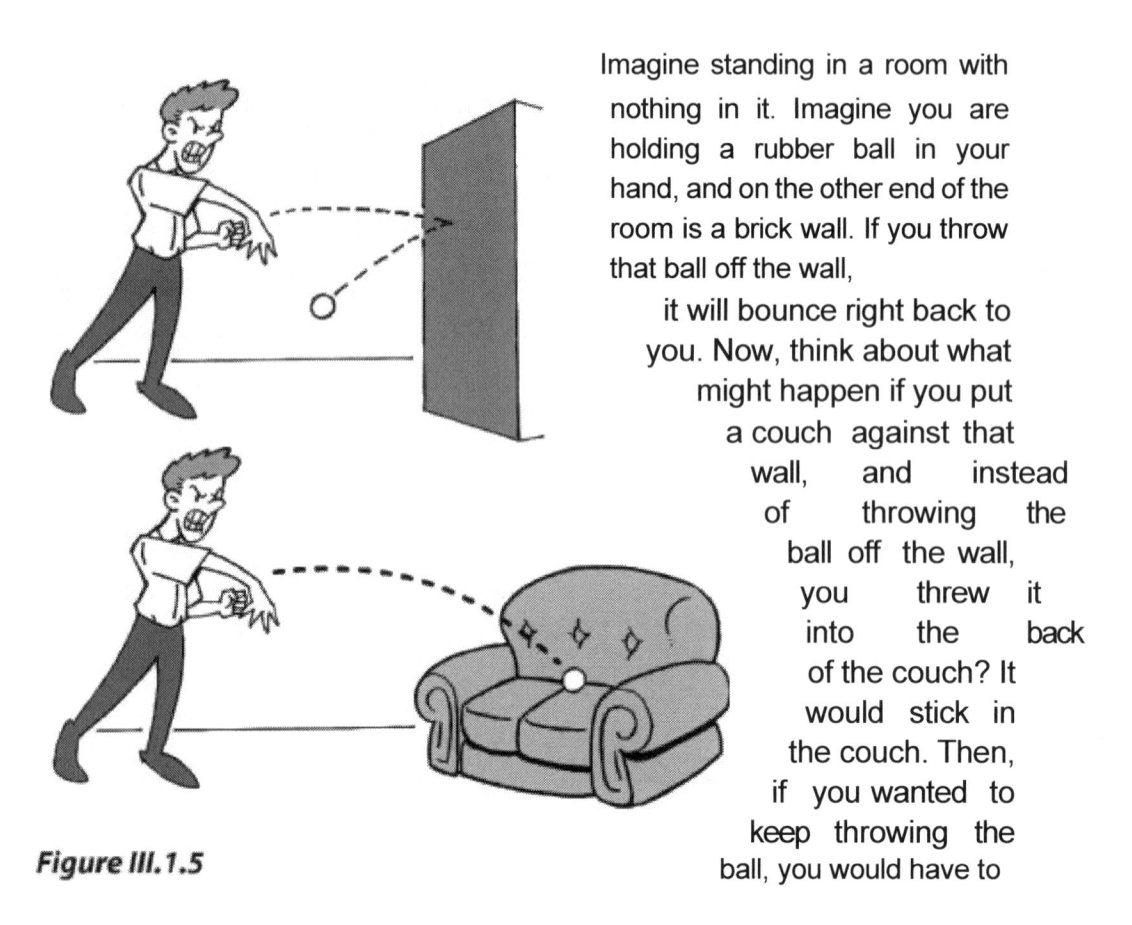

Imagine standing in a room with nothing in it. Imagine you are holding a rubber ball in your hand, and on the other end of the room is a brick wall. If you throw that ball off the wall, it will bounce right back to you. Now, think about what might happen if you put a couch against that wall, and instead of throwing the ball off the wall, you threw it into the back of the couch? It would stick in the couch. Then, if you wanted to keep throwing the ball, you would have to

Figure III.1.5

walk all the way over to the couch, pick up the ball, and walk all the way back to the other side of the room, and do it again. And it would stick again. And you would walk, and eventually you would get tired of doing this.

If you were throwing the ball off the wall, however, it would keep coming right back to you, and you wouldn't get tired so easily, so you could keep doing it all day long. That's how it is in an argument. When someone says something that angers us, and we reflect the content of what they say, we are like the brick wall. We can keep going back and forth easily all day long. The argument escalates and escalates until an eruption is about the only option left to end the conflict.

If we can be like the couch, however, we can avoid "throwing back" at someone. Imagine what that might do to our conflict. At a minimum, it would lessen our conflict. There is a problem, however, and it is this: How the heck are we supposed to be the couch? The answer that most people come up with is to use silent treatment. "I know," We've heard many people say, "I'll just shut down and won't say anything at all" (Silent treatment is, as you will see later on, manipulative and a part of the continuum of violence.) But that is NOT being the couch. After all, when is the last time that you were ignored and thought, "Oh, I'm okay with someone ignoring me."

If we truly want to be the couch, we have to acknowledge what is going on with the other person. To be the couch, we must validate the process. Validating the process means we want to confirm how a person is feeling in that moment. Sometimes we think we are validating how a person feels, but what we are actually doing is glossing over how that person really feels. All too often, we have heard people say things along the lines of, *"I **did** validate him/her, so he/she should have been . . . "* What we hope to make clear is this: *simply acknowledging or validating a person's feelings does not equate being the couch.* To "be the couch" as we use the phrase, one has to make the other person *completely feel* as though he or she was heard.

Consider what it is like if you were the one who was talking to another person: would you want that person to simply acknowledge your emotional state, or would you hope the person also heard what you were trying to communicate? Seek first to understand others – and the more you understand, the more ability you will have to truly "be the couch."

Try not to say, "I understand"

We strongly recommend that you avoid telling others that you "understand." More often than not, when we tell others that we "understand," we bring out a defensiveness in them that has them arguing for why we do not, in fact, understand.

This can be tricky, but stick with us.

When we tell others that we "understand," we can come across as belittling and condescending. The bottom line is we may never fully understand what is going on inside someone else, and that's okay. We know ourselves that we do not always have the exact words to describe what emotions we are experiencing; and it is the same thing for others.

If you need to use the two words, "I understand," try this context:

A huge difference exists between saying, "I understand exactly what you're going through," and "I understand you're going through a tough time." In the context of the first statement, the person is purporting to completely understand what the other person is experiencing. In the second statement, the person is only alluding to understanding that the other person is having a difficult time, not that he/she can understand all aspects of that experience.

A similar way to understand this is to consider the idiom: *"Been there. Done that."* When we say something along these lines, we are invalidating a person's experience. When a person experiences something, he or she does so from his or her own distinctive ability to think, emote, and experience; so each human experience is truly unique. For example, two people could experience sky diving, but if one had a lifelong fear of heights and the experience represented a monumental achievement over fear, and the other person always enjoyed heights, then the two experiences end up being vastly different.

We may all share some sense of what each other are going through; we can even experience the same event at the same time – but we see it from our own perspective, and we all have our own unique experience from every situation.

We may not be able to fully understand each other, but what we can do is be there for each other – even if that means just sitting there while the other person experiences things internally.

Cognitive-Behavioral Therapy (CBT)

Cognitive-Behavioral Therapy (CBT) can sound intimidating to someone who has never heard of it before, so we are going to give you a behind-the-scenes look at how simple it can actually be to understand (though it is still tough at times to actually practice).

Cognitive means *"thinking"* and behavioral refers to *"actions;"* hence, cognitive-behavioral therapy refers to teaching people about their thoughts (self-talk) and their actions. CBT is about helping people look at the ways in which they talk to themselves and evaluate whether or not what they are saying to themselves is in fact helpful for them. CBT is predicated on the assumption of a statement made by a philosopher (Epictetus) almost 2,000 years ago. Epictetus said,

"People are not disturbed by things, but by the view of which they take of them."

The point, as modern-era psychologists Albert Ellis and Aaron Beck described, is that events cannot make us mad, glad, or any other emotion. Events cannot cause emotions – instead, what causes emotions is what we tell ourselves, or our "self-talk." Think about it: after a break-up, how is it that the two people involved can feel so differently? They both experience the same event: a break-up. One person says, "This is what I need," and feels relief; the other says, "I can't be without this person," and is devastated. One event, two totally different reactions: it's the self-talk, not the event itself that impacts feelings.

The ABC model of cognitive-behavioral therapy is helpful for breaking down our internal thoughts (Ellis & Dryden, 2007). The A stands for "Activating event," or the situation over which we got angry. The B stands for our "Belief" about the event, or in other words, the B stands for our self-talk. And the C stands for "Consequence," or the feeling that we had as a result of our thoughts. So A can represent the breakup. B can represent for one person, the self-talk of "This is what I need," and that person's feelings or C becomes relief. For the second person, A still represents the breakup, but the B is completely different. For the second person, the B is "I can't be without this person," and therefore, the second person's C (or consequence) is feeling devastated.

Events cannot make people feel a certain way. If they could, all people would react the same to every event. Instead, it is always our life experiences and perceptions (which make up our self-talk) that contributes to how we experience situations. It is always our self-talk that determines how we feel.

Important Fact!

Just because it is true that our thoughts determine our feelings does NOT mean that it is easy for us to control our thoughts. Controlling our thoughts can be difficult and takes a great deal of practice. However, with practice, we can become very good at using effective self-talk.

The Core of CBT:

We all talk to ourselves (this is called, "self-talk"). What we say to ourselves determines how we feel about things. Outside events, according to CBT, cannot make us feel a certain way; the only thing that can influence how we feel is our own thoughts (i.e., our self-talk).

I. CBT can be understood through the ABCs

    1. "A" stands for "activating event" (i.e., the event that got us emotional)

    2. "B" stands for "belief" (i.e., what we told ourselves – or our belief - about the event)

    3. "C" stands for "consequence" (i.e., what we ended up doing – our actions – as a result of what we told ourselves)

II. CBT therapists say things happen in order: A then B then C

III. An event then, cannot make us feel a certain way

IV. An example of how this plays out is:

Scenario 1

A = Traffic jam
B = "This shouldn't be happening! I can't stand this!"
C = Anger

Scenario 1 Again *(but looked at with a different belief about the situation)*

A = Traffic jam
B = "It's unfortunate that I am in this, but I can handle it."
C = Frustrated (but not as angry as the first time)

By changing our self-talk (or "cognitions"), we can change how we feel about things. Changing self-talk is not always easy. Changing self-talk does, however, result in different feelings. No part of CBT is designed so that people will become like robots and not have feelings toward things – what CBT does do, however, is help people think about things in less-extreme terms – which helps us to react to events better.

Get rid of the "should!"

Whether we use it on others or ourselves, the word "should" can be a harmful one. The word "should" implies that things need to be a certain way – that there is only one way to do things, and when it comes to human interactions, that is simply not accurate.

Try eliminating the word *"should"* from your vocabulary this week. Watch what happens. You will find yourself less demanding and more accepting of others, and less demanding and more accepting of yourself. By eliminating the word "should," you will put yourself in a position to be clear about the things you *want* versus the things that *have to happen.*

Shame and Anger

In the work that we have done through the years, we have found time and again that the following dictum is, in fact, a truism: *People who live in shame act out of shame.* In other words, when people have low self-worth, they are less likely to want to make decisions from their higher selves. If, for example, a person feels like a "no-good-piece-of-nothing," then that person has little motivation to make good choices; because he or she would be living out the self-fulfilling prophecy that has been internalized.

The penal system has traditionally been predicated on shame. We shame people for the crimes they have committed. As a society, we call people who act out of violence "scum-bags," and "monsters." We have, traditionally, looked to shame people convicted of violent crimes until they "realize the pain they have caused." Whereas this approach is in line with a safe, "either/or" world of "good people" and "bad people," what it doesn't leave room for is everything in between the "either" and the "or."

It has been our experience that there are two types of shame: shame-forward and shame-backwards. Shame-forward points to the feeling of embarrassment or thoughts of dishonor that we get about something that we might potentially do. An example of shame-forward is a person thinking about hurting someone, but experiencing a sense of shame ahead of time. Shame-forward can be healthy because it can stop us from doing potentially harmful things to others.

Shame-backwards, however, is the experience of shame in the traditional sense of the word. Shame is the painful emotion that arises when we become aware that what we have done is dishonorable or improper. It has been our clinical experience that shame-backwards is unhealthy for the very reason that makes the dictum mentioned above a reality: People who live in shame act out of shame. People who experience intense and chronic feelings of shame about what they've done integrate the experience of shame into their identities, and move forward in life looking backwards with regret. We believe it is difficult to move forward in a healthy way if the focus is continually on the past.

Novices to the subject of shame traditionally rely on the elementary argument that, "if we get rid of shame, then we are excusing the hurtful things others do." Excusing behavior, not providing consequences, or not holding people accountable for their actions, however, are not the same as shaming people. In no way, shape, or form do we ever condone or excuse any acts that stem from anger. We do, however, aim to not only explain it, but also, through this program, help people learn about why they do what they do so that they can in turn, take complete control of their actions.

To live in shame is to act out of shame, but to learn from shame is to make new, healthful decisions that impact us personally, as well as those who are around us. We invite people to learn from shame, not to dwell in it.

Scale of Consciousness

In 1995, Dr. David Hawkins, building on the work of Dr. John Diamond, published a map of consciousness. Consciousness simply means awareness, so this map is essentially a scale of human awareness. Here's an overly simplified summary of the parts that we have found in our own work to be relevant to anger:

5 Love
4 Anger
3 Anxiety
2 Depression
1 Shame

Notice that shame is on the very bottom of the scale. That means that the lowest form of consciousness (awareness) that human beings live in is *shame*. Above shame is *depression* (but not much higher). Above depression is anxiety. Now, and this is important to understand, above anxiety is *anger*. What that means is this: we would rather be angry than anxious, depressed, or living in shame.

This is very empowering to understand when we consider how many times in our lives we have used anger to cover up feelings of shame, sadness, or anxiety. Think about how many times in our lives we have experienced anger and didn't know why. The scale of consciousness helps us understand: *our bodies unconsciously would rather be angry than experience these other emotions.*

Look at the scale again and notice that love is higher than the other emotions. In other words, love is more conscious than anger. We used the term "love" to simplify other parts of the map that are above the negative emotions . Forgiveness , understanding , peacefulness , knowledge , and love are all above anger, anxiety, depression, and shame; and the good news is this: we do not have to go up the scale in order. What that means is once we understand this scale, we do not have to simply become unconsciously angry to get rid of our feelings of shame, anxiety, or depression. Instead, we can move beyond those negative emotions by a different approach: love, forgiveness, peacefulness, understanding, and knowledge.

Body Awareness

Stopping Anger Before it Starts

One key that we have found to stopping anger before it starts is body awareness. By *body awareness*, we mean awareness of the body's feeling hunger, thirst, fatigue, physiological anxiety/depression, fear, or stress. Teaching people about how they respond to their bodies' needs is a key first step in dealing with anger.

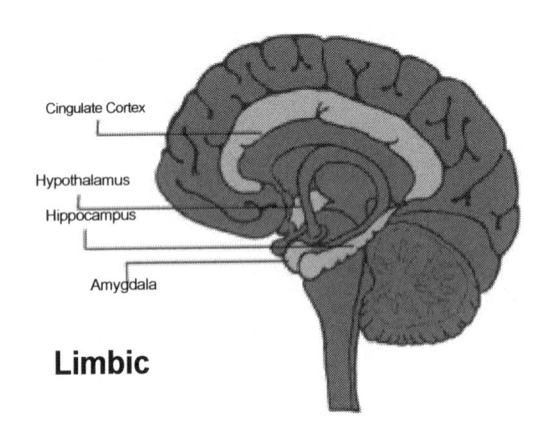

Figure III.3.1

The limbic system (shown left) is the area of our brain devoted to emotions. Deep in the limbic system is the hypothalamus. The hypothalamus is primarily responsible for alerting the body to things like hunger, thirst, fatigue, and sex.

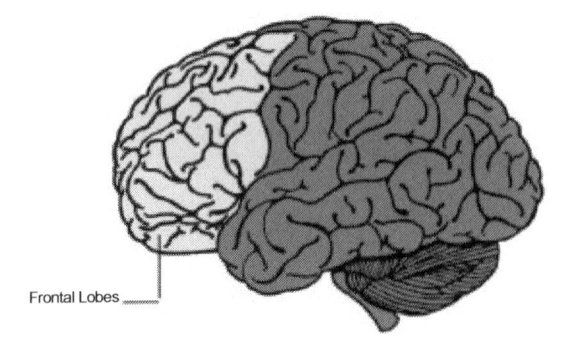

Figure III.3.2

The frontal lobes make up the area of our brain involved in higher level thinking. Notice that the limbic system and frontal lobes are two different areas of the brain.

When we experience hunger, thirst, and fatigue, we are, in a sense, operating primarily out of the limbic system (specifically the hypothalamus). Blood flow and neural activity is not the same in every part of the brain at every moment. Therefore, when we are operating primarily out of the limbic system, we are not using our higher-order thinking (frontal lobes) in the same way as we do when our bodies are satiated. When the body is satiated physically, blood flow and neural activity (and this is oversimplifying it) are freed up to be more available to the frontal lobes.

Mind-Body Congruence

Our bodies and minds work in unison. When our bodies don't function well, we tend to make up stories in our minds that match the way our bodies are feeling – and those stories can be extremely creative. Imagine for instance, that we devour three energy drinks in a row. In a very short time, our bodies will mimic physiological anxiety. Our hearts will begin to beat fast, our hands may tremble, and our stomachs may feel nauseated – and all of this will amount to us not feeling great at all. Now, think about what happens when we don't feel great: we tend to need to make up a story so that our minds match what our bodies are feeling; when that happens, we call that experience mind-body congruence.

Mind-body congruence is not always negative, but it becomes negative when we have to create a negative story to match an uncomfortable physiology. For example, if after we drink back-to-back-to-back energy drinks, we begin to feel all the symptoms of anxiety, then we are likely to create a negative story in our minds to match what our body is experiencing. If we have a readily available negative story to draw on, we will go to that (i.e., if something was already on our mind before we drank the energy drinks, it will likely be amplified) – but if we do not have a present story to tell ourselves that matches our body, we will search our minds for the most accessible story. For example, we may look to past arguments or problems that were lurking in the background, and bring them to the foreground.

For example, let's continue with the idea of drinking the three energy drinks in a row. Now let's imagine that we do not have an immediate story present to be upset about; mind-body congruence suggests that we will find something to be upset about, because it is easier to have a story to be upset about than to sit in our physiological discomfort and just accept it. The antidote then, is to do exactly the opposite: accept our uncomfortable physiological states without creating a story to match.

Understanding this concept is crucial to eliminating anger caused by physiology before it even begins. For example, take the role hunger has played throughout your own relationships; consider what countless needless arguments could have looked like in your own life had you accepted that your body was experiencing agitation simply because it was a way to signal that more food was necessary.

Imagine how different those arguments could have looked had you or your loved one not created a new story to be angry about, and simply accepted the feelings of discomfort as symptoms of hunger.

Just as we create a story to match the physiological feelings of hunger, so too do we create stories for any other physiological needs that we have. In addition to the physiological needs, we also create a story to match our feelings of fear, anxiety, and depression. The stories we tell ourselves determine how we feel, and vice versa. Learning to be in control of our thoughts can literally change our physiology. After all, not being in control of our thoughts also affects our physiology. Consider the following example:

Anytime we experience low blood sugar (one does not have a chronic disease or experience something linked to any specific illness to experience low blood sugar), we develop symptoms.

Some symptoms of low blood sugar are:

- Racing heart
- Irritability
- Trembling
- Feeling shaky

When we experience any of those symptoms, we are also experiencing identical symptoms of anxiety. How do we distinguish anxiety, for instance, from low blood sugar? One way to distinguish between anxiety and low blood sugar is to take care of our blood sugar first. If we know that our blood sugar is where it needs to be, then we can rule it out as a cause of anxious feelings. The same is true with any physical complications that can mimic anxiety.

The point is this: to take control of our anger, we need to find a way to understand what is occurring in our bodies. We need to be mindful of what impact food, drink, medicine, or substances have on us. And being aware of what is going on inside our bodies is not a one-time thing: we must evaluate what is happening physiologically with ourselves *every day* of our lives. The more we can understand what impact food, drink, medicine, substances have on our bodies, the more we can understand that many times we are not actually angry at the things we think we are angry at. Instead, we are simply trying to find a way to cope with the uncomfortable things that are happening to our bodies.

Nothing excuses behavior, but plenty explains it.

The goal of psychologists and counselors is not to excuse behavior, but to attempt to explain it. We have seen that when people understand their behavior, they are more likely to be able to change it. Oftentimes people believe that if we give others a reason for their behavior, that it is the same thing as excusing it. To the contrary, we believe that explaining and excusing are two entirely different concepts. As such, the focus of this workbook is largely about bringing motivations for behavior to the foreground.

When people come from violent backgrounds, for instance, it makes sense that they replicate the violence that they learned. It makes sense that people will act in ways that are consistent with what they learned about the world. Our job (and if you are doing this workbook – your job) is to ask the question: Do you want to continue on the path that you are on, or do you believe it is time for you to take a new path? If you've landed in an anger management program, or even if you've allowed your emotions to get the best of you from time to time, then the answer can be a resounding "Yes, I want to take a new path."

The exercises in this book are geared toward helping you become more aware of why you do what you do, and they are intended to help you create an entirely new path for yourself; a path that is marked by psychological freedom. By answering the questions in each exercise honestly, you will have an opportunity to understand a great deal about yourself.

Becoming What We Hate: The Concept of the Shadow

The potential for everything great and everything terrible lies in all human beings. What we do with that potential is up to us. Sometimes we are happy with who we are; other times we step back and realize we have become the very thing we hated in the past. Carl Jung was a famous psychologist who taught about the shadow. The shadow is the part of ourselves that we either do not like or simply refuse to recognize as a part of who we are. What we do not want to face about ourselves, we hide in the shadow of our psyches.

The *shadow* is the part of us that we stuff deep down. Sometimes the shadow is made up of negative things, sometimes it is made up of positive things; it is always, however, by definition, outside of our awareness. The shadow can drive our behavior. Sometimes we have the qualities that we hate about others, and sometimes unwanted qualities drive our behavior without our knowing it. For example, if people hate those who are domineering, and "domineering" gets stuffed into the shadow, then they are likely to become passive. But, when they become passive, they are likely to build up resentment for others, because they may feel like they can never say what they want.

Additionally, they will avoid being assertive because of their "fear" of becoming domineering; hence, domineering will remain in the shadow.

Figure III.3.3

The shadow could be as real as the picture above. On the outside we may work hard and talk about how terrible "lazy" people are, but lurking in the shadow projections deep inside us is a part of us that wants to be lazy. Maybe we want to be lazy and just not work so hard; maybe we have a fear of being lazy, so that drives us – but the concept of the shadow is this: *in everything and everyone, the potential for the opposite resides.*

All of us can learn about the shadow in our lives by listening to the types of things that we say when we are judgmental toward others. This is matter of being mindful. For example, if you have already created an entire story to explain to yourself who and what kind of person someone is, then the person you think you know is merely a product of your mind that might or might not reflect reality. Now, if you read or hear a story about that person that does not fit your imagined characterization, then you might face a dilemma: How can you reconcile your characterization with the anomalous action reported in the story? That is, what do you do to understand behavior that doesn't fit your idea?

Maybe the best way to handle your misconceptions and misperceptions is to acknowledge that you might have misjudged the person, that you took an incident from the person's past, for example, and magnified it into a full biography of the person. It might also be appropriate for you to realize that just as you would not want to be judged by a single incident in your life, so too, do others probably want to be seen as more than any set of behaviors or statements. Everyone is more than any one incident and behavior might indicate. With mindfulness, as we judge others, we can learn a great deal about ourselves.

But I Barely Did Anything . . .

We have heard many tales of people who were sentenced to prison for hurting someone else after anger got the best of them and they lost self control. Time and again, we have heard people say something like *"But I barely hit her; I don't know why she got so upset about it."* What people fail to understand is this: The act that gets us in the most trouble is not always the worst thing we have ever done. The act that gets us into trouble is usually the one that is like that final drop of water that causes a pitcher to overflow.

Like water overflowing a pitcher, there is a point at which there is simply just too much water for the container. Behaviors that we do may be tolerable for days, weeks, months, and even years, but at some point, our behaviors take us over the edge. We may believe that we "barely did anything,"

but we easily forget that the little things we've done for a long period of time have added up to something that is no longer containable.

We have seen countless people be simply unaware that they were scary when they were angry. We have talked with many people who believe that because they intended something else in their minds, that others "shouldn't" have been intimidated. Unfortunately, others respond to our behaviors, not our intentions — just as we respond to other people's behaviors, not their intentions.

For behaviors to add up, they have to start somewhere, and for us, that's where the continuum of violence comes into play.

Continuum of Violence

All behavior, all action, is on a continuum. Every human being is on a continuum of potential, including a continuum of violence. The potential to do every horrible act that others have done is inside all people (but remember only the potential is there; no one has to act on that potential). The reason movie sequels contain more blood, more sex, and more violence in each subsequent film is that human beings have something called psychological tolerance. Like the tolerance that develops for substances, we also have a psychological tolerance that increases with life experiences. Once we reach a certain level of psychological tolerance, it takes more to get us to the same level of gratification; and we get immediate gratification in the release of anger (we might regret what we did one second later, but in the moment we release the energy, we feel an instant sense of gratification).

| Passive aggression (silent treatment) | Name calling (objectifying) | Hitting / kicking (physical violence) | Killing others |

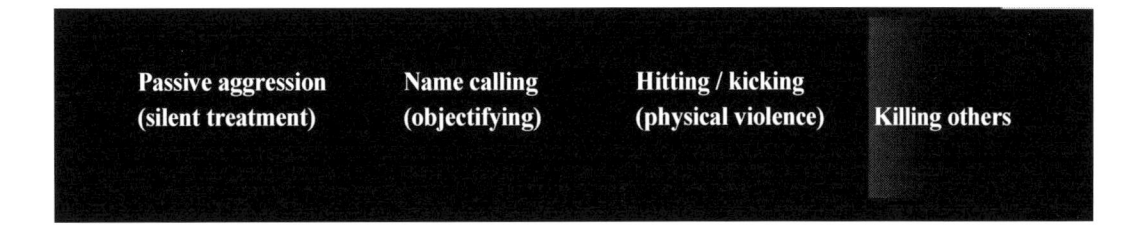

Figure III.5.1 The continuum of violence

We believe it is important for all of us to recognize where we are on our own continuum of violence. If we see people who commit violent acts as "monsters," then we can sit back in the safety of our comfortable worldviews and never assess where we are in terms of our own expression of violence.

The continuum of violence ranges from aggression that is passive on one end to killing someone on the other end. The continuum starts with passive aggression (by doing things like manipulating others with silent treatment), and it moves a bit further along to hollering at someone, and further still toward putting another person down and objectifying that person (i.e., calling people names – everything from "jerk" or "bitch" to body parts). The next step on the continuum involves a push or a shove (and is usually justified by something along the lines of, "I had to get her off me"), then the pushing or shoving intensifies to pushing someone down a flight of stairs; the continuum escalates to punching or kicking another person, then it moves to hitting someone with an object. Finally, a person, not a vilified "monster," but an every-day-human-being, can find himself on the far end of the continuum where he or she is physically stabbing someone repeatedly.

At some point in our lives, we may find ourselves alone and with our head down, wondering how it ever got that far; until we finally face the truth that we allowed things to get that far because we never took the time to become aware of where we were on the continuum - because if we had taken a step back, we likely would have been able to pause and say to ourselves, "What am I doing? This isn't where I truly want to be." By recognizing where we are on our own continuum, we can have the opportunity to change it.

As long as we see those who escalate violence to murder as "monsters," we will continue to deny or downplay the role that anger and violence plays in our own lives. By seeing anger and violence as something that is "out there," we will likely never take the time to recognize you, me, and every other person on the planet is on the same continuum; we are all just at different places on it at different times in our lives. Understanding the continuum of violence is critical for living more consciously.

I Never Hit Her Even Once

Chris was furious that he was sentenced to an anger management group. He told the group, "I never even hit her once." He swore he never would have actually hurt her. And apparently, that could have been true; so what did Chris do that warranted his needing anger management?

One day when he and his wife were in an argument that continued to escalate, Chris pulled out a 12-inch carving knife and stabbed the air mattress that they had nearly forty times. When he turned around dripping in sweat and anger, his wife was terror-stricken by seeing him holding the knife over his head and witnessing the rage he was capable of. She had seen him get angry before, but never like this. She had no idea if he was going to keep stabbing things and move forward until he stabbed her.

His wife had seen him get angry many, many times before, and each time Chris seemed to get a little angrier, shout louder, and push the violence further. So when he stabbed the bed – it's true that he didn't literally stab his wife – but how was she to know he wouldn't have stabbed her if a neighbor had not come flying through the door when he heard the screams? She couldn't know. Chris's wife could never know his intentions – she could, however, see his actions. This was not the first water ever added to the proverbial pitcher. He had been filling the pitcher for years: now, with his actions, he overfilled it.

When he began anger management, he didn't believe one act of violence warranted his having to attend the group, but not too long into the group, he saw how much anger had controlled him almost all of his life; and how, if left unchecked, he could have easily slid down the continuum of violence into the depths of places he would have never imagined he could go.

Chris also recognized that his wife did not see his intentions that day, but his actions. Whereas he believed that his intentions would have never been to hurt her, the fact is, in retrospect he saw that from her perspective, based on his actions, she could have never responded to his intentions, because she had to respond to his actions in the moment. He realized how scary it would have been for her to see him repeatedly stabbing the mattress, and what it might have looked like from her eyes when he turned in sweat and rage holding tightly to the knife.

Chris is a man who eventually recognized where he was on the continuum of violence. He saw how he was escalating. Chris is also a man who eventually stopped blaming others for his own behaviors. Because of his awareness and his learning to act from a place of awareness, Chris was able to make significant changes in his life. The question for you is:

Can you recognize where you are on your own continuum of violence?

Being the Puppet:
Probably the Best Reason to Get a Grip on Your Anger

A puppet is easily controlled by someone else. Consider the marionette: Someone else pulls the strings, and the puppet goes this way and that – wherever the person pulling the strings wants it to go. Whereas being in control of the puppet can be fun, actually being someone else's puppet is not fun at all. No one likes the idea of being someone else's puppet, yet every time we allow someone else to determine how we feel or what we think, we are essentially becoming that person's puppet.

For years, we have made people aware that every time they allow someone else to say something and get them angry, they have essentially become that other person's puppet. It's tough for a lot of us to admit, but we often hand over our power to others and allow them to take the reigns and control our lives. Sometimes we allow other people to control us, and other times we allow a concept like "respect" to control us. Consider how some people will do whatever it takes to "be respected." In those instances, they are allowing the concept of respect to control them.

Puppet Power

Roger could not stand to be disrespected. He was so controlled by seeking the respect of others that he would risk everything he had and was just so that others wouldn't do anything "disrespectful" in his eyes.

One day, Roger learned about "being the puppet" and "giving away his power," and the affect on him in the moment was significant. He shared this with his anger management group:

"All of my life I have fought anyone who ever did anything disrespectful to me. I have hit people I never thought I would hit – girlfriends, even my own wife. I have been so hung up on not being 'disrespected,' that I didn't realize how disrespectful I have been. I guess I've just been a pawn, or as doc says, 'a puppet,' and honestly, I'm tired of it."

Roger realized he was a puppet to "disrespect" and that he frequently gave away his power – even to complete strangers; but Roger is not a success story yet. Two days after he announced those words in front of the group, Roger got into a fight with a man for not paying him back 10 dollars he was owed, and he was sent back to prison.

The fact is, wanting to change alone is not enough. If we want to make real life changes, we have to do more than just "want them;" we have to work hard to learn about ourselves and dedicate ourselves to changing. Completing this workbook will help you with that process.

Hold Onto Your Power!

Imagine that, like a superhero, your power source is centered in the middle of your chest, and that it was possible to remove it if you so chose. Would you, under any circumstances, willingly give your power away? What about if a person were rude, disrespectful, or otherwise hurtful to you – would you then give your power source away? If the answer is "no," then stop and think for a minute: Don't we regularly give our power away every time we give up our control over ourselves?

Ask yourself if there are any situations in which you would be comfortable giving your power away. Then ask yourself who is significant enough in your life to hand your power over to. What do you really gain by giving others your power? Without an awareness of how we give our power away, we are doomed to continually hand it over to others. Hold onto your power – or at least be aware of how easily you give it away.

Fundamental Exercises

You're Ready To Begin!
Two foundational principles exist to managing anger. The first is to be mindful that what is going on physically inside your body impacts how you feel mentally. The second is that what you tell yourself mentally (self-talk) impacts how you feel physically, including how angry you allow yourself to get. Knowing these two principles is vital to transforming your life.

To begin the transformation from being someone who is controlled by anger to someone who is in constant self-control, you must ask yourself:

- What state of mind am I in and how does that impact my actions?

- What is the difference between what I expect the world to be and what the world is? (i.e., cartoon world versus the real world)

- What can I do to not stuff the ball under the boat?

- What can I do to avoid being the puppet?

- What can I do to stop myself from drifting further along my continuum of violence?

Your answers to the above questions, coupled with the exercises that you are about to undertake, can transform your life.

Now it's time to get started on the exercises. Every now and then, you may want to return to the questions above and/or the information you have read on the preceding pages to refresh your perspective on where you are in your unique process of change. We will revisit those questions when you have completed the workbook. The differences in your responses from the beginning to the end will reflect how much you have grown as an individual.

Implementing Verbal Aikido

Aikido (pronounced, "EYE-KEY-DOE") is a martial art built on the idea that it is easier to redirect someone else's energy than it is to exert our own. If someone pushes an aikido artist, the aikido artist will simply pull that person; if the person pulls the aikido artist forward, instead of resisting the pull, the aikido artist will simply push that person.

The concept of verbal aikido is similar to the martial art. When a person verbally attacks a verbal aikido artist, the verbal aikido artist validates the person completely. In other words, he or she "goes with" the angry person completely until there is nothing left for the angry person to be angry about.

Verbal aikido artists realize the importance of self-awareness, self-observation, and openness to constant self-evaluation. It is not a matter of what they can "do" to others. Instead, for verbal aikido artists, it is a matter of how they can utilize the energy of other people to yield positive results.

To become a verbal aikido artist, it will take practice. Remember, the journey of a thousand miles begins with the first step. In the following two exercises, you will be introduced to a path you can take to become a verbal aikido artist.

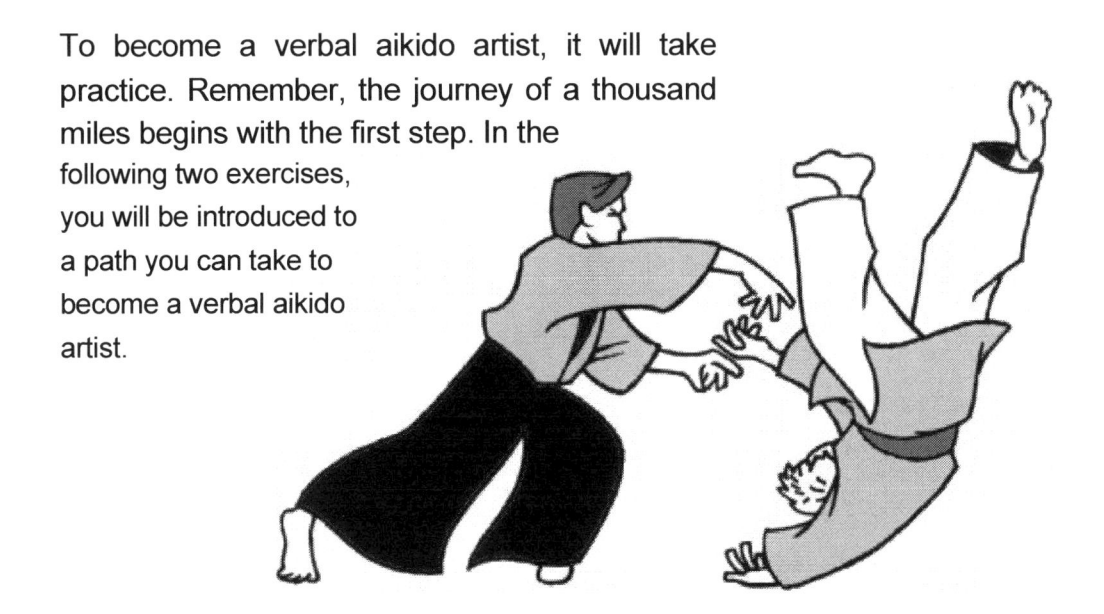

Implementing Verbal Aikido Exercise

To know how to master your anger it is important to know how you currently handle your anger. Be honest with your response to each question, because it is only by being honest with yourself that you will make any real changes in your life.

Scenario #1

1. Briefly describe the most recent conflict (verbal or physical) that you can recall:

_____
_____
_____
_____
_____
_____
_____

2. Below, write down some things that you actually said to the other person that did not help the situation:

_____
_____
_____
_____
_____
_____
_____
_____

3. What do you think that you could have said that may have been more effective?

_____

_____

_____

_____

_____

_____

4. What stopped you from saying those things that you recognize could have been more effective (try to be as specific as possible here)?

_____

_____

_____

_____

_____

_____

Scenario #2

1. Briefly describe another recent conflict (verbal or physical) that you can recall:

_____

_____

_____

_____

_____

2. Below, write down the things you actually said that did not help the situation:

_____
_____
_____
_____
_____
_____
_____

3. What do you think you could have said that might have been more effective?

_____
_____
_____
_____
_____
_____
_____

4. List the types of words (or phrases) you have used that resulted in negative outcomes with others:

_____
_____
_____
_____
_____
_____
_____
_____

5. What makes those words ineffective?

___

"When we cannot control ourselves, we seek to control others."

**Personal challenge:
Seek more control of yourself today.**

Verbal Aikido: Self-Knowledge

Communication is tricky. As human beings, we seem to have a natural tendency to blame miscommunications on others. Yes, we can blame others, but as long as we do, the power to change the communication lies outside of ourselves. When we focus instead on our own communication, we are on the path to becoming verbal aikido artists: people who are **in control of** communication rather than being **controlled by** it.

We cannot become verbal aikido artists if we do not have self-knowledge about our own communication style. Not knowing how we communicate when we are in different physical or emotional states can hurt us and others. After all, how many arguments have we gotten into in our lives simply because we were hungry or overly tired, and did not realize it?

Science behind it all:

> There's a saying in the field that when you
> are, **H**ungry,
> **A**ngry,
> **L**onely,
> or **T**ired,
> you need to **HALT!**

There is scientific evidence behind why it is helpful for us to halt (or stop and think) when we are experiencing different emotions.

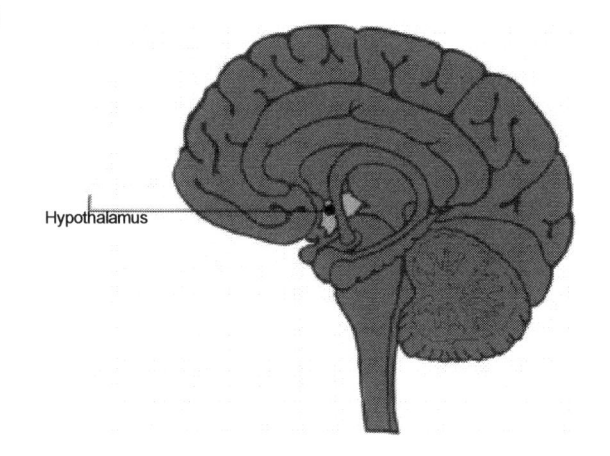

Figure IV.1 Hypothalamus

When we are hungry or tired, we are primarily operating out of our hypothalamus. Our hypothalamus is a part of our limbic system, the part of our brain that is involved with emotions.

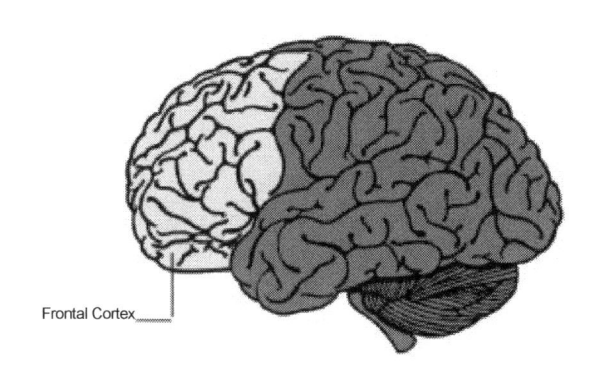

Figure IV.2 Frontal Cortex

When our physical state impacts our hypothalamus, there is less energy to engage the frontal cortex, the part of the brain involved with thinking. In order to think clearly and use our frontal cortex effectively, we must have sufficient nutrition and rest.

Go to bed angry – by all means!

There is an old saying: "Never go to bed angry." But this saying is very outdated, because how many times in your life have you fought with a loved one when you were overly tired? How different might your interaction have been had you gone to sleep instead of shouting things you later regretted? What we say is this: if you are fighting when you are overly tired, by all means, go to sleep and get a good night's rest. If you wake up in the morning still upset about the issues from the night before, then you have a much better chance of thinking clearly in the morning.

Self-Knowledge Exercises

Knowledge of how you communicate, in any state of being, allows you to gain control of your communication. Being hungry, angry, lonely, or tired, can cause you to respond without thinking clearly, thereby making it difficult to interact and communicate effectively with others.

1. How many arguments do you think you have gotten into because you were hungry, tired, or physically stressed out?

    _____

    _____

2. Now let's figure out the specifics. How do you communicate when you are: a. Hungry?

    – _____

    – _____

    b. Tired?

    – _____

    c. Stressed out?

    – _____

    – _____

    d. When you do not get your way?

    – _____

    – _____

    e. Angry?

    – _____

    – _____

f. Sad?

g. Anxious?

h. Afraid?

i. When you feel at peace?

3. Being a verbal aikido artist means being in control regardless of your state of being. Describe what you can do *differently* when you are hungry, tired, stressed out, do not get your way, are angry, sad, anxious, or afraid.

_____

_____

_____

"We are more than puppets to our bodies and emotions: we have minds that can set us free."

Personal challenge:
Be mindful of the impact your body has on your emotions.

The Stages of Change

Most of the time, making changes is difficult. Sometimes, however, making changes can be easy. Regardless of how difficult or easy change is, anytime we make a change, we go through a series of stages. Sometimes those stages can take us only moments, and sometimes they can take us years. The stages of change are:

1. **Precontemplation:** (*pre* means *before*, and **contemplate** means *thinking*) In the stage of precontemplation, we are not even thinking about changing. In this stage, a person lacks the awareness that he or she has done anything to offend or injure another person. For example, a person in this stage might be thinking: *"I did not do anything wrong."* When we are in the precontemplation stage, we are usually living from a place of unconsciousness.

2. **Contemplation:** In the stage of contemplation, we are beginning to consider a change, but we are not quite ready to make those changes. For example, a person in this stage might say something like: *"I sincerely think I need to make some changes in my life, but I'm honestly not ready to make any real changes; but hey, at least I'm thinking about it!"* People can be in the contemplation stage for a moment or for an entire lifetime.

3. **Preparation:** When we are in the preparation stage, we are starting to make small changes, and we are getting ready to make bigger or more permanent changes. For example, a person in the preparation stage might think: *"I am blaming others a lot less for where I am in my life; and now I am actually starting to make some small changes in my life."* The preparation stage "prepares" us to take some real action.

4. **Action:** The action stage is defined by actually and fully making a change. For example a person in the action stage may say something along the lines of: *"I accept responsibility for my part in this situation. I am actively living out the change I needed to make in my life."* People often believe they are in the action stage when they are trying to make changes. But trying to make changes is "preparation;" we are in the action stage when we are actively living out our change as an everyday part of our life.

5. **Maintenance:** In the maintenance stage, we are working hard to maintain the changes that we made. We are mindful on a consistent basis about the behaviors necessary for a permanent change. For example, a person in the maintenance stage might say: *"I am actively trying to maintain the changes I have made in my life… but it is day to day, and I have to really work at it."*

6. **Relapse:** In the stage of relapse, we are unable to maintain the change we made, so we revert to doing what we worked so hard to change. A person in this stage often says (prior to relapsing), *"I can't do this anymore,"* or *"I have to go back to the way I was before."* After people relapse, they tend to feel shame. Remember, when people live in shame, they act out of shame. Relapse, however, is often considered a part of the process of change; hence, the self-talk we use after we relapse is crucial. We can essentially take one of two major paths: 1. Live in shame for "not being strong enough to maintain the change," in which case we are likely to continue doing the things we don't want to do; or 2. Tell ourselves that relapse is a normal part of change, accept ourselves for what we did, and move forward in the positive direction we want.

Figure IV.3 Process of Change

> **We go through the first four stages of change every single time we make a change.**

What to watch for:

Sometimes when people learn that relapse is a natural part of change, they have a tendency to pre-plan to relapse, and simply blame their fallback on the process. But just because relapse can be a natural part of change, it doesn't mean that it definitely *has* to be a part of the process of change.

Self-fulfilling prophecies are powerful. If we look hard enough for an excuse to do what we want to do, we will definitely find one. If we look for strength to maintain our changes, we will find that as well.

Texas to North Dakota

Imagine that you are lost in the middle of Texas, and you call and ask your friend for a ride. Your friend agrees to come get you, but instead of telling your friend that you are in Texas, you tell him that you are in North Dakota. Now, that seems silly, right? After all, why would you tell someone to come pick you up in North Dakota when you are really in Texas? Probably for the very same reason that you might tell others that you are farther along in the stages of change than you really are.

If you need help from others, try reaching out and being as honest as possible about where you really are in regard to change. It might just get you the help you really need.

Stages of Change in Regard to Anger

Precontemplation

Stage 1: I'm not even thinking about changing

> Example: *"It's stupid for me to be working on 'anger management' because I am in complete control of my anger."*

Contemplation

Stage 2: I'm thinking about changing, but I'm not really ready to make any changes

> Example: *"Maybe I have some anger, but so does everybody; so why do I have to change?"*

Preparation

Stage 3: I started making small changes

> Example: *"I know I have a problem with anger, so I've started to do some things to keep myself from losing my temper. For example, "This week, when I got angry, I decided not to say the first thing that came to my mind."*

Action

Stage 4: I have actively changed

> Example: *"Things that used to bother me just sincerely don't bother me anymore. I know what triggers me getting pissed off, and I know how to handle it."*

Maintenance

Stage 5: I work hard to maintain the changes I made

> Example: *"I still think about the stuff that used to get me angry, but it's been months since I've even felt angry."*

When evaluating our own behavior, most of us say that we are in the "action stage," whereas when we evaluate other people, we say where they are according to their behaviors. The reason is that when it comes to ourselves, we can see our potential, but when it comes to others, we see only their actions.

Stages of Change Exercise – Part 1

For this exercise, we want to evaluate your stage of change according to what others can see and observe about you.

1. Give an example of a time that you were in the precontemplation stage in regard to anger.

   _____
   _____
   _____
   _____
   _____
   _____

2. Give an example of a time you were in the contemplation stage in regard to anger.

   _____
   _____
   _____
   _____
   _____
   _____

3. Give an example of a time that you were in the preparation stage in regard to anger.

   _____
   _____
   _____
   _____

4. Give an example of a time that you were in the action stage in regard to anger.

_____
_____
_____
_____
_____
_____
_____

5. Give an example of a time that you were in the maintenance stage in regard to anger.

_____
_____
_____
_____
_____
_____
_____

6. Give an example of a time that you relapsed in regard to your anger.

_____
_____
_____
_____
_____
_____
_____

7. The stage of change I believe I am in right now regarding my anger is . . .

___

8. The evidence I have to support my saying that I am in that stage of change is . . .

___

9. The stage of change others seem to believe I am in regarding my anger is . . .

___

10. What I can do to help others see me where I see me in regard to my anger?

_____
_____
_____
_____
_____
_____

Stages of Change Exercise – Part 2

Evaluating someone else:

Sometimes it's easier to see the stages of change in regard to someone else. For this exercise, think of someone you know who was doing something ineffective in his/her life (past or present), and needed to make a change.

1. First name of other person:

   _____

2. What was the other person was doing that he/she needed to change?

   _____
   _____
   _____
   _____
   _____

3. Where do you think the other person would have said he/she was in regard to change?

_____

_____
_____
_____
_____
_____
_____

4. Why do you think there is a difference between the answers for number 2 and 3?

_____
_____
_____
_____
_____
_____
_____

5. If you can see that the other person wasn't always aware of where he/she was in regard to change, can you be open to seeing that you may not be as far along as you think?

_____
_____
_____
_____
_____
_____
_____

Nag, nag, nag!

Did you know that when we talk to people as though they should be in the action stage when they are in fact in the precontemplation or even contemplation stage, that all we are really doing is nagging?

If you don't want to nag others, try meeting them where they actually are rather than just expecting that they should be where you want them to be.

Stages are something we all go through to change. We can go through these changes in a day, a week, a month, etc. Recognizing the stage you are in is essential to changing your behavior.

Personal challenge:
Change is inevitable. How long it takes to change is your choice.

Continuum of Violence

Continuum of Violence in Action

Bryan came into his anger management group and was quick to share that he wouldn't have been with the group today had it not been for his understanding of the continuum of violence.

He told the group that he and his wife got into an argument the previous night and they started yelling at each other, and then he called her a "stupid bitch." In the moment he said it, he remembered the continuum of violence, so he took a physical step back and sat down. He thought about how he escalates, how he has hit her in the past, and the conversations we have had in anger management about how we tend to forget what we fight about in a couple weeks anyway. He realized he was getting out of control.

He said his wife kept yelling at him, but something in him shifted, so he told her about the continuum of violence. He said that the two of them talked through the rest of the issue sitting down facing each other at the kitchen table. This is something they had never done before.

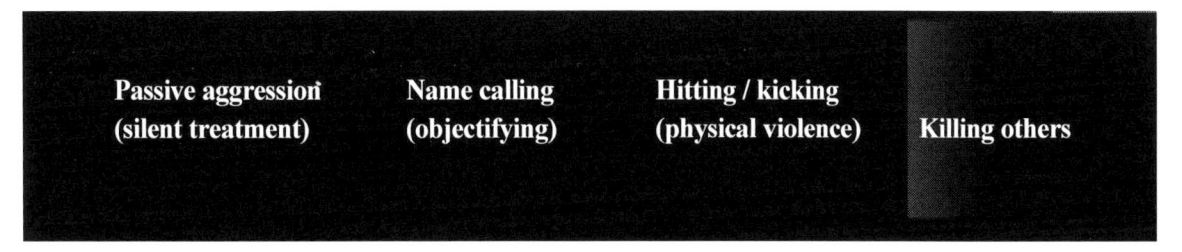

| Passive aggression (silent treatment) | Name calling (objectifying) | Hitting / kicking (physical violence) | Killing others |

Figure 9.1 The continuum of violence The continuum of violence resides in all of us. An awareness of our place on the continuum is necessary. Without an awareness of where we are in regard to our own continuum, we are likely to move further and further along it.

Small changes can be big changes.

Continuum of Violence Exercise

This exercise is intended to help you get a sense of where you've allowed yourself to move along the continuum, and challenges you to find out what you can do to stop your violence from continuing.

1. Where are you currently in regard to the continuum of violence?

   _____
   _____
   _____
   _____
   _____
   _____

2. What is the farthest you've ever been in regard to the continuum?

   _____
   _____
   _____
   _____
   _____

3. What were the factors that you believe contributed to your getting to that point on the continuum?

   _____
   _____
   _____
   _____
   _____

4. What can you do to make yourself aware of where you are on the continuum when you are actually in the moment?

_____
_____
_____
_____
_____
_____
_____

5. What can you do to stop yourself from creeping further and further along the continuum?

_____
_____
_____
_____
_____
_____
_____

6. What kinds of things can get in the way of your becoming aware of where you are along the continuum?

_____
_____
_____
_____
_____
_____
_____

7. What can you do to get around those barriers (that you listed for number 6)?

_____
_____
_____
_____
_____
_____

There is a better way: Find it and follow it every day.

Personal challenge:
Find a better way.

Shame and Anger

In 1995, Dr. David Hawkins, building on the work of Dr. John Diamond, published a map of consciousness. Consciousness simply means awareness, so this map is essentially a scale of human awareness. Here's an overly simplified summary of the parts that we have found in our own work to be relevant to anger.

> 5 Love
> 4 **Anger**
> 3 Anxiety
> 2 Depression
> 1 Shame

Notice that shame is on the very bottom of the scale. That means that the lowest form of consciousness that human beings live in is shame. Above shame is depression, but not much higher. Above depression is anxiety. Now, and this is important to understand, above anxiety is anger. What that means is this: we would rather be angry than anxious, depressed, or living in shame.

This is empowering to understand if you consider how many times in your life you used anger to cover up feelings of shame, sadness, or anxiety. Think about how many times in your life you experienced anger and didn't know why. Our bodies unconsciously would rather be angry than experience these other emotions.

Look at the map again and notice that love is higher on the scale than the other emotions. In other words, love is more conscious than anger. We used the term "love" to simplify other parts of the scale that are above the negative emotions. Forgiveness, understanding, peacefulness, and love are all above anger, anxiety, depression, and shame. The good news is this: we do not have to go up the scale in order. What that means is once we understand this scale, we do not have to simply become unconsciously angry to get rid of our feelings of shame, anxiety, or depression. Instead, we can move beyond those negative emotions by a different approach: love, forgiveness, understanding, and knowledge.

Shame and Anger Exercise

Answer the following questions to see how this map might play out in your own life.

1. Describe a time when you got angry, but in retrospect, you can see that your anger was intended to cover up feelings of **shame**.

   _____
   _____
   _____
   _____
   _____

2. How could you have handled the situation differently had you been able to see with love and compassion the other person's perspective?

   _____
   _____
   _____
   _____
   _____

3. Describe a time when you got angry, but in retrospect, you can see that your anger was intended to cover up feelings of **depression**.

   _____
   _____
   _____

4. How could you have handled the situation differently had you been able to see with love and compassion the other person's perspective?

5. Describe a time when you got angry, but in retrospect, you can see that your anger was intended to cover up feelings of **anxiety**.

6. How could you have handled the situation differently had you been able to see with love and compassion the other person's perspective?

Looking Through the Johari Window

The Johari Window, a technique created by Joseph Luft and Harrington Ingham, is an amazing tool for gaining insight into our behavior. Learning about ourselves can be a powerful and eye-opening process. Sometimes it is difficult to realize that we do some things that we don't think we actually do. This exercise can forever change the way you look at yourself.

The Johari Window consists of four quadrants that assist us with heightening our self-awareness. The quadrants help us have a better understanding of our relationship with ourselves and with others. As seen below, the quadrants create a grid or "window." Different quadrants represent different degrees of our understanding or our self-awareness.

The four quadrants are:

1. "Open" quadrant
2. "Hidden" quadrant
3. "Blind" quadrant
4. "Unknown" quadrant

JOHARI WINDOW

	Known to self	NOT Known to self
Known to others	1. Open	3. **BLIND**
NOT known to others	2. Hidden	4. Unknown

The **"Open" quadrant** contains areas of our lives that are known to both others and ourselves. For example, liking a particular sports team might be in an open quadrant, especially if you wear a sweatshirt that represents that team and are outspoken about liking that team.

The **"Hidden" quadrant** contains parts of us that we do not want others to know about. For example, oftentimes when people relapse on substances, they do not want others to know, and they go through great lengths to hide it. Things that you know about yourself, but others do not know about you are in your hidden area.

The **"Blind" quadrant** contains the areas of our lives that others can see about us, but we cannot see about ourselves. In comedy, it can be something like walking out of a bathroom with toilet paper stuck to your pants: you come out and say something that you believe is making everyone laugh, but in actuality, they are laughing at something that you cannot see. In terms of our lives, the blind area tends to be the most difficult and troublesome area for people. We may, for example, express anger in a much more intimidating way than we believe we are expressing it.

The **"Unknown" quadrant** is difficult to understand. We often do things and do not know why we do them. Uncovering the unknown about us usually takes the help of others, but it can also occur on our own through a great deal of introspection.

Spotlight on the Blind Quadrant

When one person says something one time about our blind area, it may very well be that the person is saying so out of anger. If more than one person tells us the same thing, however, or if the same person identifies something over and over again, then there is a good chance that others are seeing something that we are not.

We believe that multiple people seeing the same thing may be the best gauge to view the blind area. The problem is that we really do not want to own up to what is in our blind quadrants, so we tend to be resistant to listening to others telling us something about ourselves that we do not want to face. We spend a great deal of psychological energy defending our position or denying that we are coming across a certain way. Unfortunately, the more we deny that we are doing something that others are obviously seeing us do, then the less likely we are to make a change.

Learning to be open to what is in your blind area can change your life. We encourage you to try to listen openly to how others experience you.

Looking Through the Johari Window
Exercise – Part 1

Write down things about yourself that you believe are in each of the following quadrants.

OPEN –
(These are things that you choose to show everyone.)

_____

_____

_____

BLIND –
(These are things that others have told you about yourself that you were not aware of. You may not agree with these things)

_____

_____

_____

HIDDEN –
(These are the things you hide from others that are revealed in time)

_____

_____

_____

_____

UNKOWN –
(Think hard and make at least one guess as to what you think may be unknown to you about yourself)

_____
_____
_____
_____
_____
_____

Looking Through the Johari Window
Exercise – Part 2

> *"When help is needed, sometimes people get the help they need rather than the help they want."*

1. Do you agree or disagree with the statment in the box above?

_____

2. What are your reasons for agreeing or disagreeing with this statement?

_____
_____
_____
_____
_____

3. Give an example of a time when someone gave you the help that you needed, but not necessarily wanted at the time.

_____
_____
_____
_____
_____
_____

4. When people see things that are in your blind area, what is the best way for them to make you aware of it without having you get defensive?

_____
_____
_____
_____
_____
_____

5. How can you be more accepting to what other people see about you that you just do not agree with or see about yourself?

_____
_____
_____
_____
_____

Personal challenge:
Be open to the feedback that you receive from others.

Types of Rage

Dr. Potter-Efron in his excellent book, *Rage*, described different types of rage people experience. The different types of rage we may encounter in ourselves or others are:

Sudden Rage:

This type of rage seems to come on all of a sudden and we have a difficult time calming down from it. People experiencing this type of rage are often unsure as to why they are so angry.

Abandonment Rage:

This type of rage occurs when we believe that we are going to be abandoned, and it stems from our fear of being alone. People experiencing this type of rage have a tendency to inadvertently push others away in their attempt to "squeeze" them into staying close.

Shame-based Rage:

This type of rage occurs when we act out in rage to cover an internal feeling of shame over something. Remember that people who live in shame tend to act out of shame.

Impotent Rage:

This type of rage occurs when we believe that there is nothing we can do about a situation (i.e., we feel helpless or "impotent"). People who experience impotent rage have a difficult time letting go of the things that they cannot change.

Seething Rage:

This type of rage occurs when we allow our thoughts to spin faster and faster about a situation, and in so doing, build up a tremendous sense of animosity. People who experience this type of rage have difficulty controlling their self talk.

It is important to identify the ways in which we experience rage or intense anger. The more we know about each aspect of what is happening with us, the better chance we have to do something differently about it.

Rage Exercises

In the following exercises, identify ways in which you have experienced each of these types of rage; then, reflect on which (if any) stand out more to you in terms of what you tend to experience:

Rage Exercises – Sudden Rage

Sudden rage

Occurs when we least expect it; it comes on fast, and we are often surprised at how angry we actually get. We often have difficulty calming down from sudden rage.

What happens?

When we are faced with a threatening situation, a part of our brain called the amygdala (center of the fight or flight response) sends a message (via the hypothalamus, the center of the basic survival needs) like, *"Let's go!"* to the adrenal glands, which in turn send cortisol and adrenaline through the body. The increase in cortisol and adrenaline rapidly affects the body, making us agitated (or stressed) at the very least. Once we deem a situation to be safe, the hippocampus (center of memory) shoots a message of its own to the adrenal glands saying, *"It's cool, shut down the cortisol and adrenaline now,"* and then we calm down.

The system doesn't always work in a timely way, however. Our bodies and minds stay agitated when there is a delay between the time when the amygdala says to the adrenal glands *"Let's go!"* and the hippocampus says, *"It's cool, calm down."* As the delay continues, more adrenaline and cortisol travel throughout the body, making us more agitated.

People who have experienced trauma have a tendency to have a delay in the amygdala-hippocampal connection. What that means is that people who have experienced a trauma *may* struggle with having too much cortisol and adrenaline when startled. Their body is essentially saying that the situation is worse than it actually is. Once these two hormones stimulate their body, their mind races to create a story to match, such as *"This is terrible!"* or *"I can't stand this!"* and then they react in extreme ways.

Antidote to sudden rage

If you think you may struggle with sudden rage, try saying to yourself the words *"I'm safe,"* or something similar such as *"I'm cool"* or *"It's okay"* anytime that you are in a situation that elicits a quick reaction from you. Saying it quietly to yourself is sufficient; you do not have to attract unwanted attention by shouting it aloud in the presence of others. Over time, your brain will re-associate startling situations with less intensity, and your sudden rage will decrease.

1. In what ways have you exhibited sudden rage?

   _____
   _____
   _____
   _____
   _____
   _____
   _____

2. What phrase or set of words would be realistic for you to say to yourself the next time you are faced with a potential sudden rage situation?

   _____
   _____
   _____
   _____
   _____
   _____
   _____

Rage Exercises - Abandonment Rage

Abandonment rage

When we perceive that we are going to be left or abandoned, we lash out at others; hence we cover our fear of abandonment with anger.

What happens?

Consider that other than the death penalty, the worst punishment in any given society is considered by many to be solitary confinement. The reason is that human beings need each other. Whereas we all may long for solitude from time to time, the majority of people do not want complete isolation from everyone in the world. Evolutionary psychologists have argued that togetherness is so important to people because there is strength in numbers and humans needed each other to survive. We only have to look at how long it takes a human to be able to fend for him or herself. It takes years at a minimum, which supports the most basic reason why humans need each other.

So when people perceive themselves to be abandoned, fear shoots throughout their body. Fear is most easily covered up by anger. People who struggle with abandonment rage lash out at others when they perceive that they will be abandoned. Though it is neither rational nor logical for us to believe that becoming angry with and screaming at others to not leave us will produce the type of attractiveness to draw others toward us, abandonment rage moves us beyond reason and logic, and pushes us into acting out of emotion (primarily fear).

Antidote to abandonment rage

If you believe that you may struggle with abandonment rage, the antidote lies in discovering whether or not you are really going to be abandoned. Yes, people walk away from relationships. Yes, people can walk out of our lives forever, but the vital question to ask is, *"Am I truly alone, or am I just not with the person I wanted to be with?"* This question is so important to ask. If we believe that no one will ever be near us again, then we will likely act in extreme ways. If, by contrast, we use healthy, balanced self-talk to guide us, we can learn to see that being left by a loved one is not the same thing as being ultimately alone and unable to survive.

1. In what ways have you exhibited abandonment rage?

2. What self-talk might work for you to get through your fear of abandonment?

Rage Exercises – Shame-based Rage

Shame-based rage

When we feel we've been disrespected, dwell in guilt, or feel shame, we act out in rage to cover the feelings.

What happens?

The cycle of shame occurs when we do something we know to be "wrong" or that embarrasses us or causes others to criticize our behavior as unacceptable. To cover the sense of shame, we sometimes act out in anger. Our lashing out at others is equivalent to "exercise" in the sense that endorphins follow the adrenaline-driven action. Getting angry releases cortisol and adrenaline. The endorphins that follow make us feel better than we did when we had felt the shame. The endorphins basically act as our bodies' natural pain killers." Unfortunately, when we act out of anger, we tend to do things that we regret, thereby bringing up more feelings of shame, and hence, the cycle begins again.

When we live in shame, we act out of shame. As long as we "feel stupid" or "disrespected" or "shameful," we dwell in a realm of discomfort. That discomfort eventually boils to a certain point resulting in self-talk akin to, *"I've had enough,"* or *"I can't take it anymore."* These kinds of statements can lead to rage. When we choose not to overtly deal with the shame that we feel, covering it up with rage becomes an unconscious process. The body feels better with endorphins than it does with feelings of shame, so unless we learn to actively deal with the thoughts that surround shame, we will continue to lash out at others.

Feeling shame about the past can lead to rage. Shame-forward, or allowing the feeling of shame to stop you from doing something you are about to do, however, can be a healthful condition in the sense that it can prevent you from harming others. Shame-forward is conscience; shame-backwards is guilt. Bottled up guilt can lead to rage. Pushing things down is rarely helpful; hence, we encourage you to actively deal with anything that might be driving your behaviors.

Antidote to shame-based rage

If you believe that you may struggle with shame-based rage, the antidote is to begin to tell yourself that you are ultimately good at your core. Learning to accept that *human beings do the best they can with what they have in any given set of circumstances* is a powerful way to be rid of the kind of shame that leads to rage.

1. In what ways have you demonstrated shame-based rage?

___

2. What is the first step you need to take to deal with the shame that you feel?

___

> **Personal challenge:**
> Try to go one day without using any adjectives to describe uncomfortable situations, and then notice the difference between experiencing discomfort with many thoughts versus experiencing discomfort with fewer thoughts. (Getting to "no mind" might be tough, but we sure can limit our thoughts with practice.)

Antidote to impotent rage

If you are struggling with impotent rage, the antidote is to learn to let go. Whereas letting go is much easier said than done, when you develop the ability to practice letting go on a regular basis, you have a much more realistic chance of letting go in the more difficult situations.

1. Describe a situation in which you showed impotent rage.

   _____
   _____
   _____
   _____
   _____

2. What daily practices can you begin to implement so that impotent rage does not build up inside of you?

   _____
   _____
   _____
   _____
   _____

Rage Exercises – Seething Rage

Seething rage

When we allow our thoughts to grow a situation once we walk away from it, we experience seething rage.

What happens?

Like an underground fire, we begin to boil inside without anyone other than ourselves realizing what is happening. In seething rage, our self-talk becomes rapid, our anger multiplies. Essentially, the self-talk that we use reverts to extremes. We begin to use phrases like, *"I can't believe he/she did that!"* or *"They planned to get me all along!"* or *"They always try to hurt me!"* or *"He/she never, ever cared about me!"*

Extreme thoughts lead to extreme behavior. When human beings feel cornered, they will strike. When we use extreme words to describe (e.g., "always," "never," "have to," "must," etc.), we place ourselves in a metaphorical corner. The reason intense thoughts lead to dangerous behavior is that the more extreme a situation really is, the more pressed we are to come up with a solution. The faster thoughts race, the faster the solution needs to be found. The human body reacts in severe ways in life-threatening situations. Seething rage (rapid, extremely negative self-talk) is one way we can create a life-threatening situation out of non-life-threatening one.

> ### Time-Outs are NOT for Everyone!
>
> People frequently ask us, *"Can't we just take a time-out when we're angry? I mean, why do we have to learn all that's in this big book?"* And the answer is this: Time-outs work for some people, but they do not work for everyone. As you become more aware about the different types of rages, you will see that someone struggling with seething rage or abandonment rage will only get increasingly angrier if he/ she walks away from a situation.
>
> The bottom line is this: There is no simple solution to handling anger: it takes hard work and dedication to learning about yourself so that you can have the kind of self-control necessary to make good decisions regardless of how emotional any given situation becomes.

Antidote to Seething Rage

If you struggle with seething rage, the antidote is to begin to change your self-talk. By learning what thoughts you have that add to your anger, and what thoughts you have that can calm your anger, you can choose to use either set of thoughts repeatedly. A starting point is to use a daily mantra such as, "It's not the end of the world."

1. Describe a time when you had seething rage.

___

2. Describe the situation you wrote about above with extreme descriptions first, then tell the same situation – this time with no extreme adjectives. What difference do you notice?

___

"Knowing why we rage gives us the best chance to handle it well."

Personal challenge:
Control your anger before it controls you.

The 5 Errors of Communication™

From our crying for milk as a hungry infant to our ordering a pizza as a hungry adult, we have spent our lives communicating. Still, being able to communicate accurately with others seems to be as elusive as the fountain of youth. But why is this so? Shouldn't we be good at the process after years of practice? One reason communicating with others is difficult is that we have a tendency to not take into consideration what is going on, both for the listener and within ourselves.

We have all known people who have perceived themselves to be excellent communicators largely because others appear to agree with them. Such people usually do not realize that the other person's apparent agreement might hide a disagreement or a misunderstanding. In relationships and in jobs, some people agree simply because they lack the assertiveness to openly disagree. The fact is that few people can communicate well most of the time, and all people fail to communicate well some of the time.

Why do we fail at communication?

- Sometimes we shut people down from the beginning of the conversation.

- Sometimes we misinterpret what other people say.

- Sometimes we judge people rather than assess what is going on with them.

- Sometimes we turn people off or shut people down with key words in the middle of the conversation.

- Sometimes we make the mistake of thinking we are responsible for how other people act.

All in all, we make some pretty big errors in communication.

The 5 errors of communication *(Conte, 2009)* were developed to help people better understand when and where they fail to communicate effectively.

The Five Errors of Communication include:

- **The Error of Approach** - occurs when we confront someone in a way that makes them either shut down or respond aggressively and negatively toward us.

- **The Error of Interpretation** - occurs when we fail to listen to what the other person is really trying to say.

- **The Error of Judgment** - occurs when we judge people rather than assess what is going on with them.

- **The Error of Language** - occurs when we elicit someone else's fight or flight response.

- **The Error of Omnipotence** - occurs when we think we are responsible for another person's behavior.

Each description of the errors is intended to help bring awareness to how we communicate. Learning how to avoid the Five Errors of Communication can forever change the way we interact with others.

The Five Errors in Action

"We need to talk," Anjie said to Jake [ERROR OF APPROACH]. Jake was furious. Immediately he became defensive. "Every time she says that, we fight," he thought to himself. His mind raced to more harsh thoughts, "She's so self-righteous," he said to himself [ERROR OF JUDGMENT]. "I want to talk about what we're going to do when your parents stay here this week," Anjie said, hoping to be able to convince Jake that they needed new bedding for their guest room. "What's your problem with my parents?" Jake asked infuriated, not knowing that Anjie really thought they "needed to talk" to discuss his not allowing her to just buy things without having a conversation over it [ERROR OF INTERPRETATION].

"Me? Have a problem with *your* parents?" Anjie fired back. "You always do that! You always assume the worst! You never give me any credit! I have always put up with your stupid parents!" [ERROR OF LANGUAGE in the words "always," "never," and "stupid"]. "You're the one who always puts my family down!" Jake said, now enraged and not listening at all [ERROR OF LANGUAGE]. And the argument continued with neither side taking the time to listen to the other.

When Jake's parents came to stay, both Anjie and Jake thought that the other should say and do exactly what each wanted, and each of them took it personally when the other said or did something other than what they expected [ERROR OF OMNIPOTENCE].

It might be easy to try to turn this into a linear equation and trace it back to Anjie's committing the error of approach, but had Jake listened to what she said with compassion and openness, the miscommunication would have ended much sooner; so each, equally, played a role in the miscommunication. Even having one person in a relationship learn how to avoid the Five Errors can profoundly impact a relationship.

Will you wait for someone else in your life to learn the Five Errors, or will you take the initiative to focus on yourself and become dedicated to learning how you make them? We have found that those who spend time focusing on how others can change rarely see real changes in their lives. To the contrary, those who are able to constantly evaluate their own communication have the best chance to see their relationships (and often their lives) truly turn around. Focus on your own communication, and you will make far fewer errors along the way.

100 Five Errors of Communication Exercise

1. Give an example of a time when you made the error of approach.

_____

_____

_____

_____

_____

_____

2. Give an example of a time when you made the error of interpretation.

_____

_____

_____

_____

_____

_____

3. Give an example of a time when you made the error of judgment.

_____

_____

_____

_____

_____

_____

4. Give an example of a time when you made the error of language.
   _____
   _____
   _____
   _____
   _____
   _____
   _____

5. Give an example of a time when you made the error of omnipotence.
   _____
   _____
   _____
   _____
   _____
   _____
   _____

"We cannot fix what we don't know is broken."

**Personal challenge:
Communicate with good intentions.**

What Are We Responsible For Anyway?

A theory exists that says we all contribute to every interaction we have. This is to say that every time you talk to someone, both you and the other person have a part to play in the interaction. When two people communicate, each contributes something. Frequently we don't accept responsibility for the part we play. Many say things along the lines of, *"See, I knew he/she was to blame for that! He/she made me act like that!"* Statements like these where we tend to blame others entirely for miscommunication is a relatively immature interpretation of the interaction. A more mature position would be to consider your own behaviors.

Ask yourself:

- What did I do ineffectively when I interacted with that particular person?

- What could I do differently the next time I have an interaction with that person?

In life, we may not necessarily be responsible for the things that happen to us, but we are responsible for what we do in response to the things that happen to us. We are also responsible for how we manipulate things to our advantage. For example, we often minimize our role in incidents and interactions, whereas we tend to maximize other people's roles in similar situations. Human beings have a tendency to minimize the hurtful things they do to others, yet maximize the hurtful things others do to them.

As long as we minimize any negative or harmful behavior in our interactions, we get to convince ourselves that we are not really responsible for a detrimental relationship or a hurtful incident. If we can see the reality of the impact of what we have done, then we have the opportunity to change whatever we did that was ineffective.

Examples:

Minimizing/Maximizing:
"I might have raised my voice a little bit, but she was crazy screaming and out of control!"

"I might have raised my voice a little bit" is an example of minimizing, especially when, in the same statement, the person maximized the other person's loud voice as *"crazy screaming and out of control."*

Taking responsibility:
"I was angry and I lost self-control, so I screamed at her. I could have made a different decision. I could have chosen not to yell."

The person who minimizes what he did does not give himself a reason to change his behavior; therefore, he is likely to repeat the same type of behavior in the future. The person who takes responsibility for his/her behavior creates an opportunity to change his behavior and learn from the past.

Oftentimes, people will say, "but it's not fair, because he/she was screaming too." the reality is, however, that regardless of what others do, we are all ultimately only responsible for our own behavior. The more time you spend focusing on what others are saying or doing, the less time you have to focus on your own words and actions.

Responsibility Exercises

1. Briefly explain below a negative interaction you have had with someone.

   _____
   _____
   _____
   _____
   _____
   _____

2. Describe your role in the interaction, but **minimize** your responsibility. In other words, write down how it wasn't *really* your fault at all.

   _____
   _____
   _____
   _____
   _____
   _____

3. Now write down what you did ineffectively in the interaction, and this time, do **NOT** minimize your responsibility.

   _____
   _____
   _____
   _____
   _____
   _____

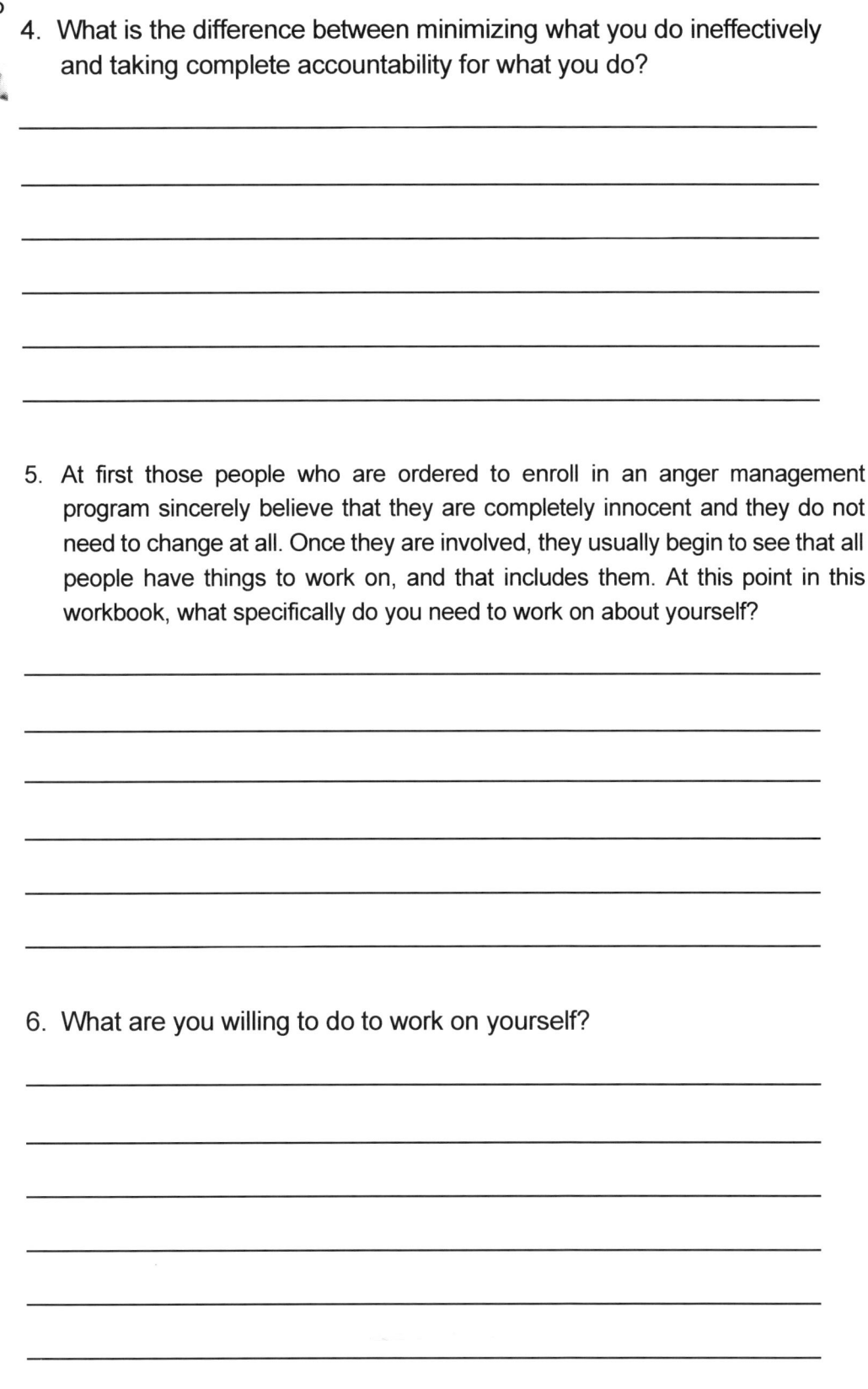

4. What is the difference between minimizing what you do ineffectively and taking complete accountability for what you do?

5. At first those people who are ordered to enroll in an anger management program sincerely believe that they are completely innocent and they do not need to change at all. Once they are involved, they usually begin to see that all people have things to work on, and that includes them. At this point in this workbook, what specifically do you need to work on about yourself?

6. What are you willing to do to work on yourself?

7. What do you believe might need to happen (or what steps do you think you need to take) for you to learn to accept responsibility more often in your life?

___

"We can only control ourselves. As long as we take full responsibility for what we do and how we interact with others, we have a great chance of being successful."

**Personal challenge:
Take responsibility for your own success.**

Wisdom in Five Years

A wise man and a foolish man were talking when the wise man said, "All my life I have changed so much. I have gone through different stages, learned from my mistakes, and now, even though I am in such a good place in my life, I realize I will always make changes; I will always be striving to be a better man than I am today." The foolish man looked at the man as though he was out of his mind and said, "Why would anyone ever want to change? I have always been right about everything. I never changed even one opinion about the world since I was 16 years-old. I know enough already. What's wrong with never changing?" The wise man simply just laughed. He knew the second was a fool.

Not many people would identify themselves with the foolish man. Still, so many of us have a difficult time admitting that we need to change; so many of us have troubles because we keep making the same mistakes. It is common for people to struggle with accepting responsibility for their part in negative interactions.

If you could go back and talk to yourself before every major mistake you made in life, what might you say to yourself? Would you want to go back multiple times to stop yourself from making the same (or similar) mistakes, or would you want to go back only once and teach yourself the wisdom and lessons that you learned, so that you don't keep repeating that same mistake?

Knowledge can be gained quickly. In the age of the Internet, anything can be looked up and found relatively fast. But wisdom comes over time. We cannot rush wisdom. The wisdom we've gained has come from years of living: we gain wisdom from making choices and learning from the experiences we had. We develop wisdom as we learn and grow; but we also sit on wisdom that we don't realize that we have.

When we step back and look at the big picture of our lives, we can listen to the voice of our own wisdom. The only constant in life is change, and dealing well with change takes an inner wisdom that all people are capable of experiencing. Wisdom is not about what other people can do differently; instead, it is about what we can do differently. To become wise takes demonstrating to ourselves and others that we are always open to change.

Wisdom Exercises

If you are in a spot in your life right now where you continue to look at how others have wronged you, or if you continue to see the faults in others but minimize your own faults, then this exercise will likely be difficult for you.

1. Imagine your life 5 years from now. Specifically, what kind of person do you want to be in five years?

   _____
   _____
   _____
   _____
   _____

2. Write down how you will be different or how you will have grown in five years.

   _____
   _____
   _____
   _____
   _____
   _____

3. Who will be the first to notice you are different?

   _____
   _____
   _____
   _____
   _____

4. How will others be able to tell that you are different in five years?

___

5. How are you different right now from five years ago?

___

6. If you had a time machine, and could go back five years, what wisdom do you think you would help yourself uncover?

___

7. In five years, what will you be able to say that you learned about who you are right now?

___

8. It takes courage to admit when we are wrong. It takes courage to look at ourselves rather than blaming the outside world for our lives. What do you need to work on most over the next five years to help yourself get to where you want to be?

9. What will stop you from working on what you need to do? What will stop you from listening to your own inner wisdom?

"Remember that the decisions you make today will impact the person you are tomorrow."

Personal challenge:
Make choices today that you'll be proud of tomorrow.

Imitation:
A Form of Flattery, a Form of Truth

A person who is trapped in anger usually has no idea how he or she comes across to others. Understanding how others see us is a profoundly important step to changing our ineffective behaviors. People who do not have any idea of how others perceive them or would imitate them tend to struggle the longest with the same issues.

When people train to become professional counselors, they have to videotape themselves in session with others. Most often, when they watch themselves on video, they learn quickly that how they are coming across to others is very different from how they thought they were being perceived. The same is true of actors. Actors are taught to practice, practice, practice, because how they are perceived is often much different from how they were attempting to portray themselves.

We don't typically have cameras following us every moment of our lives, so instead of learning from videotaped interactions, we can learn by imagining how others might imitate us. Imitation can be a form of flattery, definitely, but it can also be a form of truth. In other words, there can be some truth to every imitation. When others imitate us, they reveal their perception of us. From such an exercise, we would have the opportunity to learn a lot about ourselves.

How we see ourselves in our mind is often different than how we actually come across to others. After all, how many times have we believed that our words and actions meant what we intended, whereas others experienced our words and actions differently? When that happens, we can do one of two things: insist that the other person's experience of us was wrong, and do nothing to change our behavior, or we can accept someone else's experience of us, learn from it, and grow as individuals.

Imitation Exercises

If we are afraid to be imitated, what does that teach us about ourselves? Does it mean we are taking ourselves too seriously? If we cannot handle how someone imitates us, what does that teach us about ourselves? Are we being too sensitive? In this exercise, you are going to imagine that people are able to imitate you. We want you to try to imagine your communication with others from their perspective.

1. If the person you are currently in a relationship with (or the person from your most recent relationship) were going to imitate how you come across to others when you are angry, what would they do?

   _____
   _____
   _____
   _____
   _____
   _____
   _____
   _____

2. If your friends were going to imitate you when you are being a jerk, how would they imitate what you say or do?

   _____
   _____
   _____
   _____
   _____
   _____
   _____

3. If your co-workers/boss/employees were going to imitate you, how would they imitate what you say or do when you interact with them and others at work?

_____

_____

_____

_____

_____

_____

4. If your children (or other people's children if you do not have your own), were to imitate you, how would they replicate what you say or do?

_____

_____

_____

_____

_____

_____

5. If your relatives were going to imitate you, how would they impersonate what you say or do?

_____

_____

_____

_____

_____

_____

6. If strangers were going to imitate you, how would they mimic what you say or do?

7. If your ex-partner were going to imitate you, how would he/she imitate what you say or do?

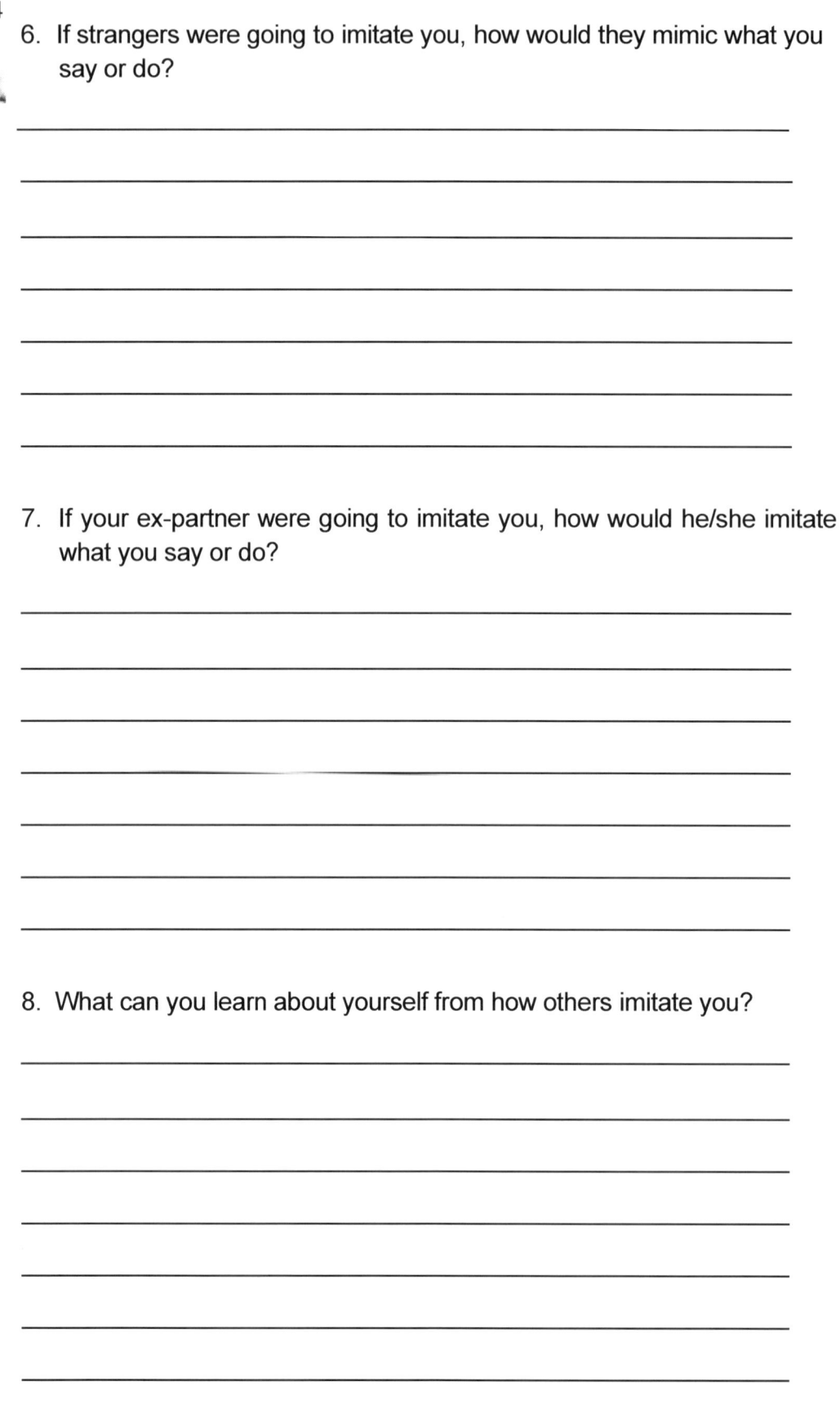

8. What can you learn about yourself from how others imitate you?

9. Are you kinder to strangers than you are to your loved ones? If you answered yes, then you are like most people. Strangely enough, we tend to be kind to strangers because we want them to perceive us the way we want to be perceived rather than the way we really are. What can you do to begin to that change?

_____
_____
_____
_____
_____
_____

"People who are closest to us see us at our worst. Why not give them our best?"

Personal challenge:
Be kind to those who are closest to you.

Hurt People Hurt

When any of us are hurting, we have a tendency to take it out on others. In other words, when we are hurt, we usually hurt someone else. If we can find and deal with the real hurt, we can stop the cycle that occurs when "hurt people hurt."

Our work has taught us that people who live in shame act out of shame. If I truly believe that I am a worthless, bad, evil, abusive, or mean person, then why should I make an effort to live differently? A cycle of shame exists when people feel hurt and shame. First they make a mistake or do something they are not proud of; second, they feel a sense of shame; third, they act out of anger to cover the shame - then they feel bad about what they've done and feel more shame, so the cycle continues.

Figure 17.1 Cycle of shame

If we don't learn to let go of the shame that we feel, we are likely to repeat the same types of behaviors that can keep us locked in the cycle of shame for a long time. Finding a way to forgive ourselves, move beyond the shame, and let go of the past is important to making big changes in our lives.

4. What things have you told *yourself* as a result of your being hurt?

_____

_____

_____

_____

_____

_____

_____

5. How has what you told yourself impacted your behavior through the years?

_____

_____

_____

_____

_____

_____

_____

6. How have you reacted to others as a result of being hurt?

_____

_____

_____

_____

_____

_____

_____

Charley's story...

As a child, Charley was abused by his parents and molested by a relative. For many years, he felt like it was his fault. He was told repeatedly that he "messed up," that he was "worthless," and that he "couldn't do anything right." Charley watched his father abuse his mother through his entire childhood, that is, until his father had a heart attack and died when Charley was 10. His mother told him his father "died because he had to stress about Charley's bad behavior all the time." His whole life, Charley felt shame.

As he grew up, Charley was used to being told he was "worthless" so many times, that that he began to act with devaluated worth. He found himself selling drugs to middle school children when he was in his twenties; he found himself beating up an elderly man over a trivial parking lot incident by the time he was 30. He said his wife called him a "bastard" because "that's what he is," and before he knew it, he became violent with her. He would push his wife, stand overtop of her, and constantly intimidate her – and he consistently blamed her for "why he had to act that way." In short, Charley was living almost entirely in shame.

When Charley began to release some of the shame he felt as a child, the releasing had a reverberating effect, and with time and effort, he began to see the good in himself. Once he saw the good in himself, others started to notice it as well. For Charley, it took him many years to find his authentic self and be the man he always had the potential to be.

From Charley's story, the real question is for you: *What shame do you need to rid yourself of so that you can live from your deeper, authentic, and true self?*

Hurt People Hurt Exercise – Part 2

1. How can you change your perspective on your hurt to help yourself get over some of the pain you felt as a child?

   _____
   _____
   _____
   _____
   _____
   _____
   _____

2. What can you do to get over some of the pain you felt as a teenager?

   _____
   _____
   _____
   _____
   _____
   _____
   _____

3. What thought processes can you use to help you get over some of the hurt you have felt as an adult?

   _____
   _____
   _____
   _____
   _____
   _____

4. What can you tell yourself differently that could help you face the world differently?

___

5. How would you treat others if you felt internal peace instead of hurt?

___

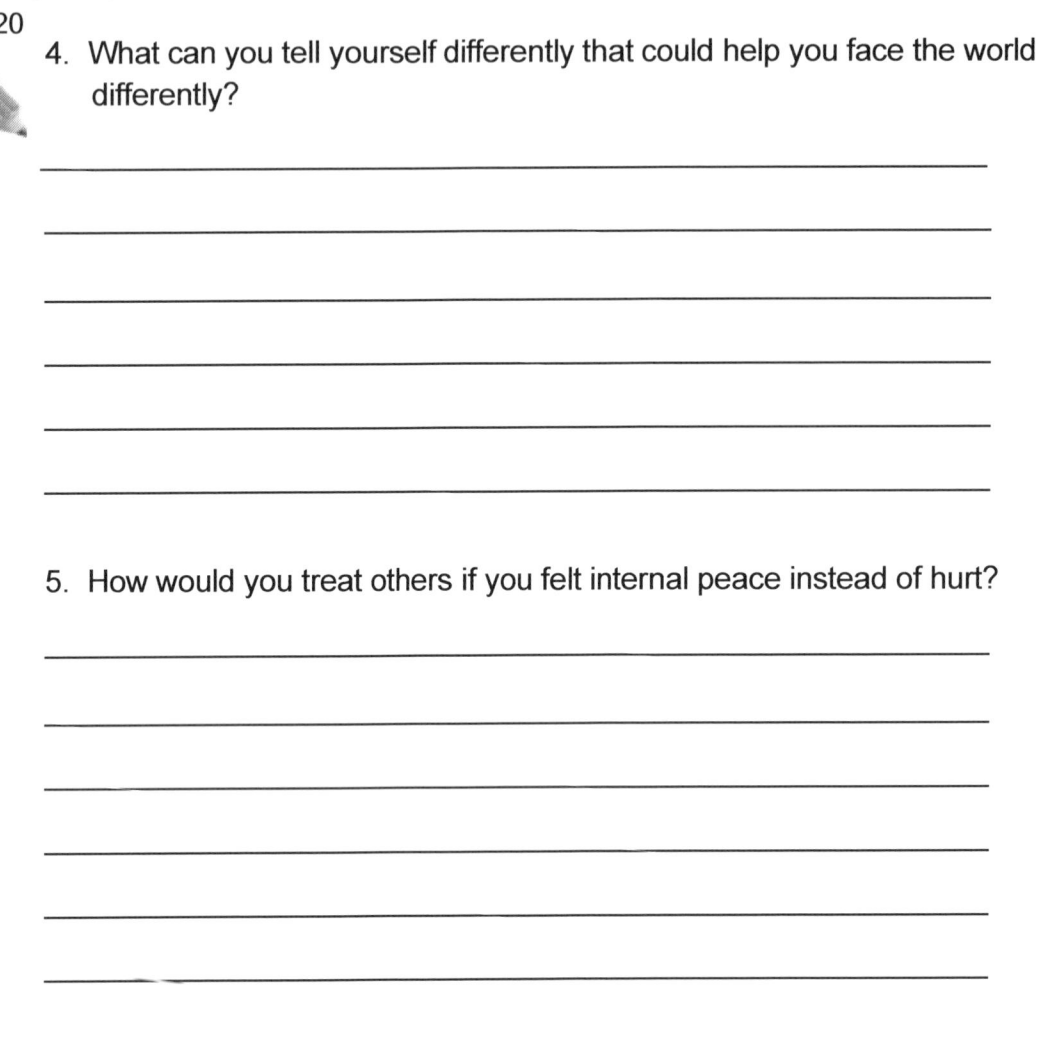

"When we live in shame, we act out of shame."

Personal challenge:
Choose to leave shame behind

Stories We Tell Ourselves About The World

Many times, there is a difference between how the world is and what we actually see. The difference is that sometimes the story we tell ourselves about the world just doesn't match up to the way things are. For example, if you routinely say (to yourself or others) that *"people are stupid,"* then you likely see a lot of examples of people being stupid in your everyday life. If, on the other hand, you routinely say that, "people are mostly kind," then you likely most often see people that way. The story we tell ourselves about the world determines in large part how we actually see the world.

When it comes to anger, we often find ourselves seeing situations from only one perspective. In fact, one sure way to stay very angry is to not allow yourself to ever see a particular situation from anything but your own perspective. The more we stay locked into our own view of the world, the less opportunity we give ourselves to grow as individuals – and by only seeing our own perspective, we certainly do not give ourselves an opportunity to stop being angry.

The Story of Hate/Love

There was once a man who seemed to eternally feel sorry for himself. Whatever happened in a day, in his view, happened "to him." One day, as he was driving to a job interview, he encountered a traffic jam. The traffic was so backed up, that people eventually just shut off their cars. The man could not believe such an event could happen to him.

"Of all days!" he lamented. *"How can this happen to me?"* He sat in his car and a repeatedly hit his steering wheel. He kept his car running and continually edged up half-inch by half-inch to a car that was completely shut off in front of him. He would press his car horn and hold it for long moments.

People got out of their cars and, as intrigued as they were as to what happened that slowed up the traffic, so too, were they intrigued to watch this man. He screamed and cursed the traffic, the people around him, and whatever 'idiot' ruined his day by making him late. He repeated to himself over and over that *"life sucks"* and that *"he can't stand it anymore!"* until he eventually wished the most intense evil on whoever was the cause of this accident. He sat in his misery, anger, and rage. He sat in hate.

A man in another car less than 100 feet ahead of him, also sat in the same traffic jam. This man was also late to a job interview. This man desperately needed a job, but when he encountered the traffic jam and slowed his car to a stop, he immediately recognized that something serious must have happened to someone for traffic to be backed up this much. He imagined that there must have been a bad accident and he began to say to himself, *"I hope everyone is okay. I really hope no one died from this accident,"* and *"I feel so bad that something like this happened to someone today."* He sat in reflection and meditation for anyone who might be hurting in that moment. He sat in love.

Although both men would be late for their interviews, the second man aligned his feeling with reality: He knew he could not change being late, but he also knew that something beyond his control had happened and that something more serious than missing an interview had happened to someone else. In a complex world with seven billion people, incidents in the lives of others will occasionally become incidents in our own lives—but those incidents are not intentionally aimed at disrupting our lives. Our involvement is coincidental, not intended as an act against us personally.

Hate and love are not concepts that are outside of us. Hate and love live within the self-talk of each of us.

The story we tell ourselves can make or break any given situation. The stories that we tell ourselves when we are being foolish only include our side, and they keep us trapped in anger. The wise are able to recognize, even in the moment, that every situation has more than one side to it. The more we practice seeing other people's stories, the broader our stories become. The broader our stories become, the better we are able to handle our anger.

Stories We Tell Ourselves Exercise

1. Describe a recent interaction you had with someone when you were really angry.

   _____
   _____
   _____
   _____
   _____
   _____
   _____

2. Describe the *same interaction* from the other person's point of view.

   _____
   _____
   _____
   _____
   _____
   _____
   _____

3. If you were to write the story of your life from this day forward, how would you write your story?

   _____
   _____
   _____
   _____
   _____
   _____
   _____

4. Adventure stories captivate us, whereas a story with no action is usually relatively boring. If you had to write about your life as though it was an adventure story, and you had to identify obstacles that will get in the way of your path, what would those obstacles be?

___

5. How will you get around the obstacles you will face?

___

6. How would you like your story to end?

___

Social Learning

We know that children learn much more from what they watch adults do than from what adults tell them. If we are smokers, then we can tell our children all we want not to smoke, but the odds are, they will smoke one day. The same is true of all of our actions and habits, both healthy and unhealthy. Even as adults, we learn more from watching others than from listening.

"Social learning" is the idea that people learn from what they see more so than learning from what they hear or are told. We are constantly learning by watching others. Others are equally learning by watching us. Sometimes we wish others weren't watching us – especially when we are at our worst. Unfortunately, the world is the way the world is, and sometimes people do see us when we are not at our best.

Intentions are different than actions. We may have all the best intentions in the world, but if our behavior isn't consistent with those intentions, then it matters little what we "intended to do." Just as you have learned a lot about people by watching what they've done, so too, have others learned a lot about you by watching your behaviors.

Science behind the idea:
Our brains are able to do all that they do because of nerve cells called "neurons." One type of neuron that we have is something called a "mirror neuron" (located primarily in our premotor cortex). Mirror neurons become active when we are just watching something. For instance, one reason we love to follow the main stars in action movies is because with every move they make, we are making the same move (in our brains).

Mirror neurons enable us to learn vicariously. Mirror neurons are the reason that athletes all over the world watch the best in their sport do what they do. By watching, their brains are visualizing performing the task. We can learn simply by watching. We can experience just by watching. Mirror neurons can drive behavior.

Social learning happens in part because even on an unconscious level, our brains are always learning when we are watching. Pretty cool, huh? Yes, but there is a downside: Children can learn harmful behavior by watching adults lose self control, become angry, or even become violent.

People see our actions, not our intentions

Regardless of how badly we might wish others could see our intentions, the reality is that people can only ever see our actions. You might have had the best of intentions in mind when you yelled at someone recently, but that person didn't see your intentions, he or she only saw your actions. Once you learn that people only see your actions, you can begin to spend less time justifying your behaviors, and instead spend more time changing the behaviors that others see. Remember: people see our actions, not our intentions, so choose to act in ways that fit with how you really want the world to see you.

127 Social Learning Exercise

In this exercise, reflect on the things that people might have learned about the world by watching you.

1. What have you learned about the world by *watching others*?

   _____
   _____
   _____
   _____
   _____
   _____

2. What have other people learned about the world by *watching you* over this past year?

   _____
   _____
   _____
   _____
   _____
   _____

3. What have people learned about the world from *watching you* over your lifetime?

   _____
   _____
   _____
   _____
   _____

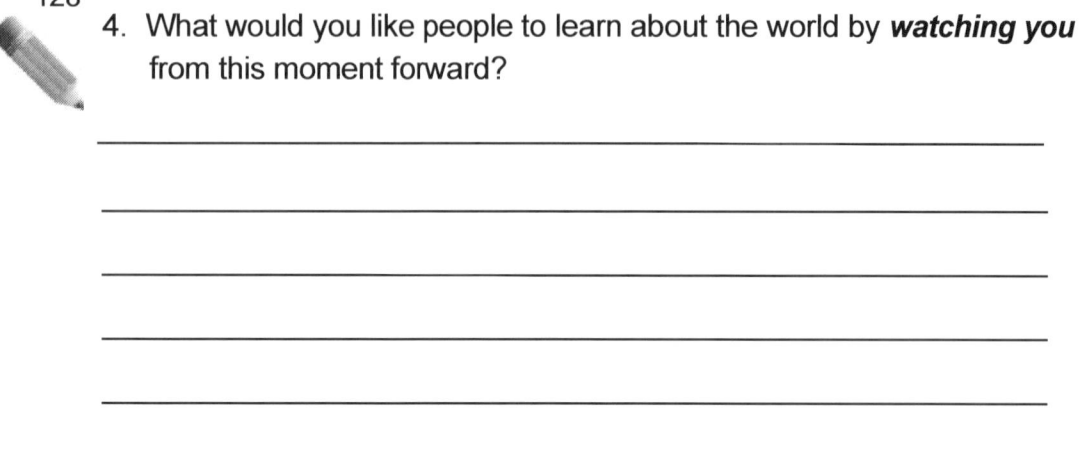

4. What would you like people to learn about the world by *watching you* from this moment forward?

_____

_____

_____

_____

_____

_____

*"We learn what we see. We teach what we do.
By watching us, others learn about the world."*

**Personal challenge:
Be what the world needs.**

Time Changes Everything

One day, age will catch up to all of us. There will be a time when our bodies no longer allow us to do what we are now able to do. Consider what happens to men. As they age, they have less testosterone flowing through them and actually do not even have the physical ability to be as angry as they were when they were younger. All people's brain chemistry changes over time, and all emotions change with time, too.

Think about something that you were mad about as a young person. Remember how important it was to you? Remember how you did not believe there could be anything else in the world other than the feelings you had in that moment? Think about how all that has faded. Think about how differently you see that situation now.

Whatever you are experiencing right now will change in some way. Human beings have about an eight-minute attention span. That means regardless of whatever is going on in our lives, some other thought, even if only briefly, will enter our minds within eight minutes. In most situations, at a minimum, thoughts regarding our basic needs (hunger, thirst, sleep) will enter our minds, albeit briefly. Over time, however, other thoughts will consume more space in our minds, and whatever we feel intense emotion around will eventually lessen.

Change is constant. Whatever perspective we have right now will be different one week from now, one year from now, and 50 years from now. The quest is for us to be able to be mindful that when our perspective changes, our emotions will change as well. Knowing this, we can be empowered to change our perspective to change our emotions sooner than later.

Cool scientific fact:

Psychologists use the term, *"fading affect bias"* to describe the phenomenon that, over time, our brain loses intensity for negative memories faster than it does for positive ones. So what does such "fading" amount to? Simply this: Now we know scientifically that *time really does change everything!*

Time Changes Everything Exercise

For this exercise, consider that one day you will have to change your perspective on life, because your body will force you to do so.

1. When I am 90 years old, I really hope that I am **not** ...

   _____
   _____
   _____
   _____
   _____
   _____

2. In 5 years, I hope that I **am** ...

   _____
   _____
   _____
   _____
   _____
   _____

3. The biggest internal conflict that I struggle with is ...

   _____
   _____
   _____
   _____
   _____
   _____

4. The internal thoughts that I have struggled with most throughout my life have been…

_____

_____

_____

_____

_____

_____

5. Something I struggled with years ago that no longer affects me in any way was…

_____

_____

_____

_____

_____

_____

"Nothing lasts forever: Time changes everything."

Personal challenge:
Learn to welcome the changes in your life.

Cycle of Violence

Tension   Explosion   Honeymoon

Figure V.4 The cycle of violence is as follows: Tension builds in the relationship. When the tension becomes too much, an explosion takes place. Sometime shortly after an explosion, people regret or feel sorry for their explosion, so they apologize and make promises of the explosion never happening again. The other person doesn't want to be in pain anymore, so a "honeymoon" ensues; but honeymoons cannot last forever. Expectations come crashing right back in shortly after the honeymoon, so the tension mounts and the cycle begins again anew.

Tension comes from many different places. Tension can develop when people develop unrealistic expectations for each other or fail to communicate with each other. People think, "I wanted her/him to do X, but they did Y instead." Consider the following situation involving a man named Jack. Jack's wife was 9 months pregnant and had just stopped working. Jack would come home at the end of the workday expecting her to have cleaned the house. When he discovered that the house had not been cleaned, he would be furious and think that he worked all day, and from his perspective, she "did nothing." Some days he wouldn't say anything, he would just let the tension build. She could sense something was wrong because he gave her limited eye contact and didn't speak to her much. The tension built….

> **Spotlight on the Tension Phase**
>
> The tension phase in the cycle of violence is very significant, yet it's often the most overlooked phase. We tend to underestimate how damaging the tension phase is because it is like pinpricks. Though annoying, we can handle individual pinpricks. When they are over, we think, "Well that was annoying but not the end of the world." Therefore, we continue to put up with them, without dealing with them, until they build up so much that we can no longer take it and we explode.
>
> Learning to address the tension when it happens is so important. The sooner that we learn how to deal with the individual "pinpricks," the sooner we can stop them from happening again. We can rely on assertiveness to deal with the pinpricks and lessen the frequency of them occurring. If however, we allow the pinpricks to happen too much, we are left resorting to aggression over assertiveness, and it's aggression that hurts others and gets us in trouble.

Explosions come when people "can no longer take it." Such explosions of anger can include everything from the most extreme cases, which result in death, to hitting, kicking, choking, pushing or otherwise being physically violent with someone, to screaming, intimidating, punching walls or throwing objects to express the anger. Explosions are serious, dangerous, and catch the attention of everyone involved.

The honeymoon is the attempt to make up for the explosion. In the honeymoon phase, promises are made that "things will never get that bad again." The promises may be heartfelt and genuine. The problem is that changes rarely come from simply regretting what one has done. Instead, real change comes from introspection, education on how to be different in the relationship, and a dedication to practicing new habits.

Spotlight on the Honeymoon Phase

When we make promises in the honeymoon phase, we tend to actually believe the promises we make. Recall from the scale of consciousness that shame is the lowest form of consciousness. When in a place of regret and shame, we tend to do whatever we can to get out of it, including promising the world. The other part of those promises is this: remember that the potential for everything great and everything terrible lies within all of us. When we are at our worst (experiencing the terrible within us), it is possible that our psyche opens us up to seeing the best (the potential for everything good inside of us), so we make promises from a place of hope.

The problem is that promises, no matter how well-intentioned, are not something we can follow through with until we create the skills that are necessary to go along with the words that we say. If we make promises from a place of hope, but remain in the same negative life patterns, then it is not likely that any real changes will be made. We need to make promises from a place of hope to begin a new process, rather than promising the results. In doing so we not only dedicate ourselves to that process of introspection, education, and practicing new habits, but we then are much more likely to follow through with those promises.

Watch out for that *foot-in-the-water-principle* that we described earlier in the workbook! Remember that if you only change based off whether or not others also change, then you will continue to place control of your life outside of yourself. Change rarely happens when we expect others to do the changing for us. If you really want to break your cycle of violence, dedicate yourself to changing yourself for you. Resist making promises to "never do things again." Instead, by your actions, show your loved ones that you are willing to look deeply at your own life. Change will happen in that case.

Our experience has shown us that as people enter an anger management program and are still in the heat of the punishment for their behaviors, they are quick to make promises, and they even seem to genuinely want to change. The problem we have equally encountered is that people have a tendency to believe that "wanting" to make a change is equivalent to *"actually"* making a change. Wanting change and actually changing are two very different things. People can earnestly want change, but it takes time to break ingrained behavioral patterns.

The cycle of violence is called a *cycle* because, if left unchecked, the behaviors can continue for a lifetime. More than half a century of research has determined that cycles can be passed from generation to generation, and whereas that can be viewed as "hopeless," we prefer to think of it as "awe-inspiring." We see an immense possibility for change in the sense that one person's commitment to positive changes has the potential to impact many others. By breaking the cycle of violence, a person can change him or herself, as well as positively impact generations to come in his or her family.

Cycle of Violence Exercise – Part 1

1. What do you think the cycle of violence looks like from the victim's perspective?

   _____
   _____
   _____
   _____
   _____
   _____
   _____

2. Why do you think people stay in violent relationships?

   _____
   _____
   _____
   _____
   _____
   _____
   _____

3. If you were working with victims of violence everyday, how do you think that might affect your perspective?

   _____
   _____
   _____
   _____
   _____
   _____
   _____

4. Write down specifically what your cycle of violence looks like.

_____

_____

_____

_____

_____

_____

_____

5. If you went to see a wise guru on some mountaintop, what do you think he or she might say to you about what you wrote above?

_____

_____

_____

_____

_____

_____

_____

Cycle of Violence Exercise – Part 2

Knowing others requires intelligence. Knowing yourself requires wisdom. The entire essence of this workbook is about gaining self-awareness. When it comes to our own patterns of violence, knowing what they are is the first step to breaking them. Consider the past incidences of violence in your relationships. Be mindful that violence can be everything from intentional silent treatment, to screaming at others, to physically hurting others. Consider patterns of behavior that have emerged in your relationships. With your patterns of behavior in mind, answer the following questions.

1. My Tension Building Phase looks like this.
   (These are things that make your tension rise.)

   _____
   _____
   _____
   _____
   _____

2. My Explosion Phase looks like this.
   (When you lose control, you look like or do this.)

   _____
   _____
   _____
   _____
   _____
   _____

3. My Honeymoon Phase looks like this. (Things that you say and promise)

_____
_____
_____
_____
_____
_____
_____

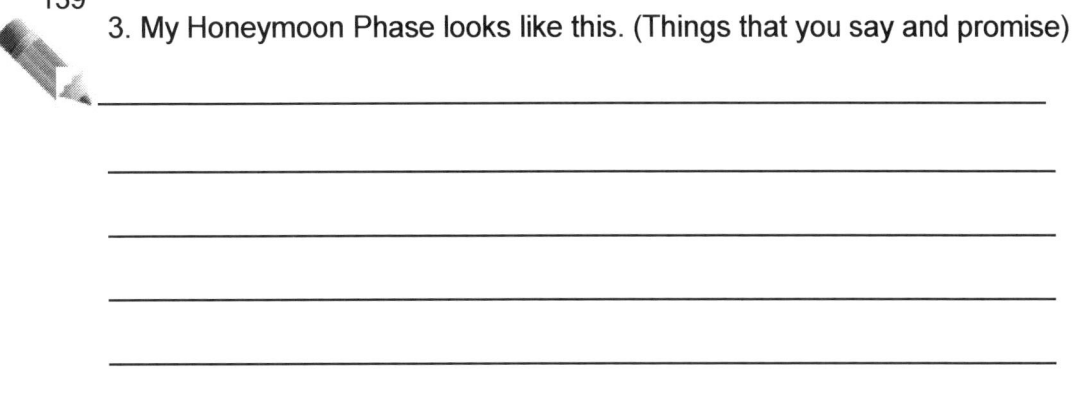

Choose to change your cycle of violence: or at least be aware that you are choosing to continue it.

Personal challenge:
Break the negative patterns in your life.

The Many Faces of Me

Trans means "across;" *action* refers to "behaviors;" and *analysis* is a really fancy term for "looking at things." Transactional Analysis (TA) is a way to look at how people interact with each other. The premise of TA is that everyone lives in and out of three different ego states (or "states of being") all the time, and the ego state of one person affects the ego state of other people. The three ego states are:

Critical Parent: Critical
Nurturing Parent: Loving

The parent is the part of us that learned to be either critical or nurturing

Adult: Rational

The adult is the reasonable part of us that is always willing to learn

Hurt Child: Wounded
Fun Child: Pleased

The child is the part of us that seems to want to either have a ton of fun, or just hold on to pain

141 Many Faces of Me Exercise

1. When I am in my Critical Parent, these are the types of things I tend to say and do.

_____
_____
_____
_____
_____
_____

2. When I am in my Nurturing Parent, these are the types of things I tend to say and do.

_____
_____
_____
_____
_____
_____

3. When I am in my Hurt Child, these are the types of things I tend to say and do.

_____
_____
_____
_____
_____
_____

The Anger Management Workbook, The Program that Changes Lives

4. When I am in my Fun Child, these are the types of the things I tend to say and do.

5. When I am in my Critical Parent, others around me…

6. When I am in my Hurt Child, others around me…

7. When I am in my Adult Phase, I am able to see others as…

_____
_____
_____
_____
_____
_____
_____

Personal challenge:
    Catch yourself being critical of others.

Types of Abuse

Abuse is a very difficult concept to address. When the word "abuse" comes up, people tend to become very cautious and defensive. We believe that the reason this occurs is that many times a person may commit an act of violence and be unaware that it is defined as such. Knowing the definitions of different types of abuse, examples of each, and figuring out which types you may have used to control others are all steps toward removing violence from your life. The types of "abuse" are as follows.

1. **Physical Abuse:** *Using physical force against your partner*

    Examples: pushing, kicking, dragging, holding down, restraining, throwing objects, grabbing, squeezing, pulling hair, twisting arm, suffocating, choking, pushing out of car

Physical Abuse

Dominic was furious with Ashley. When she said she was leaving, he stood in front of her and refused to allow her to get to the door. When she attempted to go beyond him to the door anyway, he pushed her to the ground. She tried again to leave. Again, he grabbed her arms and squeezed tightly while saying, "Why are you making me do this?"

When Dominic was arrested he adamantly insisted he did nothing wrong. He believed it was the "system that was crooked." When he first discussed the experience in his anger management group, he said bewildered, "What else could I have possibly done?" Robert, a senior group member, who also happened to be twice the size of Dominic, said, "You could have stepped aside and let her go." Dominic replied, albeit respectfully to his fellow group member, "But I didn't want her to go." The other man leaned in and said compassionately, "Brother, just because you didn't want her to go doesn't mean you have the right to make her stay. You don't get to just use force to say what you want without facing the consequences."

Robert was right. We do not get to just use physical force to emphasize what we want to say without facing consequences. More than that, however, is the very real understanding that regardless of how badly you want to, you can never make someone feel a certain way about you. Physical abuse ranges from the intentional spectrum of hitting, kicking, and pushing, to "unintentionally" physically harming another person in any way. Unintentional physical abuse is usually described by culprits as "accidental." **Regardless of a person's intentions, any physical force constitutes physical abuse.**

2. **Emotional Abuse:** *Any psychological harm*

   Examples: embarrassing her/him in front of others, creates crisis to gain attention, forcing partner to live with drugs and alcohol, constant demands on time, only allows seeing your friends and not hers/his, no relief and help with work, threatening, suicide attempts, not giving your partner any privacy, exhibiting unpredictable behavior, giving the silent treatment, physically withdrawing, constant phone calls

   Emotional Abuse

   Bryson admitted the silent treatment to manipulate Carlos. Ann admitted to a counselor that there was gratification in watching Carlos drown in his "worst fears" and negative projections. By intentionally using silent treatment, Ann was able to control Carlos and exhibit emotional abuse.

   Tony threatened Mary repeatedly. He would tell her that he was going to kill himself and that it would be her fault. He would say that if she left him he wouldn't go on, and she felt constantly trapped to stay in the relationship. By threatening Mary, Tony was able to control Mary and exhibit emotional abuse.

   Jon was open to listening to Taylor. He listened very well to what she would say. The problem wasn't his listening; it was what he did with the information. He remembered every negative thing Taylor ever told him about her family, and he would use all of it to convince her to not contact them, thereby isolating her through emotional abuse.

Amanda never respected Parker's time. She would call him incessantly at work, regardless of his asking her not to because he was already fired once due to her doing so. If Parker would even say hello to another girl in public, Amanda would scream at him and embarrass him, thereby exhibiting emotional abuse.

3. **Sexual Abuse:** *Any unwanted or unsolicited physical contact*

   Examples: Rape, wanting/forcing sex after abuse (to make sure she/he accepts apology), forcing sexual acts, forced pregnancy, withholding sex with the intent to control partner

Sexual Abuse

Bryson admitted that he would force sex on his girlfriend to make sure she would accept his apology and forgive him. He would even tell her, "You can't be mad! We already had sex. That issue is over!" He admitted that he reached a point where he would use sex as a way to "seal an argument" and move on.

When Bryson was asked by his counselor to describe any times when his girlfriend did something hurtful to him, he was quick to talk about how "she flirted with another guy at a club last year." Bryson was then asked when the last time he had sex with her was. "Last night," he said.

The counselor replied, "So you're telling me that you had sex last night, and this flirting with another guy happened a year ago?"

"That's right," Bryson said.

"Well I'm just a little confused," replied his counselor, "If having sex seals the argument so it can never be brought up again, how is it possible you still remember her hurting you any time before last night?"

Bryson saw how he believed it was okay for sex to seal the argument on the things he did that were hurtful to her, but sex certainly did not seal the argument on anything she ever did to hurt him. And Bryson's story is fairly common.

Sexual abuse happens on a continuum. The worst is rape. On the same continuum, however, is using sex as a tool to control another person, thereby engaging in sexual abuse.

4. **Financial Abuse:** *Any manipulation done through monetary means to gain power and control*

   Examples: taking money away from your partner, taking full control of banking, making all the bills in only your name, not letting partner have any money of her own, selling partner's things, destroying partner's belongings that she/he worked for, never giving enough money for your part of the bills, putting your wants before your family's needs, making partner account for every dime spent, not allowing partner to go to work, spending food money on alcohol and drugs, forcing partner to deprive children

   Financial abuse

   When Gavin first met his first wife, she was in an incredible amount of debt. He came into her life and "saved" her, as he would later report. He paid off her debts, and the two of them were married. Gavin never put his wife's name on any bank account, mortgage, or car loan with him, and he justified it by saying how "bad she was with money."

   Gavin told himself that he was taking complete control of the finances because it was in his wife's best interest for him to do it, but what he didn't realize is that his wife came to view herself as a prisoner in their home. She had to ask for money for everything from buying groceries to gasoline, and any money that was spent on anything he didn't "approve" would cause big arguments.

   Their relationship worked at first for two very important reasons:

she needed someone to help her, and he needed to feel in control. He would later admit that he felt in some way that he "owned her," because he knew how much debt he relieved for her. But it took Gavin a long time to admit to the control he had over her with money.

Gavin struggled for months with considering what he did as abusive behavior. Then, one day Gavin showed up to his anger management group and shared this:

"I hated when Doc called what I did 'financial abuse.' I used to get so angry because I always figured I was just doing her a favor. But then after I got out of prison, I had nothing, and time and again I had to ask people for money for the smallest stuff. I felt like a little kid again… And that's when it hit me – that must be how she felt – like a little kid who had to come ask 'dad' for permission to spend any money. I didn't want to be her dad. I wanted to be her husband. But I also wanted assurance that she would never leave me."

Gavin's realization was powerful because it enabled him to begin changing. Because of his talent in business, it wasn't long before he was back to making a tremendous amount of money, and his next wife's name was on everything with his; he saw them as partners, as equals… and his new relationship was the best of his life.

5. Verbal Abuse: *Trying to gain power and control through verbal attacks on partner*

Examples: yelling at, putting your partner down in general, calling names (body parts, objects, etc.), talking down to your partner, putting down your partner's appearance, threatening to take children away, cussing at your partner, telling your partner no one else would want her/him, threatening to kill, belittling things that are important to your partner

Verbal Abuse

Melinda constantly told George that he "wasn't a real man." She talked condescendingly to him, called him names, and made fun of any hobby he liked. She did all of that in hopes of gaining control over him. By making him feel worthless, she hoped that he would never leave her.

She admitted that she learned how to be in a relationship by watching her mother do the same things to her father. She hated it then, and didn't like that that's how she turned out to act in her relationship. Melinda was quick to admit that she was verbally abusive to George, but she struggled a great deal with being able to stop.

She would come in for counseling week after week and say something along the lines of, "I only messed up a couple times this week." The problem is that we remember those "mess-ups" more than we remember the moments where we finally have reprieve. The verbal abuse sticks with us for a very long time.

Melinda's story is not a success story. She dropped out of counseling still reporting weekly that she continued her verbal assaults on George. But Melinda story is an important one, because it highlights that simply being aware that you are being verbally abusive is not enough. Owning up to being verbally abusive, while an important step, is not enough.

To stop being verbally abuse, we have to take the action step of no longer trying to control others with aggressive words.

Though it is true that all people are searching for control, these types of abuse are specifically termed "abuse" because they are used in an attempt to control and dominate a partner. People rarely want to consider themselves "abusers," despite that the same people would be quick to label others who do the same behaviors as such. The label "abuser" is largely an ineffective term to use with someone because it brings up a defensiveness that tends to lead to justifying actions, rather than openly evaluating them.

We discourage labeling people in general because labels rarely tell the entire story of anyone. In place of labeling people as "abusers," we assess particular behaviors as "abusive" behaviors. All of these behaviors stem from a place of desperation. When people cannot get what they want, they do desperate things to grasp for that control.

There is a tendency for people to justify, rationalize, or minimize all of these types of behaviors. The challenge with justifying, rationalizing, or minimizing is that change is not likely to happen until ineffective and hurtful behaviors are seen for what they are. Though it can be extraordinarily difficult for some people to own up to having done some of these behaviors, we strongly encourage you to look at the definitions of each. Be honest with yourself about which of these you may have done in the past.

We may knowingly or unknowingly engage in abusive behaviors. More often than not, people have a tough time recognizing their behaviors as "abusive." In general, we have found that people's first reaction to having the word "abusive" linked with their behaviors triggers a defensiveness that leads to denial.

It is important for us that as you read the descriptions of these behaviors. Please take note, we are naming the behaviors "abusive," we are not defining people as "abusers."

Types of Abuse Exercise – Part 1

Physical Abuse:
Using physical force against your partner

Examples: pushing, kicking, dragging, holding down, restraining, throwing objects, grabbing, squeezing, pulling hair, twisting arm, suffocating, choking, pushing out of car

1. Describe any instances where you physically hurt another person in a relationship without giving any reasons or justifications for why it happened (just provide as many details of the physical part as possible, as you will have an opportunity to provide your justifications in #2).

   _____
   _____
   _____
   _____
   _____
   _____

2. Write down the justifications or "your side" to the situation.

   _____
   _____
   _____
   _____
   _____
   _____

3. After looking at #1 and #2 in print, do you believe that your justification excuses your action?

   Circle one: Yes   No

People are not arrested for thoughts, but they do face consequences for how they act on their thoughts. We encourage you to avoid the "yes-but game" (described in the Introduction) and focus instead on the actual changes that would benefit you to make.

Emotional Abuse:
Any psychological harm

Examples: embarrassing her/him in front of others, creates crisis to gain attention, forcing partner to live with drugs and alcohol, constant demands on time, only allows seeing your friends and not hers/his, no relief and help with work, threatening, suicide attempts, not giving your partner any privacy, exhibiting unpredictable behavior, giving the silent treatment, physically withdrawing, constant phone calls

1. Describe instances where you have exhibited behavior that is considered emotional abuse.

   _____

   _____

   _____

   _____

   _____

2. Write down the reasons why you believe you had to be emotionally abusive.

   _____

   _____

   _____

   _____

3. After seeing it written down, can you see that there could have been another way to approach the situation other than emotional abuse? Describe what else you could have said or done instead of doing the things that are considered emotional abuse.

___

Sexual Abuse:
Any unwanted or unsolicited physical contact

Examples: Rape, wanting/forcing sex after abuse (to make sure she/he accepts apology), forcing sexual acts, forced pregnancy, withholding sex to control your partner

1. Describe any instances where you exhibited behaviors that fall under "sexual abuse."

___

2. What justifications have you used or told yourself that have made it possible for you engage in these types of behaviors?

___

_____

_____

_____

_____

3. Do you believe these behaviors represent who you are?

   Circle one: Yes   No

4. What can you do to take measures to not engage in these types of behaviors in the future?

_____

_____

_____

_____

_____

_____

Financial Abuse:
Any manipulation done through monetary means to gain power and control

Examples: taking money away from your partner, taking full control of banking, making all the bills in only your name, not letting partner have any money of her own, selling partner's things, destroying partner's belongings that she/he worked for, never giving enough money for your part of the bills, putting your wants before your family's needs, making partner account for every dime spent, not allowing partner to go to work, spending food money on alcohol and drugs, forcing partner to deprive children

1. Describe how you have done these types of behaviors in the past (without giving justifications/rationalizations – you will have an opportunity to do that in #2).

2. What justifications/rationalizations have you told yourself that made it understandable for you to utilize behaviors that fall under the category of financial abuse?

3. What steps can you take to let go of attempting to control others through financial manipulations?

Verbal Abuse:
Trying to gain power and control through verbal attacks on partner

Examples: yelling at, putting your partner down in general, calling names (body parts, objects, etc.), talking down to your partner, putting down your partner's appearance, threatening to take children away, cussing at your partner, telling your partner no one else would want her/him, threatening to kill, belittling things that are important to your partner

1. Describe how you have attempted to gain control over a situation by using verbal attacks on a loved one.

___

2. Describe below what you believe you gained from doing so.

___

3. What steps can you take to prevent yourself from trying to gain control through verbal attacks in the future?

_____

_____

_____

_____

_____

_____

_____

_____

Types of Abuse Exercise – Part 2

1. What type or types of abuse surprises you as something being defined as "abuse?"

_____
_____
_____
_____
_____
_____

2. Elaborate on your answer to #1.

_____
_____
_____
_____
_____
_____

"Abuse cannot end until we recognize it."

Personal challenge:
End the abuse in your life.

Enantiodromia

Enantiodromia is a big word that means we have a tendency to go from one extreme to another. In regard to violence, this means that after we explode emotionally and are angry, we become overly compassionate and nice. When adolescent boys get angry at each other to the point of violence, they often get in a fist fight, only to become best friends the next day. When men are aggressive toward women, they tend to immediately jump from the extreme of violence to the honeymoon phase, whereby they constantly apologize and use as many compliments as possible. Yes, boys and men do these things, but ALL people go from one extreme to another at some points in their lives.

Consider the mother who believes, *"I'm a great parent; it's my child who's the problem,"* until she learns that she plays a role in her child's behavior. Then she thinks to herself, *"Wow, I'm a terrible mother!"* She goes from one extreme to another.

Consider the father who thinks, *"I'm a great husband and father,"* and then something happens where he loses his job, so he thinks, *"I'm a terrible husband and father.* He goes from one extreme to another.

Consider the young person who is brought up religious, then comes to learn that some part of what he/she was taught about religion is not true, so that person begins to not believe in anything. He/She goes from one extreme to another.

Consider the person who is in love and thinks that the other person is the greatest human in the universe – until they break up – and then that other person becomes the worst person on the planet…. He/She goes from one extreme to another.

It does not have to be big events for us to go from one extreme to another. We do it all the time. We have a tendency to think in terms of extremes, *"It's terrible,"*

"I can't stand it any more," "You never…" "You always…." But life is rarely lived in the extremes. We create the extremes in our minds. For the most part, we live in the middle, but tell ourselves that we are on the extremes. We all want our lives to be meaningful, purposeful, and exciting. But if everyone were really living in the extremes in every situation – wouldn't that really just be the new middle?

Enantiodromia is a really big word, yes, but the idea of going from one extreme to another is pretty straightforward. The more time you spend bouncing from one extreme to the other, the more extreme responses you will get from others. If, on the other hand, you are able to find balance, you will likely be surprised at how profoundly that can impact your relationships.

Jeremiah the Extremist

Jeremiah came to therapy with his wife Brenda. They came in to talk about what to do about their teenage son who was beginning to isolate himself from the family. The two of them were saying that they believe they are pretty good parents and doing the best that they can. A few minutes into the session, Brenda said to Jeremiah, "Well, you kind of did yell at him yesterday," to which Jeremiah responded, "What?! Now you're turning this on me? Well then I guess I'm the problem now! I guess I'm the whole reason for every problem in the family! I guess I always mess up everything!"

Whereas it was easier for Jeremiah to go from one extreme to the other, it simply was not helpful for either the relationship or the problem-solving. Eventually, Jeremiah was able to calm down and take a more balanced approach to the conflict. By eliminating words such as "always," "never," and "everything," we too, can take a more balanced approach to the obstacles that come into our paths.

Enantiodromia Exercise

1. Write down an example of how you have gone from one extreme to another after an argument or fight with a male.

   _____
   _____
   _____
   _____
   _____
   _____

2. Write down an example of how you have gone from one extreme to another after an argument or fight with a female.

   _____
   _____
   _____
   _____
   _____
   _____

3. Write down how you have gone from one extreme to another about a fairly big issue in your life.

   _____
   _____
   _____
   _____
   _____

4. Write down how you have gone from one extreme to another regarding a relationship.

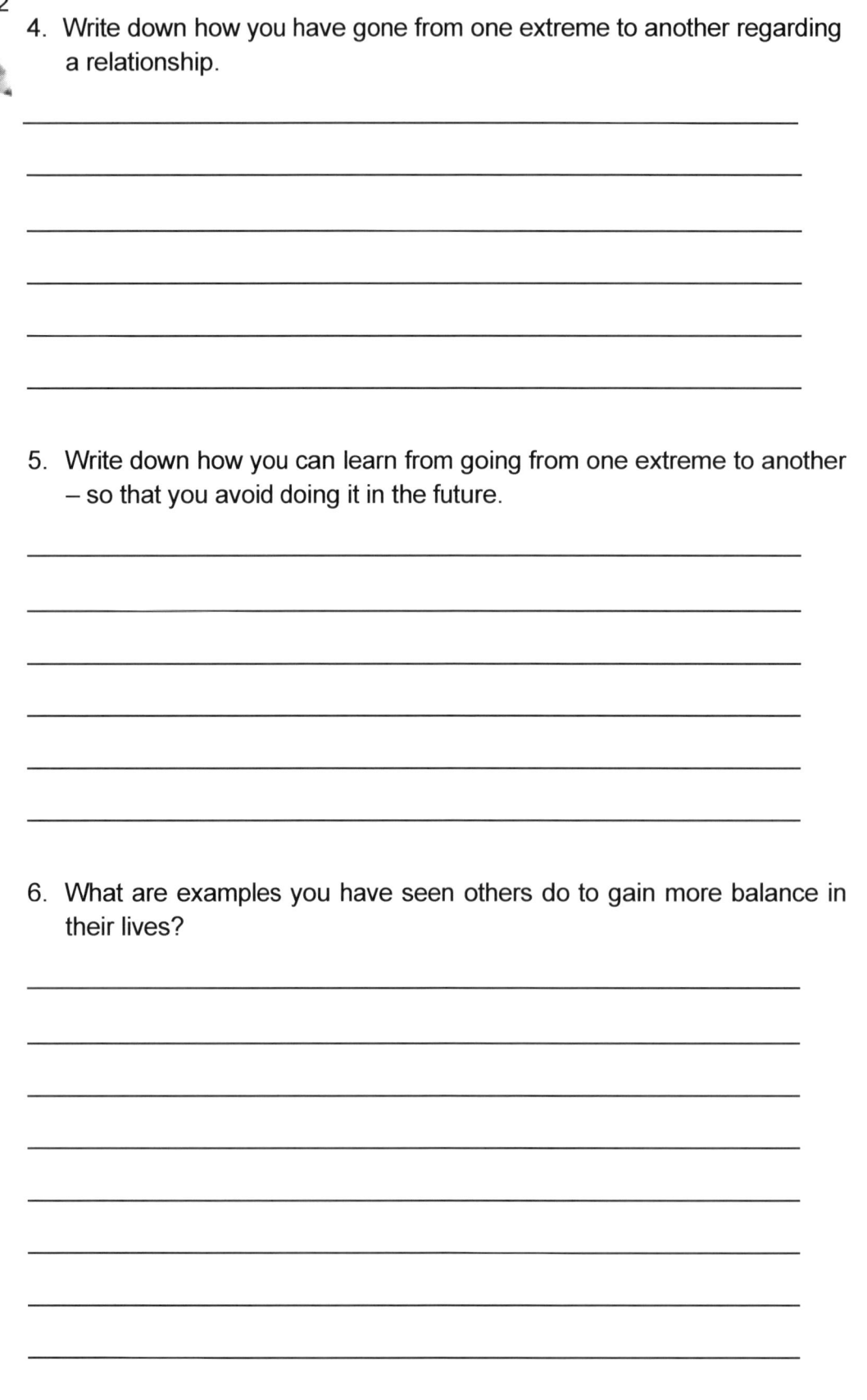

___

5. Write down how you can learn from going from one extreme to another – so that you avoid doing it in the future.

___

6. What are examples you have seen others do to gain more balance in their lives?

___

7. What can you do specifically this week to begin to get more balance in your life?

___

8. What would get in the way of you not going from one extreme to another in the future?

___

9. How can you get around the obstacles that would prevent you from gaining balance in your life?

___

I'm the bad guy!

Stacey dragged Craig into therapy to get help for their parenting. Craig was clear with the therapist that he "did not have the problem," and that he was simply there because Stacey made him come to the session. Craig told the therapist that he did nothing wrong as a parent, and Stacey constantly enabled their child, and was therefore the root of all their problems.

As the therapist questioned the two of them more, he uncovered that Craig yelled and intimidated their son, often taunting and challenging the 11 year-old to fist fights. As Craig heard himself explain what he does, he began to accept that he might in fact have some things to work on in regard to his parenting style. Craig's energy shifted quickly, and he went from being vocal to shutting down. When the therapist questioned him, he threw his hands up in the air and exclaimed, "Oh I guess now I'm the bad guy! I'm the whole reason why our child is not doing well in school!! I guess it's all my fault now! No, no, I see it. I do. That's fine."

Craig did what a lot of people do in similar situations; they go from one extreme to the other. He moved from believing he did nothing wrong as a parent to believing he was entirely the problem. His behavior in turn influenced Stacey's behavior, and she was fast to add, "See, I knew you were the problem. That's why I brought you here!" It took some work for the two of them to each see the role that they played in the situation. It took effort on both of their parts to learn to avoid moving from extreme blame to extreme praise and vice versa. When they did find the balance, they learned how to focus on what they could realistically control: themselves.

The challenge with moving from one extreme to the other is that we are bound to bounce back to the other extreme at some point.

The Anger Pattern

We all experience patterns of behavior in our lives. We have patterns of behavior that we get used to, so we keep doing the same things over and over again, even if what we are doing is not effective for us. Consider what happens in the cycle of violence. In that cycle, we experience mounting tension until it erupts in an explosion of aggression, after which follows a honeymoon phase. Until we learn about that pattern, we do it over and over again.

We have patterns of when we do certain things. We have patterns of how we communicate with others. We even have patterns of how we get angry. The general pattern that we get into when we are angry is called The Anger Pattern. As long as we do not understand the Anger Pattern, we are doomed to repeat it. To understand the anger pattern gives us a chance to change it. The Anger Pattern is:

A. An event happens that was not what we wanted/desired or expected.

For example: Someone suddenly cuts us off in traffic.

B. Rapid or subconscious negative self-talk occurs.

For example, "He/she shouldn't have done that!" or "Oh no!"

C. Chemicals and hormones are released in the body causing agitation.

For example: Cortisol and adrenaline are released in the body.

D. Negative self-talk perpetuates and intensifies the anger.

For example: We say things to ourselves like, "That shouldn't have happened. or "I can't stand it." **(Similar to the rapid subconscious negative self-talk, but occurring repeatedly)**

E. More chemicals are released in the brain that agitate the body more.

F. We make ineffective choices that lead to doing things of which we are not proud.

   For example: We scream something at the person while others are watching.

G. We feel shame about our behaviors.

   For example: We wish we wouldn't have screamed at the person.

H. The shame we feel determines how we see future events. We eventually feel we need to cover the shame with anger. That perpetuates the Anger Pattern.

Anger Pattern Exercise

1. Describe a situation that angered you recently.

_____
_____
_____
_____
_____
_____

2. Describe the difference between what you expected to happen versus what actually happened?

_____
_____
_____

3. Describe where you felt it in your body when you became angry at that situation.

4. Describe the types of negative things you told yourself when you continued to get angrier and angrier thinking about that situation.

5. Describe what you **did** (your behavior) about the situation that you were not proud of.

6. Describe **what you told yourself** after you felt shame about what you did.

_____
_____
_____
_____
_____
_____
_____

7. Describe your behavior after you felt shame about what you did.

_____
_____
_____
_____
_____
_____
_____

8. Describe where along the path you can do something to break this anger pattern.

_____
_____
_____
_____
_____
_____
_____

Our lives can become circles for repeating the same things over and over again. One day, when things get bad enough for us, we choose to change that pattern. Pattern changes take time, but they can happen. It took time to create a pattern of behavior, and it will take time to change – but it CAN happen.

What are you taking from this exercise?

___

Personal challenge:
Rock bottom will come if you wait for it: Don't wait for it!

How *I Am* in Relationships

We all have a tendency to maximize the negative things others do in our relationships, whereas we seem to conveniently minimize the negative things that we do in those very same relationships. We are naturally biased in favor of ourselves, so it makes sense why it is difficult for us to evaluate ourselves accurately in relationships. We all seem to believe that we are doing things correctly in a relationship, and if we are messing up, it's "not really that bad."

Lots of people consider themselves to be "nice guys." Those people who would do anything for a friend or a stranger. You might consider yourself to be one such person. You have probably observed, however, that being a "nice guy" to the people closest to you can be difficult. As long as any of us are nice to strangers, we get to see ourselves as "kind people." Then we use confirmation bias, that is, we consider only the evidence that we are truly "good" or "kind," and ignore any evidence to the contrary in an effort to prove to ourselves or *confirm* that we are "good guys." But even the term "good guy" implies that someone else must be the "bad guy." When we are the "good guy," then the "bad guy," unfortunately, usually ends up being whoever is closest to us.

The only way to know how we really are in a relationship is to evaluate ourselves objectively. The best way to evaluate ourselves or understand how we come across to others is to accept feedback. The problem is that if we have conditioned someone to see that we will be overly sensitive about what they are telling us, or if we have intimidated them, or even shut them down when they tried to give us feedback in the past, then we are *not* likely to get honest feedback. After all, would you give someone honest feedback if you knew that person could hurt you physically or trap you mentally?

I Am Exercises

Just to be clear before you move on, if you *genuinely* believe you are perfect in your relationship, then there is a good chance you are either dreaming right now, or you have already passed on to the next world. Take the time now to assess whether or not you seek only feedback that is favorable to your self image as the "good guy" by answering the following questions.

1. What kind of feedback have you heard about yourself from romantic partners in your life?

   _____
   _____
   _____
   _____
   _____
   _____
   _____

2. What kinds of things have significant others asked you to change?

   _____
   _____
   _____
   _____
   _____
   _____

3. In what ways have people in your current or past relationships said you can be too controlling?

   _____
   _____

4. Do you believe you need to be in control most of the time?

5. From the other person's perspective, is it difficult for your loved one to give you feedback?

6. Do you find that you are sensitive to what your loved one has to say?

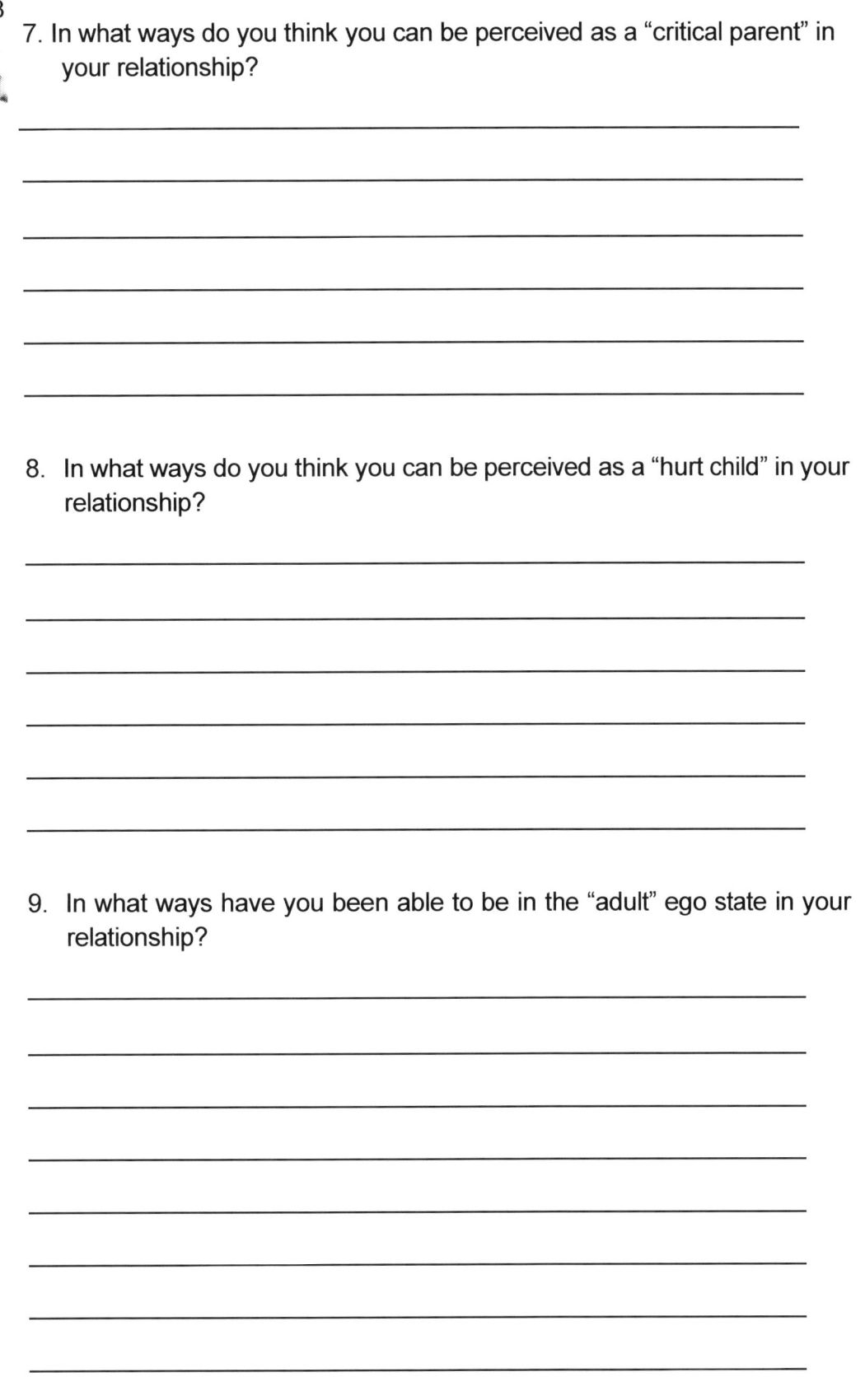

7. In what ways do you think you can be perceived as a "critical parent" in your relationship?

_____

_____

_____

_____

_____

_____

8. In what ways do you think you can be perceived as a "hurt child" in your relationship?

_____

_____

_____

_____

_____

_____

9. In what ways have you been able to be in the "adult" ego state in your relationship?

_____

_____

_____

_____

_____

_____

10. In what ways have you been considered the "fun child" in your relationship?

11. Have you been the fun child too much or too little?

12. In what ways have you been considered the "nurturing parent"?

13. Have you been the nurturing parent too much or too little?

_____
_____
_____
_____
_____
_____
_____
_____

You and you alone, have the ability to change your life.

Personal challenge:
Take a good look at the role you play in your relationships.

Why Forgive?

One of the toughest things that we can ever do is forgive people who have hurt us. Even though it ultimately hurts us to hold onto anger and hurt, for some reason, it seems so hard to let go and forgive others.

Sometimes we forget how much we have hurt others. Whatever we have done, we somehow find a way to convince ourselves that it wasn't as bad as whatever the person we cannot forgive has done to us. Two very powerful questions we all might want to consider are: *Do we believe we deserve forgiveness for the things that we have done? If we do, why don't others?*

Anytime that someone in a group says, "Everyone deserves forgiveness," someone else inevitably throws out Hitler or Stalin or Osama Bin Laden and asks, "Everyone?" The problem with throwing out extreme examples is that in doing so we are deflecting the need to face the people we are choosing not to forgive right now.

The effects of failing to forgive can be both psychological and physiological. It is common for people who choose not to forgive others have higher blood pressure, faster heart rates, and they have greater muscle tension. Whereas the past can be unbelievably painful, choosing to not forgive others only hurts us, because we are the ones who end up living in a state of turmoil

Story of the two monks

Once, an old monk and a young monk were walking along when they came to a shallow river. A girl was standing at the foot of the river, and she looked sad. The monks asked her what

was the matter, and she said she didn't want to get her dress wet. The older monk at once picked her up and carried her across the river and set her down on the other side.

Now the two monks continued on their way in complete silence. About an hour into their walk, the younger monk finally turned to the older monk and in anger said, "We took a vow to never touch a woman, let alone carry one. How could you have done that?" To which the older monk replied, "My brother, I set her down an hour ago, why are you still carrying her?"

Choosing to *not* forgive someone is analogous to carrying around a giant boulder all day. Whereas we might be physically strong enough to lift it, it certainly interferes with our day. The journey through life while carrying a rock becomes physically exhausting. The same is true when we hold onto anger. The more we hold onto anger, the more we become both emotionally and physically drained.

To choose to forgive someone, however, is analogous to dropping the rock. The sooner we learn to let go, the sooner our own journeys become much lighter. Consider dropping the rock for the sake of the other person, but at a minimum, consider dropping the rock for yourself.

Why Forgive Exercise

1. How has **not**-forgiving someone who hurt you affected your life in the past?

2. How is **not**-forgiving someone who hurt you affecting your life right now?

3. Identify someone who you have had (or have) difficulty forgiving. What did that person do that you cannot let go of?

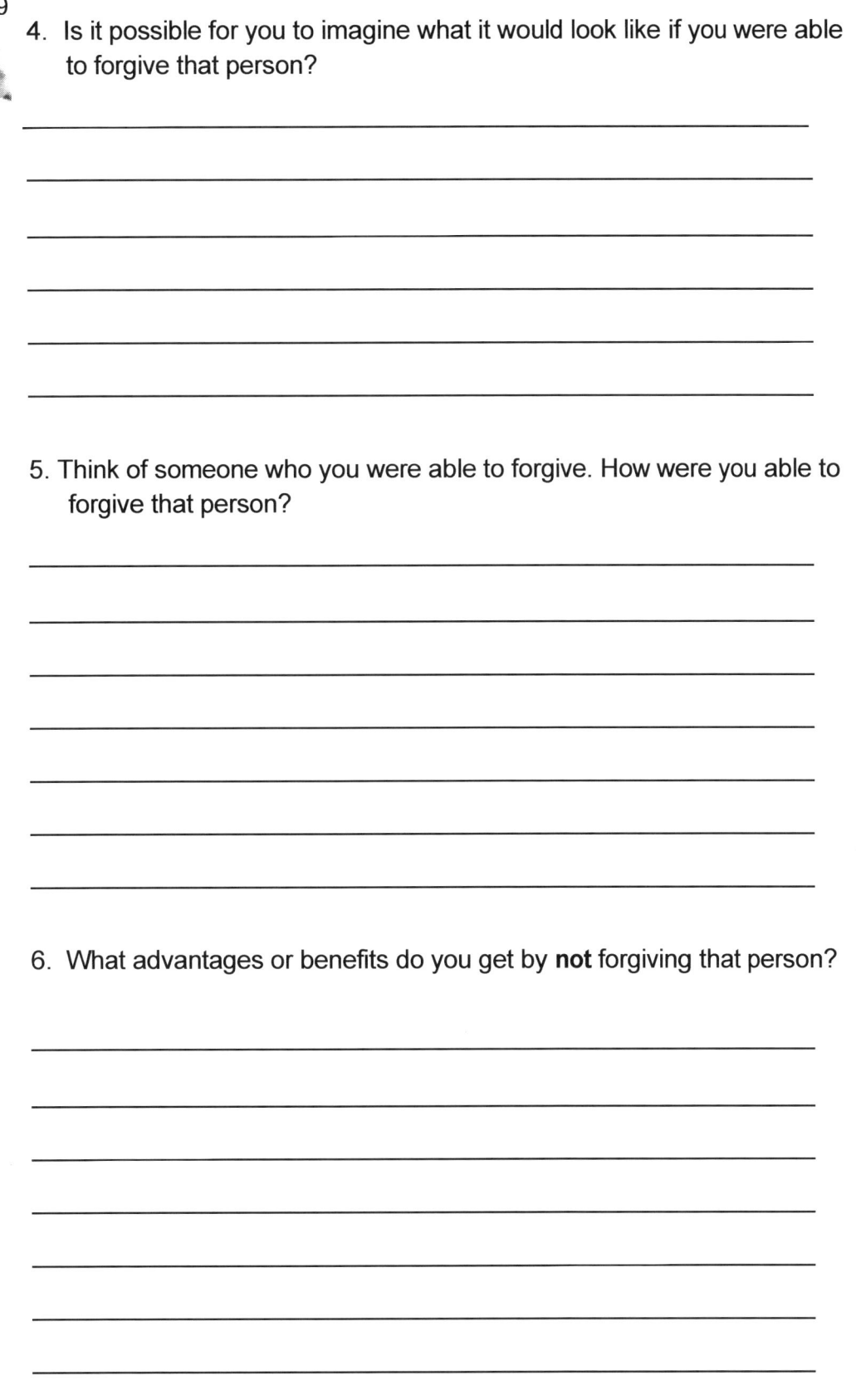

4. Is it possible for you to imagine what it would look like if you were able to forgive that person?

_____
_____
_____
_____
_____
_____
_____

5. Think of someone who you were able to forgive. How were you able to forgive that person?

_____
_____
_____
_____
_____
_____
_____

6. What advantages or benefits do you get by **not** forgiving that person?

_____
_____
_____
_____
_____
_____
_____

7. What steps can you take to forgive the person you have struggled to forgive? In other words, what will it take for you to genuinely forgive that person?

8. If you can identify someone you would like to forgive you, how and why would you suggest that that person forgive you?

9. What does it feel like when someone harbors resentment and anger toward you?

I forgive for me

Jim was angry. Jim was a genuinely tough individual. Covered in tattoos from head to toe, Jim even looked like a scary individual to approach. Regardless of his feelings of anger or his appearance, Jim was a good person who was open to learning about himself, because more than anything, he wanted to change. For the first time in his life, he was ready to stop repeating the same mistakes he always made. When Jim did this "Why Forgive?" exercise in the anger management group, he took the group leader up on the personal challenge below: he chose to forgive someone. When he came back to the group the next week, he told us something incredible.

"I took Doc up on this personal challenge to forgive someone. So I was sitting in the hospital next to my mother who's in a coma, and I know she's dying. And I've hated this lady a long time. This woman beat the shit out of me for years... I mean she was vicious. Even as an adult she treated me like shit. I've held onto this hate for her through my whole life, but I trust you; I do. So I tried it. I leaned in and told her," he paused for a while as he said this. He fought through holding back tears, and he continued telling us what he said, *"'Mom, I forgive you for everything.' Now she couldn't say anything because she's in a coma, but I knew I said it. And the moment I did, something happened to me. I don't know what happened, but I know I felt lighter. I still feel better. It's like something left me that moment. Something I held onto for years."*

"Forgiveness has a powerful psychological effect on your body."

Personal challenge:
Regardless of how difficult, choose to forgive someone.

Ageless Wisdom

Sometimes we sit around and think about things, and we think about those things until they seem bigger and bigger (*idle speculation*). Sometimes we feel certain we are right about something (*certainty*), only to learn later on that we were wrong. Sometimes we are so rigid that we believe there can only be one way to actually look at something (*inflexibility*), only to find out later there was another way to see it. Sometimes, even when we are right, we let our thoughts inflate our egos so much that we are difficult to be around (*conceit*).

Speculation: To speculate means to think deeply or ruminate about something. We have all heard the sayings, "You think too much," or "You're reading too much into it,." Sometimes that's exactly what happens when we sit around and think about something deeply. The problem with speculation, according to the wise Confucius, is that to speculate really means to "assume." To assume sometimes presents a problem: After all, how often have our assumptions been wrong?

"The Master must be freed of four things: idle speculation, certainty, inflexibility, and conceit."
-Confucius

Certainty: How can we subscribe to the philosophy that *we can always learn* when we are certain about things? Continuous learning and certainty do not go hand in hand. Confucius suggests that to be able to grow, to open ourselves up to new knowledge, we must let go of our need to be certain about things. There is a great difference between saying, *"This is what I believe today, but I am open to learning something new tomorrow that could change my mind,"* and *"I know this is how things are and nothing can ever change my mind!"*

Inflexibility: Along with certainty, people can become very rigid about their beliefs. Even people who view themselves as "open-minded" can be very rigid when it comes to accepting someone's beliefs who they perceive to be "closed-minded." So, truth be told, says Confucius, we are all closed-minded; it is only the wise who learn how to be flexible in their openness to learning new things.

> **Interesting fact:**
>
> Skyscrapers are built with flexibility so that they will sway a specific amount in the wind. Architects have learned that if they constructed skyscrapers to be completely rigid, they would be more vulnerable to being torn apart in high winds.
>
> Is there an analogy here for us?

Conceit: There is a big difference between confidence and arrogance. Confidence is knowing you can do something; arrogance is telling others that you can. Even if we are 100% right about something, we can come across in a way that pushes others away. How much do we all admire the one who achieves much, but remains humble? Confucius warns that conceit adds nothing to our victories, but does terrible things to our character.

Ageless Wisdom Exercise

Now let's learn how speculation, certainty, inflexibility, and conceit have impacted your life.

1. Describe a time when you speculated about something only to find out later that your speculations were wrong.

   _____
   _____
   _____
   _____
   _____
   _____
   _____
   _____

2. Describe a time when you were very certain about something, only to find out with time and experience that your attachment to certainty was a downfall for you.

   _____
   _____
   _____
   _____
   _____
   _____
   _____
   _____

3. Describe a time when you were inflexible about something, and your inflexibility ended up hurting you.

_____
_____
_____
_____
_____
_____
_____

4. Describe a time where you felt conceit (conceit = arrogance) about something, only to learn later that being humble would have served you better in the same situation.

_____
_____
_____
_____
_____
_____
_____

"Learning from our mistakes is hard. Not learning from our mistakes is more difficult."

Personal challenge:
Be more open to the views of others.

A Picture of Me:
An Exercise in Self-Awareness

Who we are is many things. Sometimes who we are changes with experiences in our lives. We invite you now to take a moment to think about your life. Think about who you are. Just for a brief moment, sit back and look up from this page, and think about who you really are.

This exercise can help you get a better sense of who you are; and as you will see, it will also give you a different way to view others. We will provide an explanation at the end of the exercise, but first, we are inviting you to answer the following questions with the very first ideas that come to your mind.

A Picture of Me Exercise

For this exercise, answer the following questions as quickly as you can:

1. What makes me angry is…

_____
_____
_____
_____

2. I hate it when…

_____
_____
_____
_____

3. When I get angry I…

4. My worst trait is…

5. My life really changed when…

6. I feel most lonely when…

7. I am afraid…

8. I cannot forgive…

_____
_____
_____
_____

9. I tend to deny…

_____
_____
_____
_____

10. I am happiest when…

_____
_____
_____
_____

11. Sometimes at night I…

_____
_____
_____
_____

12. I used to laugh more because…

_____
_____
_____
_____

13. I feel like a phony when…

14. I would give anything to…

15. I would be more lovable if…

16. When I am alone, I…

17. It hurts me when…

18. I never seem to…

_____
_____
_____
_____

19. My mother and father…

_____
_____
_____
_____

20. If only I had…

_____
_____
_____
_____

21. I regret…

_____
_____
_____
_____

22. I never seem to…

_____
_____
_____
_____

23. Sometimes I…

24. I wish…

25. I love…

26. It would be best if…

27. I believe…

Now look back at your answers.

What answers stand out to you?

_____

_____

_____

_____

_____

What answers surprised you, if any?

_____

_____

_____

_____

_____

What can you learn about yourself by reviewing your answers to this worksheet?

_____

_____

_____

_____

_____

_____

_____

Sometimes when people think others might see or hear their answers to questions like these, they answer the questions how they *think* others would want them to answer. Answering quickly, without thought, without having to impress anyone, can teach us a lot about ourselves. There is no right or wrong when it comes to self-awareness: there is only learning.

However you answered these questions, one fact is true: you know that who you are is much more than *how you answered them* in this moment. None of us like to be defined by our worst moments, by our lousiest ideas, or by our embarrassing moments. Yet, all of us, at one time or another, judge others by those very same standards. What do our judgments about others tell us about ourselves?

Despite the fact that we tell ourselves stories about others, even when we only have a little bit of information about them—none of us like it when others do the same to us. We hate to be judged on one or two pieces of information. Therefore, we might just want to consider no longer judging other people on one or two things as well.

We are all vast and deep. We are all much more than what can be seen on the surface. As much as it can be fun to joke around about the depth of others, the truth is, all people have substance. The more that you can learn about the depth of others, the less you will hold onto anger toward them.

"There is always more to know about ourselves as well as others."

Personal challenge:
Judge others in the way that you would want to be judged.

Blinders Off

Blinders are used on horses to prevent them from seeing anywhere but right in front of them. Anytime that we fail to see things from others' perspectives, it is as though we are wearing blinders. People might look pretty ridiculous if they wore blinders, yet every time we fail to see anything other than our own point of view, "psychological" blinders are exactly what we are wearing.

The world is big. The world is more than what we see at any given moment. The blinders we place upon ourselves can limit our vision. When we are in pain, we have a tendency to be locked into our own perspectives. Freedom from this pain releases us from our blinders to see the bigger picture.

Have you ever noticed that you have a better perspective on other peoples' problems than your own? If so, you are not alone. It is easier to see what other people can do more effectively when not saddled with their blinders. It seems easier to come up with solutions for others than it is for us to come up with solutions for ourselves. A key to becoming more self-aware, however, is to find a way to see ourselves from the outside-in.

Learning to see the big picture, outside of the moment you are in, can make all the difference. No one moment can last forever. It is also true that, by definition, no interaction can be one-sided. There is always more than one way to see things. When we are open to the big picture and can take on another's perspective, we can learn interact with others more calmly.

challenge is letting go of our own perspective. we are up for it, is to try to see ourselves the way others see us - and try to experience ourselves the way others experience us. The more difficult that is for us to do, the bigger the blinders are that we are choosing to wear.

> **Interesting thought from the world of counseling:**
>
> Professional counselors and therapists have to attend something called "supervision" while they are going through their training. As we noted earlier in this book, counselors in training counselors-in-training usually videotape the meetings with her clients, then after meeting with the clients, counselors-in-training go and show that videotape to their supervisor. The term "supervision," is used because, in a sense, the supervisor has "super" vision of what's going on – after all, the supervisor is seeing things from an outside perspective.
>
> Anytime we are involved in an interaction, our whole brain is also involved in the interaction. What that means is this: experiences include cognitions (thinking about things), affect (our emotions), and behaviors (our actions). A supervisor watching a videotape of an experience between two other people (a counselor and a client), has a much better chance at remaining detached emotionally, and thereby has an ability to see both people's perspectives. In fact, counselors who have been supervisors for some time seem to have more of an ability to step outside of themselves during their own counseling sessions.
>
> What we can take from this supervisor analogy is this: The more we learn to step outside of our own situations and evaluate them from a variety of perspectives, the more effective we can be in every interaction.

Blinders Off Exercise

For this exercise, try to suspend your own perspective and genuinely see yourself from the outside. The more difficult it is for you to do this exercise, the more you know that your blinders are blocking you from changing. If this exercise is too difficult for you, consider asking someone you trust to give you feedback about what you could have done differently. If the person says you were "completely right in the situation," then the odds are that he/she does not feel comfortable giving you honest feedback.

1. Write about an explosive situation with someone else that ended up with negative results, BUT, write about it **from the other person's perspective ONLY.**

   _____
   _____
   _____
   _____
   _____
   _____
   _____

2. After looking at the situation completely from the other person's perspective, how do you see the situation differently?

   _____
   _____
   _____
   _____
   _____
   _____
   _____

3. Imagine that there was an incident report written about the situation that got you involved in anger management (or if there was one, refer to the actual report). If you were to consider this report from another's perspective, what part(s) of the report would have been true about your behavior?

_____
_____
_____
_____
_____
_____

4. If you knew that you would have to live out the moment that got you involved in an anger management course over and over again for all of eternity, how do you think you would have handled the situation differently?

_____
_____
_____
_____
_____
_____

5. What do you think you can do to begin to see others' perspectives in the moment, rather than waiting until after the moment is over?

_____
_____
_____
_____
_____
_____

A Very Unhappy (but true) Story

A client was once asked to report on a scale of 1-10, with ten being "perfect" and 1 being "terrible," what kind of husband he was. He reported that he was a "10." He said that he was absolutely perfect, and that his wife was just "crazy." He didn't believe that he had any problems at all, and he believed that therapy or learning about himself was "a waste of his time."

Later that week, the same man was arrested for beating his wife unconscious. He sat on her shoulders and repeatedly struck her in the head. He told the police that she "made him do it" because she didn't listen to him. In his eyes, he had nothing to change, so he changed nothing.

Years in prison did not change his perspective. Though he always maintained that it would be wrong for anyone to ever hit him, he also always maintained that if he felt someone deserved a beating, it was okay to do so. He lived with blinders on, unhappily, for the rest of his life.

> **The next time you face a situation where you get angry, consider imagining that however you respond, you will have to live that response out for infinity.**

> **Personal challenge:**
> Be mindful that others see your actions, not your intentions.

Memory and Anger

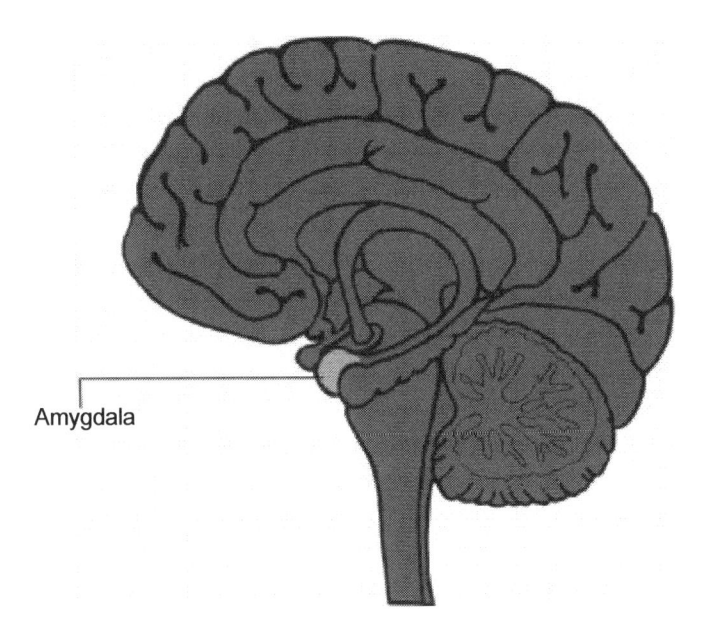

Amygdala

Memory is a combination of creating and recreating events. For many, many years, we had believed that memory was like a video recorder: all we needed to do was play things back to see them just as they occurred. Here in the 21st century, we have discovered some powerful truths about memory. Our memory is not like a video recorder. Our memory shapes us constantly – and what we remember shapes how we see new things and make new memories.

To understand memory completely, we have to understand the context in which memories are made. The term *"state-dependent learning"* means that the state of mind in which we learn something is the state in which we are most likely to recall it. If we get information in a highly emotional state, when we revert to a normal emotional state, we are more likely to lose at least a few of the details. Many factors contribute to the very important bottom line: memory is imperfect.

This is important to understand, especially considering what transpires in highly emotional situations. Think about trying to recall the details of an argument in which you had been involved. It is likely that you and the other person involved have different opinions as to the specifics of that argument and will recall the events differently. Psychologists have performed studies for years that demonstrate the fallibility of memory, particularly in emotional situations. Ironically, those who insist that they are "right" are often the most inaccurate about a memory.

Our memories are very important to us. We are, to some extent, mostly comprised of memories. After all, how do we even begin to describe anything about ourselves without our memories? Because our memories hold so much weight with us, we have a tendency to believe that they are always accurate. The trouble seems to occur when we tend to believe that because our memories are important, they are always accurate. When we cling to the ideas that our memories are mostly accurate, even when they are not, we set ourselves up for trouble.

Bob and the memory cue

With every memory comes some sort of association. For example, imagine the case of Bob. Bob and his high school girlfriend broke up at the drive-in outdoor movie theater in his hometown when they were seniors in high school. Bob went on to date many other women in his life, sometimes viewing himself as "in love," and other times thinking that "the right one is still out there somewhere."

One day Bob took a job at the factory in a town across the country from where he grew up. Every day on his way to work, Bob passed a drive-in outdoor movie theater that sparked old memories. Bob got to thinking about his ex-girlfriend from high school. He found that he thought of this girl nearly every day, and the more he thought of her, the more he "realized" that because he thought so much about her, he must still be "in love" with her.

Bob contacted his ex-girlfriend from high school via the Internet. He told her how he thought of her all the time. But when they met in person, Bob found that he actually didn't like her very much. In fact, he found that he did not enjoy her company much at all. This of course left Bob very confused. After all, he had thought about her so much, didn't that mean that he was truly in love?

Then Bob read something about memory cues. He read that the more frequently a memory is cued, the more important we believe that memory to be. And all of a sudden it hit him: he wasn't really longing for his high school girlfriend because he missed the relationship; he had thought of her frequently because he had frequently passed a movie theater that triggered his memory of her.

Like Bob, we may experience memories as significant, when, in fact, those memories are simply just cued more frequently for us.

We have the ability to wire and rewire our memories. We essentially create our own realities. Think about the following situation: A couple fights because one person screams and belittles the other. The person who was put down remembers the situation one way; whereas the person who screamed remembers it a different way. Which experience is the correct memory?

Who is to say whose experience is the "correct" one? We create our experiences based on the perspectives we take. What we know going into a situation influences what we remember out of a situation. What if we could change our perspective? How would changing our perspectives change our future memories? At a minimum, we should be able to see how we play a role in creating every memory we have.

Our ability to create memories leads us to ask four questions:

- What kind of memories have I created?
- Are they positive or negative?
- Why have I created them?
- What story have I created about my past?

Imagine a world in which people were less attached to being right about their memories and more open to the possibility that they could be wrong. It would likely be a less-angry world. People would have far fewer arguments over what really happened. Although we could imagine what a world would look like if this happened, the truth is, we can only control our own actions. How different would you be if you became less attached to being right about your memories?

Memory and Anger Exercise

1. Describe an event in which you got very upset/angry.

   _____
   _____
   _____
   _____
   _____
   _____

2. How else could you have remembered this event?

   _____
   _____
   _____
   _____
   _____
   _____

3. What is another side to the experience you described above? How would someone else describe this event?

   _____
   _____
   _____
   _____
   _____
   _____

4. What types of things do you see in your everyday experiences that can trigger a memory of this event?

_____
_____
_____
_____
_____

Memories are not perfect. The more you believe your memory is accurate, the more prone you are to memory errors.

Personal challenge: Be less attached to being right.

Learning from Mistakes

When the poet H.W. Longfellow said, *"Let the dead Past bury its dead,"* he was saying that the past is over and we should just be done with it. What a great line, because as long as we are dwelling on the past, we are not living in the present.

There is a difference between dwelling in the past and learning from it. Most people are quick to quote the old maxim, *"Insanity is doing the same thing over and over again and expecting a different result."* In reality, few people seem to show that they are actually learning from their past mistakes.

Once a situation is over, there is nothing we can do to "undo" it. But whereas we cannot undo situations, what we can do is make more effective choices once we've already messed up. Consider what stage actors are taught: *"if you mess up, just keep going."* The best actors do not dwell on their mistakes. Rather, they continue and recover their composure to perform well.

We will always make mistakes. Making mistakes helps reassure us that we are human and currently alive. Some people can dwell on mistakes for the rest of their lives, whereas others can move beyond mistakes easily. Whether we hold onto or let go of mistakes, all of us can learn from our mistakes. Like stage actors, we can train ourselves to adapt and to overcome mistakes.

Legend of the parallel worlds

A legend exists that tells of two parallel worlds. The original persons from our world each had a counterpart in the other world. Every time one of the originals in this world made a mistake and dwelled on it or ignored it, the counter person in the other world would learn from it and become wise. Each of the originals in our world who made mistakes and learned from those mistakes had counterparts in the other world who dwelled on the mistakes or ignored them, and suffered.

The parallel worlds were intermixed and confused so that descendants of both spread. It is said that the people in our modern world who repeat mistakes are descendants of those who refused to learn from their mistakes in the parallel world, whereas the wise of our world are descendants of those who learned from every mistake they ever made in the parallel world.

The final part to that legend is that one day a group of people will be born who will learn what is often called the Great Secret: that, regardless of our ancestors, we all have the ability to learn from our mistakes. When that group of people learns the Great Secret, they will change the fortunes of both worlds, thereby changing the fate of all the future descendants.

Learning from Mistakes Exercise

1. What types of mistakes do you make when you are angry?

_____
_____
_____
_____
_____
_____

2. What have you done to try to calm down in the past that just didn't work?

_____
_____
_____
_____
_____
_____

3. Describe a time when you felt like you were at your "wits end" and had no patience with someone. What did you learn from that experience?

4. What have you learned from past mistakes that can help you become more patient?

5. What mistake made out of anger have you learned the most from?

6. What mistake have you repeated the most in your life?

_____

_____

_____

_____

_____

_____

_____

7. What is it about that mistake that you are having trouble learning?

_____

_____

_____

_____

_____

_____

_____

8. What could you do to teach others so that they could learn from your mistakes?

_____

_____

_____

_____

_____

_____

_____

What to watch for

Your eyeglasses can't work for me!

Oftentimes we believe that because we have learned something a certain way, others need to learn it that way, too. Steven Covey once used the great analogy of eyeglasses to explain why that cannot happen.

Just because a certain prescription of eyeglasses works for you, that doesn't mean that someone else can see better with the same prescription. People need to wear eyeglasses with their own, unique prescription – one that works best for their own eyes. All too often, people will try to force what works for them onto others. So be mindful the next time you try to teach someone else to learn from your mistakes, because a great difference exists between teaching others and then letting go, versus teaching others and getting upset when they don't follow your path exactly.

> **By teaching others we teach ourselves.**

> **Personal challenge:**
> **Welcome what you can learn from mistakes.**

Forget fixing things: Let's discuss how to mess them up!

Okay, so we all have tried to fix our lives at some point. We all have tried again and again, promising ourselves that things would be "different" this time. Sometimes we sit and think about how we need to change. Actually, sometimes we spend a lot of time *realizing* that we need to change, but we are not quite sure exactly what we need to change. Maybe for too long, we have been looking for solutions to fix things. Maybe we need to stop looking at solutions, and instead start analyzing exactly how we mess things up.

One sure-fire way to mess up a sports performance is to stay up late, indulge in alcohol, and show up at the event late and exhausted. In a similar way, there are some sure-fire ways to mess up a relationship, and we all have likely done some of those things from time to time. By identifying what we can do to mess up a relationship, we can more clearly understand what *not* to do. At the very least, by understanding what types of behaviors harm a relationship, we can recognize that if we *choose* to do those behaviors, we cannot blame others for why our relationships don't work out. If we know how to mess things up in a relationship and we *still* choose to do those things, we have only ourselves to blame.

Successful athletes in every sport spend some time watching their performances so that they can figure out exactly what they are doing incorrectly. They are attempting to determine how they "mess things up." As they identify what they mess up, they also identify exactly what they need to do more effectively.

In a similar way, we can analyze our own behavior; we can look at what we do incorrectly and attempt to understand where we have messed up. By identifying where we have messed up, we can then be empowered to choose either to keep it or change it. We cannot, however, continue to use the excuse that "I don't know how I keep messing up."

Forget Fixing Things Exercise

1. Write down some ways to mess up or disturb a relationship.

   _____
   _____
   _____
   _____
   _____
   _____
   _____
   _____
   _____

2. Write down some ways to mess up children.

   _____
   _____
   _____
   _____
   _____
   _____
   _____
   _____
   _____
   _____
   _____

3. Write down some ways to ruin a good friendship.

_____

_____

_____

_____

_____

_____

_____

_____

4. Write down some ways you can mess up your job.

_____

_____

_____

_____

_____

_____

_____

_____

5. Write down some ways you can be hurtful to those who are closest to you.

_____

_____

_____

6. Write down some ways that you can sabotage yourself.

> *"Now you know exactly what it will take to make mistakes that you will later regret."*

Personal challenge:
Consider learning from your own wisdom.

Why Are We So Violent?

We do not wake up to be violent. We do not create ideas of violence out of places of peace. Violence is learned. At some point in our lives, we learned about violence. Parents, family members, friends, television, video games, and stories told within earshot are just some of the places young people begin to learn about violence.

We are social beings, and we learn a great deal by watching and listening to others. In the fraction of a moment, images can be ingrained in us that last a lifetime. Things can become buried deep inside of us that forever impact the way we view not only what is acceptable in terms of violence, but also what is possible.

Roots of violence

Everyone in an anger management group despised a particular member. When the man would share, he would seem to deny responsibility for what he did. The other group members got frustrated. He found a way, time and again, to put the responsibility on his victims for why he did what he did. The day we processed this particular exercise, everything changed for both this man and the group.

The man shared his early experiences with the group that day. What he told us all was this: "When I was little, I lived with my grandfather because I don't even know my parents. My grandfather was a mean drunk. When I was five years old, he would come home drunk, pick me up by my neck, and closed-fist punch me in the face. I remember how he used to get drunk with his friend, and they would make me stand in the corner outside our brick house. The two of them threw their beer bottles at me," as he said this last part, he pointed to the

> scars on his face. He went on to tell us other horror stories from his childhood. We learned a lot about the roots of his violence that day.

> What happened to him does **not** excuse what he did to others – but it very much *explains* it. Once we can get to the root of why we do what we do, we provide ourselves with an opportunity to change it.

All too often people believe that they will never be like those who hurt them. Unfortunately, with regard to harmful or unhealthy behaviors, many of us repeat what we have been taught. We become like the people whose behaviors repulsed us. Then one day we enter the contemplative stage when we realize that we, too, are capable of needless anger and senseless violence.

Finding the roots of our own violence never excuses the pain we have caused others. However, finding the roots of our own violence allows us to discover the map that will lead us to the treasure of peace in our lives. By identifying where our violence originated, we can re-evaluate how we view that experience. Experiences shape us. Violence that we see, can morph into violence that we become; but awareness of the origins of our own violence can help discover the map we need to find a new way to define ourselves.

215 Why Are We So Violent Exercise

1. Write down 2 places where you may have gotten your ideas about violence.

a.

b.

2. Suppose someone came to you for advice, and he/she told you the exact things that you wrote for "a" and "b." Write down at least one idea of what you could tell this person to help him/her see a different perspective. What could you say to this person to help him/her take a new outlook on the situation?

3. What stops you from following your own wisdom?

_____
_____
_____
_____
_____
_____

4. What can you do to implement a more peaceful approach to others this week?

_____
_____
_____
_____
_____
_____

> There were reasons for what we have done.
> Likewise, there are reasons for us to change.

> **Personal challenge:**
> **Avoid passing along the anger that was shown to you.**

Accountability

Accountability means to be responsible for one's actions. We are not always responsible for what happens to us in life, but we are always responsible for how we choose to respond to what happens to us. When people learn to accept accountability for their actions, they stop blaming others for what they do. When people accept responsibility for their actions, they begin to make more effective choices.

Somebody pick up the phone!

When the phone rings, what do we have to do? Nothing. We do not HAVE to do anything. When a phone rings, all it means is someone is trying to get ahold of someone else... and considering it could be a wrong number, that person might not even be trying to get ahold of us; so when a phone rings, we don't HAVE to do anything, but we can choose to answer it if we want.

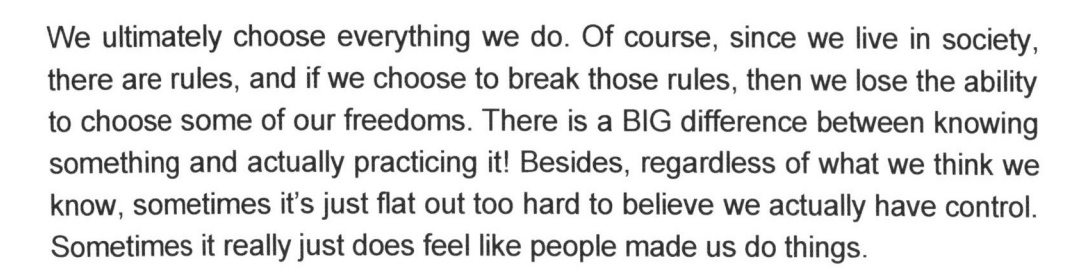

We ultimately choose everything we do. Of course, since we live in society, there are rules, and if we choose to break those rules, then we lose the ability to choose some of our freedoms. There is a BIG difference between knowing something and actually practicing it! Besides, regardless of what we think we know, sometimes it's just flat out too hard to believe we actually have control. Sometimes it really just does feel like people made us do things.

Accountability Exercise

Below, try not to think of the "correct" answer, and instead just go with the first thing that comes to mind. The more honest you are, the more you will learn about yourself.

1. The last time I got angry was...

   _____
   _____
   _____
   _____
   _____
   _____

2. Why I CHOSE to get angry was...

   _____
   _____
   _____
   _____
   _____
   _____

3. What I CHOSE to do about that anger was...

   _____
   _____
   _____
   _____
   _____
   _____

4. What I could have CHOSEN to do was…

5. A similar situation that could occur this week, or sometime soon, might be…

6. If the situation I just wrote about in number 5 does come up, a *really poor choice* I could make would be…

7. However, a *good choice* for me to make might be…
_____
_____
_____
_____
_____
_____
_____
_____

Personal challenge:
Observe how your choices impact other people.

It's Your Choice

Accountability comes down to choices. Sometimes we choose to do something because it is easiest. Sometimes we choose to do things because, "That is the way I've always done it." The easy choices and those we have repeated the longest tend not to cause us anxiety. We are at ease with the things we have been doing forever, despite the fact that some of those choices repeatedly have a negative outcome.

The choice to change, and the choice to make better choices, can be uncomfortable. It can be scary to venture in a new direction, not being able to fully anticipate the outcome. If you are reading this book, however, it is unlikely that you are happy with your current circumstance. Maybe it is time for you to begin making the hard choices that will lead to better outcomes.

Remember, the best things in life, rarely come easy. The best choices are not always easy, the comfortable choices are not always best. Making difficult choices, though frightening, can have great outcomes that can last a lifetime.

The choice to change

Norm did not show up on time for his anger management group. We took role at the beginning of the group, and he was not there. In the middle of the two-hour group, the gentlemen were able to take a ten-minute break. After the break, Norm was sitting in the group, and when we commented on his being late and coming in during the break, he got extremely angry.

Norm became aggressive and furious that anyone would dare accuse him of lying. He stormed out of the group and said that the "system was corrupt." The next week he returned, still angry, still talking about how the system was corrupt. I met him outside the group and told him that he could be as angry as he wanted to be, and that I would even help him "fight the system"; the only stipulation that I had was that he and I call his parole officer and have the three of us sit down to watch the surveillance video from the previous week's group. That way we wouldn't have to spend a moment arguing over whether he was there or not, we would just see him in the room on the tape, and the controversy would be over. Norm's face changed drastically.

Norm said, *"There's a video of the group?"* I said very calmly, *"Of course, and as everyone who starts the group is informed, both in writing and verbally, there is no audio. But even if you forgot, yes, there is a video. Now let's go call your parole officer and have the three of us sit down and watch it together. That way, together, we can fight the corrupt system."* He said, *"Please don't call him. I'm sorry. I thought I could sneak in at break and just get angry and get away with it."*

Norm had learned to use anger in his life as a way to avoid taking responsibility, as a way to avoid accountability for anything he did. As long as he could get angry at others and blame others for his anger, he never had to own up to his part in anything. The problem with doing so is that Norm was 68 years-old when this happened. You see, the longer we wait to hold ourselves accountable for our own lives, the longer we will continue to repeat the same mistakes over and over again.

That moment changed things for Norm, and this story has both a happy and a sad ending. The happy part was that, even at 68, Norm was able to make serious changes in his life (I'm not sure why that particular event impacted him as much as it did, but it certainly appeared to do so). The sad part was that less than a year after making those changes, Norm passed away from an unrelated accident.

It's never too late to make a change; but it sure feels better to make changes sooner than later.

It's Your Choice Exercise

After the following statements, circle whether you agree or disagree with the statements and write why you agree or disagree:

1. "I cannot choose things that happen to me, but I can choose how I react to those things." **Agree or Disagree.** Why?

   _____
   _____
   _____
   _____
   _____
   _____

2. "Every time I am in a hurry, it seems like others hold me up on purpose." **Agree or Disagree.** Why?

   _____
   _____
   _____
   _____
   _____
   _____

3. "I may have done something to make someone think I needed anger management, but I shouldn't have to be punished as harshly as I have been." **Agree or Disagree.** Why?

   _____
   _____
   _____
   _____

4. "Women get away with way more things than men do." **Agree or Disagree**. Why?

_____
_____
_____
_____
_____
_____

5. "Men get away with way more things than women do." **Agree or Disagree**. Why?

_____
_____
_____
_____
_____
_____
_____
_____

6. "If there weren't so many stupid people in the world, I wouldn't make so many mistakes. It's the stupid people that make me act the way I do." **Agree or Disagree**. Why?

_____
_____
_____
_____
_____
_____

7. "I should get a break when I mess up." **Agree or Disagree**. Why?

___

8. "Whether or not I do well with my anger doesn't just depend on me." **Agree or Disagree**. Why?

___

9. "It is unfair for me to make changes in my life when other people in my life are refusing to make changes." **Agree or Disagree.** Why?

___

10. As you reflect on your answers from 1-9, what can you learn about yourself?

_____
_____
_____
_____
_____
_____

> If two people are each convinced that the other person "should" be acting differently – which one is right?

> **Personal challenge:**
> Open your heart to accepting the knowledge of others.

Family Tree

Learning about our family history can be vital to helping us understand why and how we came to be where we are. The past does not determine the future – however-and this is important to understand – the past certainly influences and shapes the future. If we do not learn about the past, about family influences, or about family patterns of behavior, we are likely to continue to repeat the same unhealthful aspects of it throughout our lives.

Every family can say that someone in their genealogy struggled with anger, addiction, or some form of mental difficulties. The reason is that we are all human and we all struggle with things from time to time. By identifying who struggled and when, we can gain insight into our own struggles. Remember that patterns remain patterns until we actively choose to change them. We can use family history as an excuse to continue to act in emotionally unhealthful ways, or we can use family history as a motivation for personal change. In the end, what we choose is ultimately up to us.

Family Tree Exercise - Part 1

Draw a family tree. Use squares to represent the men in your family tree. Use circles to represent the females in your family tree. Use lines to show how your family tree developed. For this exercise, put checkmarks or little notes next to people who struggled with anger.

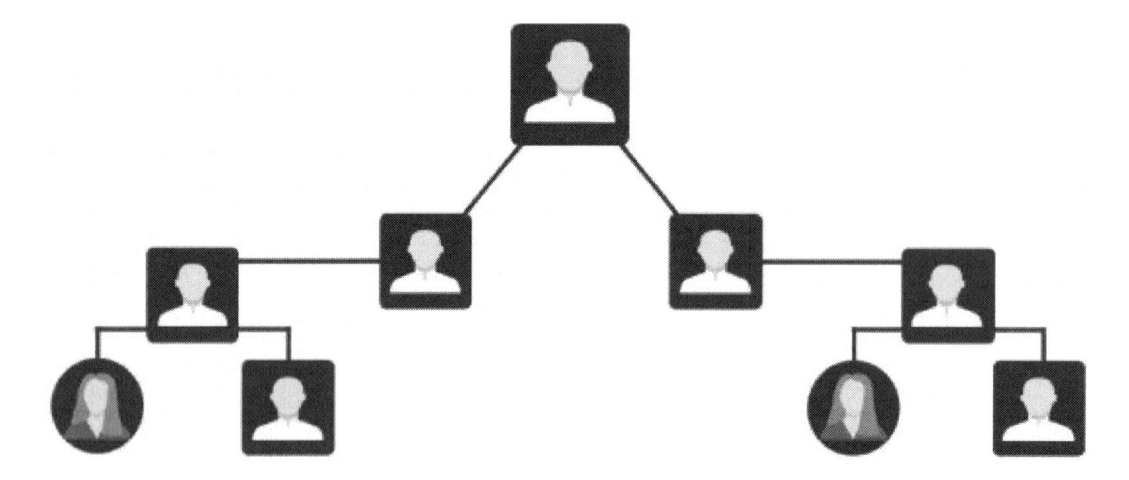

Your Family Tree:

229 As you look at the family tree that you created consider the following questions:

1. What patterns of behavior in your family history stand out to you?

_____

_____

_____

_____

_____

_____

2. Who are you most like?

_____

_____

_____

_____

_____

_____

3. Do you use your similarity to someone in your family as an excuse to act a certain way? (In other words, *"I love my dad, and he had a temper. I'm just like him, so I'll always have a temper."*)

_____

_____

_____

_____

_____

4. Can you mimic the positive qualities of that individual without taking on the negative qualities as well?

___

5. What kind of behavioral patterns do you want future members of your family to see in you?

___

6. What kind of behavioral patterns do you want future members of your family to mimic from you?

___

Recall that the cycle of violence is:

Tension   **Explosion**   **Honeymoon**

Tension builds up to an inevitable explosion in an abrupt outburst of anger. Once an explosion occurs, people jump to the "honeymoon" phase where they make promises to never explode like that again. The promises are usually well intentioned, so people believe that change is going to happen, but without learning about their own behavior and dedicating themselves to changing it, people are more likely to continue the cycle.

We have all learned our patterns of violence from somewhere, and more often than not, we learn them from watching others in our family when we are young. This does not excuse our behavior, but it does contribute to explaining it.

The fact is that behavioral patterns are passed down from generation to generation in families. As conventional wisdom teaches us, however: *We are doomed to repeat mistakes if we do not learn from them.* We cannot break familial patterns of violence until we stop and really look at the role that we play in our own cycle of violence. Every moment we spend focusing on *what others do* in our cycle of violence is a moment that we are not working on ourselves; so continue to remind yourself to focus on the one person in the world you can actually change: you.

Family Tree Exercise - Part 2

1. Write down how the cycle of violence was passed down through your family tree.

   _____
   _____
   _____
   _____
   _____
   _____

2. Write down how that cycle can be either passed on or broken.

   _____
   _____
   _____
   _____
   _____
   _____
   _____

Personal challenge:
No matter how hard, respond to someone in a positive way.

Diagramming Who I Am

Sometimes it is easier for us to interpret information when it is presented to us in a picture. Diagramming who we are in a picture can help us to "see" where we are in regard to our ego states.

Recall the following types of ego states:

Hurt Child
When we tend to feel sorry for ourselves

Fun Child
When we seek fun over responsibilities

Adult
When we think rationally and make good decisions

Nurturing Parent
When we are loving and caring

Critical Parent
When we are critical, demanding, and nagging

A person who believes he/she cannot succeed because others do not like him/her, and likewise is equally critical of others, would diagram him/herself like that below. Such a person would rate high in the Hurt Child and Critical Parent ego states and be about mid-range in the Adult ego state. Remember that ego states fluctuate, but in general, we can diagram ourselves in regard to our "baseline" of how we normally think and act.

HC

Diagram Exercise

Use your answers to the questions below to help you plot your own Diagram:

Most of the time when I get upset, I tend to go to my HURT CHILD / CRITICAL PARENT (circle one). Explain.

_____

_____

_____

_____

_____

_____

_____

_____

True or False:

I can help others get out of their hurt child by yelling at them and by being in my critical parent. **T or F**

I can help others get out of their critical parent by yelling at them and by being in my critical parent. **T or F**

It is helpful for my relationship when I go to my hurt child and start feeling sorry for myself. **T or F**

1. When I operate out of my _____ (CP, NP, A, FC, or HC), I bring out other people's _____ (CP, NP, A, FC, or HC).

2. When other people operate out of their _____ (CP, NP, A, FC, or HC), I then operate out of my _____ (CP, NP, A, FC, or HC).

3. When I get into an argument, my personal diagram looks like this:

Personal challenge:
Practice saying, "This is NOT the end of MY world but an opportunity for me to begin a new world."

Being Whole

Fritz Perls was a famous psychologist. He taught that in order to be authentic with others, people have to learn how to be authentic with themselves. To become authentic, Perls taught, we have to uncover the layers of who we are. He compared the layers to an onion. He came up with five layers that we have to peel back to thoroughly reveal our authentic selves. Revealing our authentic or true selves is necessary for us to experience any genuine change.

Here are the layers:

Phony Layer: The phony layer is where we reside when we are not being genuine. When we live in the phony layer, we often act the "way we are supposed to act," not the way our instinct tells us to act. Typically, we see the phony layer represented by saying things like, "I'm good," when someone asks us how we are, even though we don't feel good on the inside. The phony layer is the part of us who tries to be who we think others need us to be.

In terms of anger, constantly having to prove how tough we are would represent the phony layer. Anyone who attempts to "prove" to someone else how tough he/she is, is not being genuine. Think about it, if you already know you're tough, why prove it to anyone? It would not be for yourself; it would only be for the other person (i.e., to be who you think that person wants you to be).

Phobic Layer: Most people are told it's not okay to admit that they are afraid. Fear is often seen as a weakness. The ironic about fear being seen as a weakness is that without we cannot have courage and bravery. Courage and bravery occur only when we act in the face of fear. Perhaps the greatest fear most people can ever face in their lives is looking deeply inside them.

We all like to believe that we have the answers to the world. We all like to believe that our opinions are the "correct" opinions. When it is time for us to really look at ourselves, we have a tendency to distract ourselves, or otherwise we turn away from truly learning about ourselves. When we allow that fear-of-learning-about-ourselves to take over, we are living in the phobic layer.

> ### The Phobic Puppet-Master: Respect
>
> Being in the Phobic layer has nothing to do with physical toughness. In fact, even the physically toughest people in the world can live constantly in the phobic layer. So many tougher people would hate to be called someone's "puppet." Yet, even though we don't want to be a puppet to the idea of "respect," we allow ourselves to be a puppet to respect all the time. In other words, respect is like a puppet master, and it can make us jump, dance, and move however it wants. For example, consider the tough guy who demands no one "disrespect" him. If anyone disrespects him, however, and he reacts, he becomes a puppet to the idea of respect.
>
> Ironically, the fear of letting go of "respect" as a person's puppet master is exactly what keeps people being controlled by respect. The more we demand respect from others, the more we are controlled by respect ourselves. Facing our phobias can help us break through to the next level.
>
> *"Only the truly weak seek to control others; the strong control themselves."*

Impasse: The layer of impasse is the "place of great ambivalence." Ambivalence means "uncertainty." When it comes to the layers of human beings, the following statement can sum up the concept of the impasse: "We want to change, and we don't want to change." The reason we are ambivalent is that change is difficult. Sometimes change is so difficult in fact that we get stuck, and that's just what the impasse is: the stuck point.

Implosive Layer: To implode is to "burst inward." In sense, bursting inward is exactly what we are doing in the implosive layer. In the implosive layer, we are facing the fear of learning things we don't want to know or see about ourselves. In this layer, we are fighting through the fear we have that tells us to turn around and simply live a closed-off life.

In the implosive layer, we take the time and effort to delve deeply into ourselves. We listen openly to what others have to say about us. We avoid the jump from "I'm all great" to "I'm all terrible," and instead, we take an honest look at who we are. The implosive layer is a time of serious introspection or a time to look within ourselves with the intention of coming out wiser than when we went in.

Explosive Layer: The explosive layer is about not only understanding ourselves more, but also communicating accurately with the outside world. The explosive layer occurs when we take what we learned about ourselves in the implosive layer and make contact or a connection with others. In the explosive layer, we live consistently with who we really are, rather than living according to what those around us want to be.

At first glance, it's easy to say or believe that we are being who we really are. But as we look more closely, we have to ask ourselves: Are we fulfilling our true individual potential? Are we living from a place of truth? To live in the explosive layer is to live from a place of truth for ourselves.

Being Whole Exercise

It takes courage to move from the phony to the explosive layer. To begin the process through the layers, take time to answer the following questions as honestly as you can.

1. **Phony Layer** – The part of us that is phony or fake. This is a tough question. In what ways are you phony or fake? In other words, in what ways are you not genuine or maybe even not honest with yourself?

   _____
   _____
   _____
   _____
   _____
   _____
   _____

2. **Phobic Layer** – The part of us that is afraid of change. In what ways are you afraid of changing? More specifically, what are you afraid of learning about yourself?

   _____
   _____
   _____
   _____
   _____
   _____
   _____

3. **Impasse** – The part of us that stops us, the "stuck point." What does or would keep you stuck when you try to change? What stops you from changing?

_____
_____
_____
_____
_____

4. **Implosive Layer** – The part of us that looks long and hard at our lives. What things about yourself do you have to face? What do you find when you really look inside yourself?

_____
_____
_____
_____
_____

5. **Explosive Layer** – The part of us that wants to make great changes and genuinely move forward. What great changes will you make? What will your life look like when you live genuinely all the time?

_____
_____
_____
_____
_____

Good People / Bad People

From the first stories we hear as children of heroes and villains, we are taught to distinguish between "good" and "bad." Some people argue that people are inherently "good," whereas others argue that people are inherently "bad." Other people would argue that people are not born "good" or "bad," but "good" and "bad" people are made that way by the world. Regardless of your stance on "good" and "bad" people, almost everyone has an underlying idea of what makes up each. Discovering what we identify as the characteristics of a "good" person or "bad" person can help us sort out how we judge ourselves and others. Further thought about these character traits allow us to become more effective in our lives.

The challenge we can run into with labeling people "good" or "bad" is that we tend to minimize or excuse the hurtful behaviors of those we label "good," whereas we tend to zero in on or maximize the hurtful behaviors of those we label "bad." The reality is, however, that we already have labeled ourselves, as well as others, as either "good" or "bad," so what we ask you to do in this exercise is figure out how you have come to the conclusions you have about who is "good" and who is "bad."

The Middle Ground and Peace

It is easier for us to put people in categories. Categories make us feel safe and secure. "Good" and "bad" are two categories that simplify the world for us. The problem with bouncing back and forth from "good people" to "bad people" in our minds is that we leave little room for the middle ground. When we see the world in terms of black/white, good/bad, and right/wrong, we leave out room for understanding.

The fact is that we will all make mistakes. Despite all of us making mistakes, it is more rare for us to see ourselves as "bad guys." Instead, we tend to see our own side of the mistakes we make. Failure to see others' perspectives leaves us trapped in our own worlds. If our worlds are filled with pain, then we are essentially trapping ourselves in our own pain.

An elephant can be a nice representation of balance, because an elephant can cross a river without being either swept downstream by the current or stuck in the mud below. The elephant takes the middle path. A middle ground for us is to resist seeing the world in terms of black/white, good/bad, right/wrong, and instead begin to see people's behavior in terms of "effective versus ineffective." If our behaviors have been viewed as "ineffective," then we have an opportunity to do what it takes to learn a little bit more about ourselves and to become a little bit more "effective" in our lives.

Good People / Bad People Exercise

From what you have always believed regarding "good people" and "bad people," answer the following questions.

1. What does a "good" person look like?

   _____
   _____
   _____
   _____
   _____
   _____

2. What kinds of decisions do "good" people make?

   _____
   _____
   _____
   _____
   _____

3. Who are some "good" people who you have known throughout your life?

   _____
   _____
   _____
   _____
   _____

4. What about them made them "good" people?

5. What is a "bad" person?

6. What does a "bad" person look like?

7. What kinds of decisions do "bad" people make?

_____

_____

_____

_____

_____

_____

8. Who are some "bad" people who you have known throughout your life?

_____

_____

_____

_____

_____

_____

9. What about them made them "bad" people?

_____

_____

_____

_____

_____

_____

_____

10. What kind of person are you?

_____
_____
_____
_____
_____
_____
_____

11. What kinds of decisions do you make?

_____
_____
_____
_____
_____
_____
_____

12. What kind of person have other people called you?

_____
_____
_____
_____
_____
_____
_____

13. How could you be more ethically effective?

_____
_____
_____
_____
_____
_____

14. What would it take for you to become the kind of person you would like to become?

_____
_____
_____
_____
_____
_____
_____

> **Personal challenge:**
> **Recognize when you are thinking in terms of "black" and "white."**

Shame

When people feel ashamed of who they are, they tend to not care what they do or whom they hurt. When people feel shame, they tend to feel embarrassed. When people feel embarrassed they tend to react out of anger. Anger is a secondary emotion. It stems from hurt. When people learn to deal with the hurt they are feeling, they will lessen their chances of reacting out of anger. It is difficult for many people to admit or express that they are hurting, so they continue to cover it up with anger.

Imagine how different things would be if we could learn to express our hurt rather than cover it up with anger. Imagine how different our conversations would go. Imagine how many fewer conflicts we would engage in and how far fewer moments of suffering we would have. When we hurt, we suffer. When we act out of anger to cover the hurt, essentially, we are adding to our own suffering.

A Tale of Shame

Mike lost his job due to an injury. He couldn't do the job he had always done. He was trying to get disability payments, but in the meantime, he wasn't able to provide any income for his family. Mike said he "didn't even feel like a man anymore." He found himself drinking more, constantly irritated, short-tempered, and more frequently yelling at everyone in his family.

Mike lost his job and some physical ability – and that hurt. The shame he attached to not being able to do what he used to do led him to acting in ways that made it very difficult for his family to be around. His injury existed; it was real. He lost his job; that was hard. What he did to act out of shame was worse. By being angry, lashing out, and constantly putting his loved ones down, he avoided facing the shame he felt, and he created new reasons to feel shame.

Mike's pain was understandable. But what if he had chosen to do something differently about his pain? What if he had chosen to deal with the shame until he felt understood? Mike could have made very different decisions with the shame he felt, especially considering this:

Mike's wife came in to talk to the therapist. She said, *"I love Mike. He is the epitome of a man to me. I see how hard it is for him to be hurt and not be able to do the things he used to, but I don't see him as any less of a man than he was before he got hurt. I wish he could see himself the way I see him – but he doesn't, and because he can't deal with it, he's becoming a tyrant at home. Now we all walk on eggshells at home trying not to upset him. Please help us."*

Mike met with the therapist soon after. Now Mike faced a really hard choice: have pain, not be able to work, and be a tyrant to everyone OR have pain, not be able to work, and be the kind of husband and father his wife and children would be proud to have.

What decision do you think he made? More importantly, what decision would you make?

The fact is that people can relate to pain, but people are afraid of anger. People are willing to sit with us when we are in pain, but people want nothing to do with us when we are in a state of anger. Pain is understandable. Ill-expressed anger is harmful. There is nothing wrong with the feeling of anger. In fact, anger tells us something about what is going on with us. There is a big difference, however, between letting anger guide us to learning more about ourselves and allowing anger to overtake who we are.

Anger (What the outside world sees)

Hurt (What we feel on the inside)

When hurt is on the inside, anger is what we show on the outside. By understanding this, we have a chance to learn how to express the hurt we are feeling and completely change the way others relate to us. When we express anger, especially when we get out of control, people respond to the anger we are expressing. Rarely, do others attempt to ignore our aggressive behaviors and deal directly with what actually contributed to our pain. Learning to express the hurt is difficult, but the results are profoundly different.

Expressing Anger	Expressing Hurt
Example: Someone lies to us.	**Example:** Someone lies to us.
The hurt is: Feeling shame and inadequacy	**The hurt is:** Feeling shame and inadequacy
The anger is: We scream at the person and tell them how horrible he/she is	**Instead of anger, we express the hurt:** We tell the other person that we are hurt by his/her actions or that we feel embarrassed by his/her lying to us
Result: The person no longer wants to tell us much of anything because of how we reacted. The person responds to the anger we show, rather than addressing the hurt that he/she contributed to	**Result:** The person actually hears what we are communicating and can respond to the hurt that he/she contributed to, rather than just reacting to our anger

Shame Exercise

Shame is defined as the painful feeling that comes after doing something dishonorable. Shame is a painful emotion. Shame causes us hurt. From a place of hurt, we act out of anger to cover up the pain we are feeling. Unfortunately, the anger can lead to doing more things that we regret, which in turn leads to more shame. Think about one event from which you feel a lot of shame. Living in shame can produce a cycle of shame. In this exercise, we will explore the feeling of shame that you have around any particular event.

1. Identify a behavior that has you feeling shame.

   _____

   _____

   _____

   _____

   _____

   _____

2. List some reasons why you believe you might need to hold on to a feeling of shame.

   _____

   _____

   _____

   _____

   _____

   _____

3. List 3 reasons why it would help you to forgive yourself.

_____
_____
_____
_____
_____
_____
_____

4. List at least two ways of how you can start this week to forgive yourself.

_____
_____
_____
_____
_____
_____
_____

5. What would it take for you to genuinely forgive yourself and move on?

_____
_____
_____
_____
_____
_____
_____

6. In what way can you make up for some of the wrongs you have made?

   a. _____

   _____

   _____

   _____

   b. _____

   _____

   _____

   _____

   c. _____

   _____

   _____

   _____

> *"To err is human. To forgive yourself is healthful."*
>
> **When we live in shame, we act out of shame. We must move beyond the shame and learn from our mistakes if we are to become the most that we can become.**

Personal challenge:
Act from a place of peace.

The Diretion of Our Energy

Our energy determines a great deal of who we are, including how we interact with others. Most people have known someone who "drains our energy." Most have also known someone who "picks up our spirits." We impact people with our energy, just as much as others impact us with theirs. More often than not, people choose to focus on other people's energy and forget to look at their own energy.

We all bring energy to situations, and we all leave energy behind after we exit situations. What we often fail to realize is that our energy in large part determines how others approach and respond to us. People feed off of each other's energy. For example, if we bring a lot of energy to situations, we can overwhelm others, both in positive and negative ways. People in turn, will respond according to the energy that we exhibit.

There are primarily four different types of energy that we can bring to or leave behind in situations. There are, however, a myriad of types of energy that fall on a continuum between and among these types of energy. In other words, we might not fall exactly into any one box, sometimes we are somewhere in the middle.

The four main types of energy are:

High/Positive Energy: When we function from this type of energy, we can bring energy to others that can be everything from passionate and enthusiastic to manic and unrealistic.

High/Negative Energy: When we function from this type of energy, we can exhibit behaviors that involve things like rage and intimidation.

Low/Positive Energy: When we function from this type of energy, we are more likely to be calm, clear, and peaceful.

Low/Negative Energy: When we function from this type of energy, we are more likely to exhibit signs of sadness that can range from self-pity to depression to hopelessness.

Direction of our Energy Exercise

When it comes to anger, high/negative energy can be a dangerous. The higher we go into negative energy, the more likely we are to lose control. Finding the place from which you operate most is important. Once you can identify the type of energy you bring to and leave behind in situations, not only will become self-aware but you will then be able to make a conscious choice to stay the same or change.

	Positive	Negative
High	Manic Behavior Unpredictable; very difficult to maintain stability	Rage Little, if any, control
Low	Calm; Clear; Peaceful	Depressed; Bored; self pity

1. What does your behavior look like when you are in each of these blocks?

a. High/Positive

_____
_____
_____
_____
_____

b. High/Negative

c. Low/Negative

d. Low/Positive

2. What block do you primarily operate out of?

　

3. What do you notice about your arguments when you are in HIGH/NEGATIVE (rage) or LOW/NEGATIVE (depressed)?

　

4. How can you move yourself from one block to the next?

Personal challenge: Steer your energy in the direction of compassion.

Finding a Solution

Sometimes when we feel lost, the one thing that we are missing most is an answer to our problem. Unfortunately, what we find is that answers to problems cannot come until we figure out exactly what the problem is. The more clearly we can identify the problem, the more likely we are to figure out what we can do.

We have a very difficult time trying to fight what we cannot see. All too often we find ourselves swinging blindly as we try to make changes in our lives. We frequently find ourselves unhappy or not satisfied in our current condition, yet we are still not quite sure why or where to begin. Better identification of the problem may lead us to determining what the solution may be, but knowing the possible solution is certainly only half the battle. We must also identify what obstacles can get in the way of our succeeding.

Quick fact:

For years, sports psychologists have helped the most elite athletes in the world understand that clear goals are much more likely to be met than unclear goals. So if we just talk about changing "someday," or how we "would love to see some changes in our life," we are not likely to make any real changes. If, however, we lay out precisely what we need to work on AND include a specific plan for working on that issue, then we are much more likely to meet our goals.

Finding a Solution Exercise

Imagine that as you sleep tonight a miracle happens, so that whatever problems you are dealing with are magically solved. When you wake up, you find that your life is exactly the way you want it to be.

1. What is it that you would notice about your life that would be different?

   _____
   _____
   _____
   _____
   _____
   _____
   _____

2. What is it that you would notice about yourself that would be different?

   _____
   _____
   _____
   _____
   _____

3. Even if you didn't get that miracle, what could do this week to make your life the way you want it to be?

   _____
   _____
   _____
   _____
   _____

4. What stops you from working on the things you need to be working on?

_____
_____
_____
_____
_____

5. What kind of strengths have you found in yourself from the past that have helped you get through tough situations?

_____
_____
_____
_____
_____

6. On a scale of 1-10, rank where you want to be in regard to being in a different spot in your life.

1	2	3	4	5	6	7	8	9	10
Chaos				My life is fine					I'm at peace

7. What can you do to move up the scale two numbers by the end of this week?

_____
_____
_____
_____
_____

8. What potential barriers can get in the way of your moving up the scale two numbers this week?

_____

_____

_____

_____

_____

9. How can you get around those barriers?

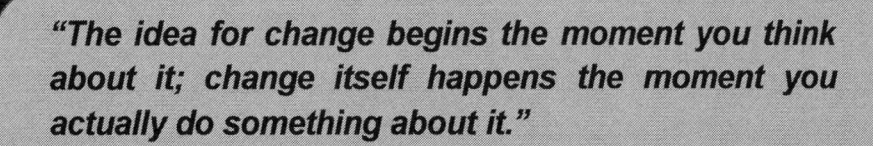

_____

_____

_____

_____

_____

> *"The idea for change begins the moment you think about it; change itself happens the moment you actually do something about it."*

Personal challenge:
Start the solution to your problem in this moment.

Excuses

We have all made excuses for our behavior. Getting caught and facing consequences is not easy for children, nor does it get easier for adults. To get around being in trouble, people will make every excuse they can, and people can get very creative in the process. The reasons people use excuses may be everything from not wanting to accept the consequences to an effort to avoid acknowledging the world the way it actually is.

When it comes to anger, we often have "valid" excuses that we tell ourselves for why we acted out of anger. Unfortunately, the consequences that stem from us acting out of anger are usually more than what we are prepared to face. Regardless of the excuses we make, at the end of the day, we are ultimately responsible for whatever we do. More importantly, as we make excuses, we simply delay making the changes we need to make.

Sometimes the easiest way to recognize the excuses we are currently making is to laugh at ourselves in terms of the poor excuses we have made in the past. Another way to move beyond excuses is to identify how others' excuses are obvious; and then reflect on how it may be just as easy for others to see our excuses, as it is for us to see theirs.

Outrageous Excuses

A student was once angry at his teacher for not accepting the excuse he turned in for missing three weeks of classes. The student's anger grew until his teacher acknowledged the anger, and then calmly pointing to the dates written on the excuse itself said, "I think I'm just surprised to see that it says here you spent three weeks in the emergency room. I guess I'm just having a tough time believing that, as it says according to the dates on this piece of paper - that the hospital didn't admit you and they just kept you in the E.R. for three weeks – especially when it says here that they treated you for a separated shoulder." Caught, the student then apologized for trying such an excuse.

A man missed his anger management group and brought a doctor's excuse the following week for why he missed. He was angry that the group facilitator did not accept his excuse, so he screamed at her and told her how "the system is unfair and corrupt." Then, she calmly pointed out that it was curious how the excuse seemed to be legitimate - except of course the part of it where he had cut out the section that had the "date of service" on it, and had taped in a scrap piece of paper with a date written in an entirely different color pen. Cutting out the date and replacing it with a different one was not the slickest move, but at the time, the man was struggling with addiction, and months later he admitted that he was embarrassed he tried it.

If these two examples of excuses seem a bit outrageous, then keep in mind that some of the excuses you and I have used have also sounded outrageous to others at times. Excuses may seem reasonable to us when we make them up and deliver them, but when we are in a more clear space in our lives, our excuses begin to seem as ridiculous to us as they actually were to others when we tried them.

Mailbag of Excuses

When we want to find an excuse to keep acting the way we are acting, we will find it. It is almost as if we have an entire mailbag filled with excuses for ourselves. If one, two, three, ten, or even twenty excuses don't work, then we seem to always be able to find more. The fact is that confirmation bias will keep us looking for the things that we want to see in the world. Regardless of the excuses that we can come up with (and both creative and desperate people can come up with countless excuses), the bottom line is **"if nothing changes, nothing changes."**

Whatever the excuses may be, at the end of the day the question we all have to ask ourselves is this: *Are we still acting in ways that are harmful to ourselves and others?* If we are, and we really don't want to change, then we will find and use one of our excuses out of our mailbag of excuses. If we are content with our poor choices, we will find a reason to keep acting the way we are acting, and we will even find a way to keep believing what we want to believe, regardless of how much we are hurting ourselves and others. Choose to throw away your mailbag of excuses, and you will see an amazing change happen.

Excuses Exercise

1. What kinds of memorable excuses have you made up in your life?

_____

_____

_____

_____

_____

2. What kinds of excuses have others made to you about their behavior AFTER they hurt you?

_____

_____

_____

_____

_____

3. How did you know they were making an excuse?

_____

_____

_____

_____

_____

_____

_____

4. What kinds of excuses do you make to stop yourself from doing what is best for you?

_____

_____

_____

_____

_____

_____

_____

5. Why do you think we make excuses for things?

_____

_____

_____

_____

_____

_____

6. What excuses do you continue to use that stop you from growing as an individual?

_____

_____

_____

_____

_____

_____

> "Despite popular belief, we actually can fool ourselves sometimes. The question is, 'Why would we want to?'" Excuses only stop us from changing.

> Personal challenge:
> Be honest with yourself in every moment.

Spiritual Guidance

The most intelligent and wise people in the world have one profound common factor: they talk openly about how much more they have to learn about themselves and the world. One common factor of all the great spiritual leaders in history is that there are stories of all of them taking time to go off alone to learn about themselves and about how they could positively impact the world. We can learn from their approach. It is not their wisdom by which they identify themselves, but rather their quest for wisdom and understanding.

The Room with A Thousand Demons

Once, a pupil visited his teacher in the great mountains. The teacher told him of about a transformative ritual that he was set to attend, and he invited the student to join him. The student, honored to join his guru in any ceremony, readily agreed, so the two of them set out on a journey immediately.

"Where are we going?" the student asked his teacher.

"Oh, I didn't tell you? We are going to the room of a thousand demons," the teacher replied with a smile on his face.

The student gulped when he heard the name of the place. "A room with a thousand demons?" he asked. "Why do they call it that?"

The teacher stopped, looked at the pupil in the eyes, and replied, "It is a called a room of a thousand demons because in it are one thousand of your worst fears. Anything you have ever or will ever be afraid of lies within this room. It is terrifying, yes, but those who go through the room will reach enlightenment."

The student, hoping to gain enlightenment, but now more terrified than ever, asked his teacher, "How is it possible to make it through this room with a thousand demons?"

The teacher, very intently commanded, "You put one foot in front of the other until you reach the other side."

We can learn to be self-reflective and intentional. By continuing to learn about ourselves and living with purpose we allow for positive change to occur. In our experiences, we have heard people say, *"I already do everything that I need to do,"* or *"I already know all I need to know."* They are basically admitting that they know very little about themselves and the world around them. The more honest you are, the more you will grow and the wiser you will become.

Spiritual Guidance Exercise

1. If you were a spiritual leader who had the responsibility of teaching many people, what types of things would you teach them about how to treat each other?

   _____
   _____
   _____
   _____
   _____
   _____

2. Of the things you described in number one, which is the most difficult for you to follow through with?

   _____
   _____
   _____
   _____
   _____
   _____

Spiritual Guidance

269

3. Why do you think it is so difficult for you to follow through with that? In other words, what stops you from living out that in your life?

_____
_____
_____
_____
_____
_____
_____

4. What shift do you need to make to start living by the things you believe in most?

_____
_____
_____
_____
_____
_____
_____

5. List a few ways in which you doubt yourself on your ability to change.

_____
_____
_____
_____
_____
_____
_____

6. What can you do to begin to work through that doubt?

_____
_____
_____
_____
_____
_____

> **Even the greatest of spiritual teachers had fear and doubt at times: the difference was the ability to face that fear and doubt – and still trust . . .**

> **Personal challenge: Find the courage to face your fears and doubts.**

Family Groups - *Rules and Roles*

All families have rules. Rules guide families on how people can behave. If someone says, "There were no rules in my family," then the rule was, "Do whatever you want." All families have rules. Rules can be framed positively, as in "please do this," or negatively, as in "do *not* do that." The rules provide the boundaries for the family. Once the boundaries have been set, it's time for each family member to take on a role. Roles can be different, and people rarely choose their own roles. Nonetheless, roles can be very difficult to ever shed. Learning about our rules and roles of the family in which we grew up can help us tremendously. With this awareness and knowledge, we can choose to hold onto or let go of whatever rules and roles are not helpful for us.

Rules

Sometimes it's easy to think about the rules we had in our family growing up. Sometimes, we have to really think about what the rules were. The reason that sometimes we remember the rules easily and sometimes we don't is that families have **two kinds of rules: overt** and **covert**. Overt rules are the rules that were spoken: "No talking with your mouth full!" is a common overt family rule for many families. Covert rules, on the other hand, were the rules that no one ever spoke out loud, yet everyone knew. Things like, *nobody talks to dad when he comes home angry* or *no one tells mom anything that might upset her* are examples of covert or unspoken rules.

The rules that families have are so powerful that we often pass those rules down through the generations without ever questioning them. Regardless if we liked the rules or not, regardless of whether the rules were beneficial or not, we all tend to simply just do what we were taught. We may have hated the rules, we may have ardently disagreed with the rules, but, because the rules were what we knew, we ended up integrating them into our own families anyway. Until now!

Roles

Think about a play. In every play, there are characters that make up the story. Each character has his or her own role. In families, the same thing is true. Every family member plays a specific role in the family. People can take on different roles through the years, but switching roles is very difficult. It's the reason why even after years of being away and making huge changes, a family member can come back home to everyone treating him or her exactly as they remembered that person before he or she left. Essentially, the family expects that the person keep the same role he or she always used to play.

To go along with family rules, each family develops what are called "roles." The roles that each person plays in a family are different. Some people take on the role of *family hero*, others take on the role of *scapegoat*. Roles can range from *enabler* to *enforcer*, from the *golden* to the *black sheep*. The roles are varied, but where families get stuck is this: once a family gets used to certain roles, if someone goes away or stops playing the role everyone was used to, the family will work to either get that person back to that role, or substitute a new person to take on that old role.

Spotlight on the Scapegoat

Consider the family that blames a particular child for all their problems. That child fulfills the role of "scapegoat." Families that tend to blame a 'scapegoat child' might transfer blame onto a new 'scapegoat' if the usual one moves away (for school, incarceration, marriage, etc.). the absence of one scapegoat member of the family doesn't prevent the family from having a scapegoat.

When it comes to roles, it is almost as if families need to have family members maintain particular roles. As long as a family can blame all of their problems on a particular child, then no one else in the family has to look at him or herself. The rest of the family is free to believe that they are normal and fine, and it is only the scapegoat that causes problems. But the fact is that every family member contributes to interactions.

Family therapists have found that as long as families' see their problems as the result of one person's behaviors rather than as a result of the families' interactions, then change is not likely to occur, and families' will continuously find a scapegoat to blame. When families' can have each member (especially parents) take responsibility for what they do ineffectively, then families' can learn to function in ways that completely eliminates the need for a scapegoat.

273 Family Groups Exercise – Part 1

For this exercise, write about your family of origin (the family you grew up with).

1. What are some of the **rules** that your family created?

   _____
   _____
   _____
   _____
   _____
   _____

2. How did these **rules** impact you and your family's behaviors/actions toward each other?

   _____
   _____
   _____
   _____
   _____

3. Describe what your role was within your family.

   _____
   _____
   _____

4. What was it about this role that you disliked? Did this role cause you to behave in ways that went against what you believed about yourself?

_____
_____
_____
_____
_____
_____

5. What was one thing you did to change this role?

_____
_____
_____
_____
_____
_____
_____

6. What roles did other members of your family play?

_____
_____
_____
_____
_____
_____
_____

7. How did these roles shape the functioning of your family?

_____
_____
_____
_____
_____
_____
_____

8. Who in your family was usually to blame for the family not doing well?

_____
_____
_____
_____
_____
_____
_____

9. What would happen if that person was no longer in that role?

_____
_____
_____
_____
_____
_____
_____

10. What family member do you personally blame the most for things not going well?

_____
_____
_____
_____
_____

Family Groups Exercise – Part 2

For this exercise, write about your current family (the family you have now or who you refer to as your family).

1. What are some of the **rules** that your family created?

_____
_____
_____
_____
_____
_____

2. How do these **rules** impact you and your family's behaviors/actions toward each other?

_____
_____
_____
_____
_____
_____
_____
_____

3. Describe what your **role** is within your family.

_____
_____
_____
_____
_____
_____
_____
_____

4. What is it about this role you dislike? Does this role cause you to behave in ways that go against what you believe about yourself?

_____
_____
_____
_____
_____
_____
_____

5. What is one thing you can do to change this role?

6. What roles do other members of your family play?

7. How do these roles affect the functioning of your family?

8. Who in your family right now takes the heat for the family not doing well?

9. What would happen if that person were no longer in that role?

10. Who do you tend to blame in your current family situation for existing problems in the family?

Personal challenge:
Create healthy dynamics for your family.

Toxic Relationships

William Glasser was a great psychologist who, among many other things, taught about the following relationship habits. Some habits help our relationships; other habits seem to hurt our relationships. It is only when we can recognize our own *ineffective* habits that we have the opportunity to change them.

It's often much easier to recognize other people's bad habits than it is to see our own. Despite not liking other people's negative habits, however, all people have some bad habits. Hardly anyone enjoys being nagged, threatened, or blamed for things; yet, everyone has, at some point, nagged, threatened, or blamed others. In other words, without knowing it, people often do to others the very things that they do not want done to themselves. We believe that the only way to begin changing negative habits is by first identifying them clearly."

This exercise can help you identify what habits are ultimately deadly to relationships, and what habits are very helpful for relationships. With awareness around what types of habits help and hurt relationships, you will have a better chance to choose to engage in the types of habits that you want.

Take a look at the following two lists.

Seven Caring Relationship Habits	Seven Deadly Relationship Habits
1. Supporting	1. Criticizing
2. Encouraging	2. Blaming
3. Listening	3. Complaining
4. Accepting	4. Nagging
5. Trusting	5. Threatening
6. Respecting	6. Punishing (guilting)
7. Negotiating differences	7. Bribing, rewarding to control

Toxic Relationships Exercise

1. Which of the **Seven Deadly Relationship Habits** do you find yourself doing the most?

2. How do you do those things? (For example, what does your "nagging" look like?)

3. What are you trying to gain by using those habits?

4. What do you think would happen if you were to trade one of your deadly negative habits for a positive caring one around the same issue?

_____
_____
_____
_____
_____
_____

5. Which of the Seven Caring Relationship Habits do you do the most?

_____
_____
_____
_____
_____
_____

6. How can you enhance how you do that habit even more?

_____
_____
_____
_____
_____
_____

7. How can your awareness of your habits impact your relationships?

_____
_____
_____
_____
_____
_____
_____

> Whereas it can be easy to pick out what others do wrong in relationships, it's often tough for us to see what we are doing ineffectively.

Personal challenge:
Confront your darkest habits head on.

Life Map

Imagine your life as one big map from start to finish. Reflecting on what has already happened we can fairly easily identify road blocks and stumbling points. It's not difficult to look at what has already happened and find a way to make a map out of it. For example, look at the following life map:

Life Map: The Tough Years

START >

        Elementary school >   Junior high >   Not getting a job
          (was bullied)   (heart broken)   I applied for…

As we look back on our lives, we can see that there were obstacles we thought we would not be able get beyond, only to see later that in fact we *did* make it through those tough times, and possibly even did quite well. Our experience allows us to see those pieces of our past in a different light. How much differently would those tough times have been for us had we known what was coming? How much different would our lives have been had we known then what we know now?

Perhaps we cannot predict the future, and there really is no real way to know exactly might come our way; however, the more we plan to meet different types of obstacles, the more prepared we will be to face them when they come our way.

Life Map Exercise

Many of us have been taught to prepare for our future. Teachers, spiritual leaders, parents, and advisors of all sorts have told us that to neglect preparing for the future is a means to failure. What we prepare for is often much less of a problem than the challenges that creep up unexpectedly in life. We cannot know what is coming, but what we can do is learn a method of how to be prepared for life's difficulties.

> **No More Troubles…**
>
> Once, a man (who had battled alcoholism for 12 years) decided he was done drinking. He loudly proclaimed, "I will never drink again!" When someone asked this man what he was going to do when the temptation came back for him to drink, he boasted, "I will never be tempted again. I know I don't want to drink ever again." But the other man persisted, "You have to prepare for what might come up though…" but before he could finish his sentence, the proud man decreed that "nothing will ever come up, so I don't need to prepare," and he did not want to hear another word about it.
>
> Almost needless to say, within one week this man was drunk on the side of the road. When the other man saw him and asked what happened, the drunk man responded, "My best friend died. Who could have seen that coming?"
>
> Because he failed to prepare for anything, he was prepared for nothing.

Life Map Exercise – Part 1

Below, you will make a goal-map for your life. A goal-map is chance to identify what you want and what obstacles might get in the way of your accomplishing your goals in regard to anger. Remember that only a foolish person believes that the rest of his or her life will be obstacle-free or anger-free. In the map below, identify potential road blocks to your getting to your life goals.

My life goal regarding anger is to:

_____
_____
_____
_____
_____

1. What is the potential road block?

_____
_____
_____
_____
_____

2. What can I do to get through or get around the road block?

_____
_____
_____
_____

3. What would stop me from doing what I wrote for number 2?

4. How can I get around what I wrote for number 3?

5. What specific plan can I make to follow through getting beyond whatever would stop me from achieving my goal?

Life Map Exercise – Part 2

In Part 2 of this exercise consider the same questions but take it one step further and consider other obstacles. Frequently after we get past one obstacle another presents itself. We then have to focus our efforts to get past that obstacle to find yet another to overcome and then have to repeat the process again. The focus must be on accepting the challenge and dealing with the obstacle, instead of returning to old habits and poor choices.

Your life right now:

First road block. What is this road block?

What can you do to get around it?

What would stop you or get in the way from your doing what you need to do to get around it?

What specific plan can you make to follow through with getting beyond whatever would stop you from achieving your goal?

Second road block. What is this road block?

What can you do to get around it?

What would stop you or get in the way from your doing what you need to do to get around it?

What specific plan can you make to follow through with getting beyond whatever would stop you from achieving your goal?

Third road block. What is this road block?

What can you do to get around it?

What would stop you or get in the way from your doing what you need to do to get around it?

What specific plan can you make to follow through with getting beyond whatever would stop you from achieving your goal?

Personal challenge: Face the challenges that await you along your journey

My Advice to the World

Many people believe they have the wisdom and background experience to justify giving advice others. In fact, everyone probably has advice to give the world. We all have experiences that have shaped our view of the world. We have all lived through our unique circumstances. Many people believe that they have experienced things differently and further believe they have surpassed their challenges better than everyone else, hence, who better to give advice.

Giving advice is easy. Taking advice is difficult. Even when it's our own, we have difficulty following through on very good advice. Think of a time that you may have offered advice to someone and shortly thereafter chose not to follow that guidance that you offered. Why is it that we have been so stubborn to taking advice that was offered to us? There are definitely times that we could have benefitted from following through on the guidance offered to us by wise individuals. Think of ways in which you can bridge the gap in your own life between having advice and actually living by it.

The 411 on Advice

Have you ever given advice to someone and then gotten angry when he or she didn't take it? Have you ever not taken good advice from others? Did you not take their advice to "get at them personally," or did you not follow his/her advice because you simply just wanted to do something else? Have you ever noticed that people take it personally when someone doesn't follow their advice?

The truth about asking for advice is this: we rarely seek genuine advice. Mostly, *when we are asking for advice, we are asking for people to confirm what we already believe we should do.*

Need some advice?

My Advice to the World Exercise

Based on your experiences, offer your advice to the following people and situations. As you do so, ask yourself: Does the advice that I give come from a place of compassion and wisdom, or Does it come from a place of bitterness and frustration?

1. My advice to people who have committed a violent crime out of anger and have been convicted is…

   _____
   _____
   _____
   _____
   _____
   _____

2. My advice to people who have to spend time in jail or prison is…

   _____
   _____
   _____
   _____
   _____
   _____

3. My advice to men about interacting with other men, male friends and/or male coworkers is…

   _____
   _____

4. My advice to women about interacting with other women, female friends and/or female coworkers is…

5. My advice to men in general about interacting with women is…

6. My advice to women in general about interacting with men is…

7. My advice to anyone about interacting in a long term relationship is…

8. My advice to people about expressing anger is…

9. My advice to people who have to handle a conflict is…

10. My advice to someone who has to deal with someone "trash talking" is…

11. My advice to someone who tries to control his or her partner in a relationship is…

12. My advice to someone for dealing with insecurities or jealousy is…

Defense Mechanisms

On some level, we all like to know that the world is the way we think it is. We like to believe that we are right about things, at least some things. So when new information comes along that counters what we already know, we have a tendency to resist it, at least at first and sometimes for a long time. The reason we resist information that counters what we know is that we all want to feel safe. When we get new information that flies in the face of what we know or believe about ourselves, we tend to defend ourselves from this new information.

Psychologists use the words *"ego"* and *"defense mechanisms"* to help describe this process of protecting ourselves. The ego is the self, or more accurately, who we think we are. We want to feel certain about the world, so we attach ourselves to certain beliefs. Talking about the ego can be very complex, but the bottom line is that our egos are fragile. When someone says something that goes against what we know or believe, and it hurts us, it's because our egos are getting hurt.

Now, no one wants a bruised ego, so we defend ourselves. *Defense* mechanisms protect our egos. Imagine defense mechanisms like a defensive line on a football team that protects its own end zone. Defense mechanisms are there to stop information that may be too much for the ego to handle. Defense mechanisms keep us safe by helping us to stay locked in our own worlds. there is nothing wrong with defense mechanisms; after all, they keep us safe.

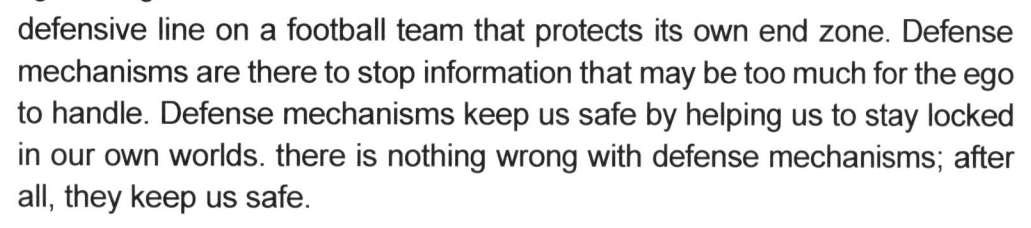

What we want to emphasize is that defense mechanisms are not wrong or bad, merely they limit the way we see ourselves and the world. The more we use defense mechanisms, the more time we stay in the fictitious world or the *cartoon world* that we have essentially created, and the less time we spend accepting responsibility for ourselves as we face the world, the *real world*, as it actually is.

Defense Mechanisms Exercise

There are many defense mechanisms, but below we will present you with eight of them. In each case, we will give you a brief description of a particular defense mechanism, then we ask you to give an example of a time when you used that particular defense mechanism. Defense mechanisms are not always easy to see, so do the best that you can.

1. **Displacement** – taking things out on the wrong people.

    Give an example of a time when you used displacement.

    _____
    _____
    _____
    _____
    _____

2. **Introjection** – unquestioned acceptance of an idea. Give an example of one of your introjections.

    _____
    _____
    _____
    _____
    _____

Defense Mechanisms

3. **Repression** – forgetting something that you did that you are not proud of. Give an example of something that you repressed.

_____
_____
_____
_____
_____
_____

4. **Denial** – refusing to accept responsibility for your actions. Give an example of a time you used denial.

_____
_____
_____
_____
_____
_____

5. **Projection** – seeing in others the things that are inside you. Give an example of a time you used projection.

_____
_____
_____
_____
_____
_____

6. **Deflection** – keeping the topic off you so to avoid dealing with what you've done. Give an example of a time you used deflection.

_____

_____

_____

_____

_____

_____

7. **Intellectualization** – coming up with a "valid" reason for why you did what you did.
Give an example of a time you used intellectualization.

_____

_____

_____

_____

_____

_____

8. **Confirmation bias** – seeing what you want to see in others.
Give an example of a time you used confirmation bias.

_____

_____

_____

_____

_____

_____

9. What defense mechanism do you believe you use the most?

_____
_____
_____
_____
_____

10. What leads you to believe that you use that defense mechanism the most (what you wrote for number 9)?

_____
_____
_____
_____
_____

Doing without questioning

A temple priest was getting ready for the sacred ceremony. The people started to gather early and watched the priest prepare. As the ceremony was about to start, a stray dog wandered close to the altar, so the temple priest took the dog and tied him to a nearby tree – then he began the ceremony. Years later, no one remembered what the priest said, but they did remember that he tied a dog to a tree before the ceremony could begin, so that – tying a dog to a tree – became the ceremony itself.

Like the people in this story who acted without questioning, so too, do we do the same thing sometimes. Anytime we act without questioning why, we are using the defense mechanism *introjection* to help us avoid having to take responsibility for why we do what we do.

Why We Do What We Do

A little girl went to her mom and asked her why she cuts the end off the roast beef. Her mom didn't know, and told her to ask her grandma. The little girl asked her grandma why she cuts the ends off the roast beef, and her grandmother said she didn't know why she did, she just knew her mom always did it. The little girl went to her great grandmother and asked her why she cut the ends off the roast beef, and her great grandmother said, "Oh, because when I was growing up, we only had one pot, and it was a really small pot!"

How many rituals in your life do you do because you "have always done them that way?" How do you feel about questioning why you do what you do? We believe that knowledge is power. The more we know about ourselves, the more we can consciously choose to act in the best possible way.

Don't Throw the Baby Out with the Bath Water!

The old saying, "Don't throw the baby out with the bath water" means that just because the water around the baby may have become dirty and needs to be discarded, there is no reason to throw out the precious baby who sits in the water; in other words, if you learn that some things aren't true, it's not a good idea to then jump to the conclusion that every aspect of what you learned is also not true. There can be truthful statements intermixed with untruthful ones.

Sometimes when people learn aspect of something they learned child was not true, they then go to the other extreme and assume nothing they learned as a child was true. For example, in schools, for many years, people taught that "honest" Abe Lincoln walked a mile to return a penny to a woman who overpaid at a store. Later on, when it was revealed that the story was made up, some people thought to themselves, "Well, if that story was a lie, then maybe everything I learned about Abraham Lincoln was a lie!" The truth is that although Abe Lincoln didn't likely walk a mile to return a penny, he still did some very good things as the president of the United States. We don't have to throw the baby or the good things out with the bath water, just the bath water.

Why We Do What We Do Exercise

We all do things just because we have always done them that way. Sometimes that works, and sometimes that doesn't. We also do things because we were told to do them that way many years ago. The truth is something else might work better. The secret is being aware of what we are doing and why.

1. Write down **three** things you do that you never really questioned.

A
_____
_____

B
_____
_____

C
_____
_____

2. What would it change for you if you began to question any of those things?

3. Is everything in life exactly the way you learned it to be?

4. What things are different from how you were taught them to be?

5. How has not questioning those things impacted your life?

6. How can you tell which things are exactly how you learned them, and which things were just how the people who taught you saw them?

7. How would it benefit you to question the things that you have been taught?

Comfirmation Bias

If you want to see someone as smart, you will. If you want to see someone as dumb, you will. If you want to see someone as disrespectful, you will.

Sometimes new information is hard to handle. It is hard to realize that what we believe might be wrong. Sometimes it is hard to handle the truth; and the truth is we are NOT always right. The more we are open to new ideas, the less angry we get when people disagree with us.

If we see only what we want to see in life, and if we hear only what we want to hear, then how will we ever grow as people? How boring it would be to only know the same information when you are 90 years old that you knew when you were 15 years old!

All human beings have confirmation bias. It is a way to protect ourselves and make ourselves feel safe about the world. Though confirmation bias is natural, it is not necessarily helpful. We can unknowingly use confirmation bias to remain trapped in our own anger and pain. To get to the heart of confirmation bias, sometimes it's easier to look for it in others.

Confirmation Bias That Others Use On Us

Julie wanted to see Mike as angry. After all, Mike had screamed, yelled, and thrown things for years in Julie's presence when he was angry. Mike completed anger management, however, and made profound changes in his life.

Even though Mike worked hard to make changes in his life, Julie would look for Mike to get even the slightest bit upset, and then she would say things like, "See, you can't change! You'll always be angry!" To which Mike felt hurt, because he worked so hard to change. His hurt would lead to anger, and he would want to lash out. However, Mike learned well that anger is just a cover for hurt, so he would take the time to express to Julie, "Look, I am in control of my anger, but just because I have learned to control my anger doesn't mean that I will never get frustrated again. I'm asking you to try to stop looking for me to fail. I'm trying to continue the changes that I am making, and I am asking you to try to see those changes in me."

Because Mike learned to maintain control even when Julie wanted to see him as angry, eventually, she began to see that he really could and did change his ways. They are happy together today because Mike didn't blame her confirmation bias as a reason he would have to revert to anger. Instead, he understood it, remained patient, and stuck to the changes he made.

Confirmation Bias Exercise

In the following exercise, first start by seeing confirmation bias in others, then move to how you see confirmation bias inhibiting your own life.

1. How do others use confirmation bias to get in their way of seeing some positive things about you?

_____

_____

_____

_____

_____

_____

_____

2. What do you hope others could see about you if they could get beyond their confirmation bias?

_____

_____

_____

_____

_____

_____

_____

3. How do you use confirmation bias to remain stuck seeing things a certain way?

_____

_____

_____

_____

_____

_____

_____

4. How do you use confirmation bias to support your own behavior?

_____

_____

_____

_____

_____

_____

_____

5. Write down something that you were wrong about recently that you were not able to admit being wrong about.

_____
_____
_____
_____
_____
_____
_____

6. If you were to have admitted that you were wrong in the moment, how do you think your situation would have turned out differently?

_____
_____
_____
_____
_____
_____
_____

> We see only what we want to see in life.
> We hear only what we want to hear.

Personal Challenge:
Allow yourself to be open to the fact that you may be wrong.

Stereotypes Are Natural

Evolutionary psychologists have argued that stereotypes were absolutely necessary for our survival. In other words, picture that it is 10,000 B.C.E. Imagine that you and your clan come across a rocky terrain and one of the members of your group gets fatally bitten by a snake that was hiding in those rocks. Now, imagine that you and your group travel on further, but come across a different set of rocks. What very helpful stereotypes might you and your group make about the rocks that might just actually increase your chance for survival? Might you stereotype that all rocks like that have the potential to have hidden snakes in them? And if you come to that stereotype, might it not help your chances of survival?

Stereotypes have a biological basis in our brains; however, just because they can have some value does not mean that they always have a positive value. In fact, more often than not (especially since this is not 10,000 B.C.E) the stereotypes by which we live now only seem to limit our worldviews and perspectives on life.

People seem to be furious when others label them by the negative characteristics of a group to which they might belong. Yet regardless of that anger, they themselves stereotype others. Stereotyping appears to be a very natural process that we all engage in, but there is hope. Once we can evaluate what our stereotypes actually are, we can then analyze why we hold those viewpoints. Even further, we can look at whether or not holding those stereotypes is actually helpful for us or not.

People are the way they are for a reason. As psychologists, we have a job to help people uncover why they do what they do. In the process of working with the thousands of people we have encountered, we have learned profoundly that *everyone* has a story. When we learn what other people's stories are, it becomes much more difficult to judge those people. As we have learned to listen openly to individual stories in the confines of our offices, we have come to deeply see that we can never know a person's entire story by working from stereotypes.

Stereotypes are Natural Exercise

Learning about your stereotypes, where they come from, why you hold them, what the basis of them is, and whether or not they genuinely benefit you to keep them, can significantly impact your life. In the following exercise, consider the stereotypes in your life.

1. What group of people angers you the most?

___

2. What types of things about this group of people makes you upset or angry?

___

3. Where does your bias against this group come from?

___

4. What is one *intelligent* argument that explains why that particular group might do some of the things that you see them do?

___

5. How does it help you to maintain your bias against this group?

___

6. How difficult would it be for you to let go of your stereotype of this group?

___

7. How can your awareness of this stereotype help you in your life?

Stereotyping Frank

Frank was the first in his anger management group to talk about how stereotyping is wrong. He was the most outspoken regarding his anger at being stereotyped for his looks. After the conversation turned from the topic of stereotypes to focusing on another group member's individual problem, however, Frank, who was already overtly involved in the group, began to offer advice to his fellow group member. He said, "You have to understand that you're dealing with a woman here. Women…" and then he went on to use about four general stereotypes of women in hopes of offering
"help" to his peer.

Frank had no self-awareness that he was doing the very thing in stereotyping women that he believed was so wrong to be done against him. Frank, however, is no different from most people in this regard. Most people will identify stereotyping as "wrong" or "harmful," but will fail to recognize how they maintain stereotypes themselves.

Be mindful of the stereotypes you hold, because you might find yourself reacting to stereotypes rather than responding to individuals.

Can you be defined by stereotypes? Then why define others that way?

Personal challenge:
See beyond the stereotypes you hold.

Archetypes

Archetypes are patterns of behavior. There seem to be patterns of behavior in all human beings. Common general patterns can be seen in individuals. Lots of different archetypes exist. For example, there are archetypes of the Warrior, the Father or Mother, the Husband or Wife, the Wise Guru, the Explorer, the Abuser, the Peacemaker, the Scholar, the Healer, the Comedian, the Prankster, etc. Archetypes are the essentially the prototype or model for any patterned set of behaviors.

We can all express different kinds of archetypes throughout our lives. Despite our ability to express multiple archetypes, we seem to be drawn to expressing just a couple for most of our lives. For example, a person could move from predominantly expressing the archetype of "athlete" for many years, until he becomes a father. By becoming fully immersed in the role of father, that person could come to identify with the archetypal father, hence, placing his own interests and needs aside to do what is in the best interest of his child.

We tend to want to tell others that we represent the kinds of archetypes that society expects from us. For example, a man may want to express to others that he embraces the archetype of father. However, by immersing himself in substance abuse, he may more accurately fit the archetype of *puer aeternus* or "eternal boy." Figuring out what archetype best fits us can be a challenge, because there is often a difference between what we want to be seen as versus what we are actually living out. Furthermore, it is important to be self-aware of the qualities that we want to have, as compared to the qualities we genuinely exhibit.

The qualities that we have can be things we are aware of or not aware of, and they can be things that are positive or negative. The qualities we have can lead to behavior patterns that have us repeating negative things in our lives. Qualities themselves can be turned into positives or negatives, but learning to channel the energy takes insight and work. Here are some examples of qualities.

Accepting	Energetic	Kind	Protective
Greedy	Self-centered	Dynamic	Witty
Curious	Humble	Friendly	Dependable
Laid-back	Frugal	Patient	Loving
Disciplined	Obsessive	Professional	Stable
Optimistic	Pessimistic	Controlling	Naïve

Archetypes Exercise

For this exercise, try to view yourself in terms of one main archetype.

1. If you had to describe yourself in terms of only one archetype, which one do you think that might be?

_____

_____

A. What are the qualities that surround that archetype? (Examples of qualities are: strong, stubborn, intelligent, persistent, funny, impatient, etc.)

_____

_____

_____

_____

_____

_____

_____

B. What qualities do you want to be perceived as having?

_____

_____

_____

_____

_____

_____

_____

3. What qualities do you actually have that are similar or different from that archetype?

_____

_____

_____

_____

_____

_____

4. If you could be exactly the kind of person you want to be and the kind of person that young people could look up to, what qualities would you have?

_____
_____
_____
_____
_____
_____

Dealing with the negative qualities…

5. Being impatient can be positive or negative.

A. Identify ways in which your impatience has been positive for you.

_____
_____
_____
_____
_____
_____

B. Identify ways in which your impatience has been a negative for you.

_____
_____
_____
_____
_____
_____

6. Not being too serious can be positive or negative.

   A. Identify ways in which not being serious was a positive for you.

   _____
   _____
   _____
   _____
   _____
   _____

   B. Identify ways in which not being too serious was a negative for you.

   _____
   _____
   _____
   _____
   _____
   _____

7. Inflexibility and stubbornness can be positive or negative.

   A. Identify ways in which your inflexibility and stubbornness was a positive for you.

   _____
   _____
   _____
   _____

B. Identify ways in which your inflexibility and stubbornness was a negative for you.

8. Persistency can be positive or negative.

A. Give an example when being persistent was a positive for you.

B. Give an example when being persistent was a negative for you.

9. Write down what you can do this week to become more like the archetype you want to be.

___

10. Identify at least one thing that can get in the way of your becoming more like that archetype.

___

Personal challenge:
   Recognize what you are, and then become what you want.

Displacement

A man got pulled over by the police and was given a speeding ticket. He was very angry that he got caught speeding and that he had to pay a fine. He knew he couldn't say anything to the police officer because that would have gotten him in more trouble, so he went home and screamed and yelled at his family.

A woman wanted to speak up to her boss for being unfair, but she didn't have the assertiveness to say anything. She was afraid she'd get fired if she did, so she kept it all inside. When she got home she got mad at her husband for something ridiculously small and then she screamed and yelled at him.

A child gets picked on at school and does not know how to stand up to the bullies, so he comes home and takes his anger out on his family.

When we are not able to say what we want to people, we keep it inside until we are around someone safe, then we release it. Does it seem fair for any of the three people in the stories above to take it out on their families? If you can learn to express what you are really mad about or at whom you are mad, then you are not likely to take it out on your loved ones, your family or those closest to you.

Displacement Exercise – Part 1

1. Who do you tend to take your anger out on the most?

   _____
   _____
   _____
   _____
   _____
   _____

2. What about that person makes you feel comfortable enough to show him/ her the worst side of you?

   _____
   _____
   _____
   _____
   _____
   _____

3. How does it feel when you take things out on that person?

   _____
   _____
   _____
   _____
   _____
   _____

4. What could you do instead of taking things out on that person?

_____
_____
_____
_____
_____

Displacement Exercise- Part 2

Anger grows. Anger fills up like water in a cup and when it reaches the top, it overflows. Many times, we are not really angry at what we think we are angry at. Very often, when we finally express anger, it is because we have been neglecting to deal with the emotions that have been building up. We need to learn to deal with issues when they arise. We would benefit from dealing with those issues from our Adult-self. To do that, we need to have a very clear understanding of what makes us so angry.

On a scale of 1 – 10, rank how angry the following things make you:

Driving/traffic:

    1   2   3   4   5   6   7   8   9   10

Not at all angry   Extremely Angry

Being accused of lying:

    1   2   3   4   5   6   7   8   9   10

Not at all angry   Extremely Angry

Being treated unfairly:

1   2   3   4   5   6   7   8   9   10
Not at all angry   Extremely Angry

Bills / Money:

1   2   3   4   5   6   7   8   9   10
Not at all angry   Extremely Angry

Relationship disagreements:

1   2   3   4   5   6   7   8   9   10
Not at all angry   Extremely Angry

Hunger:

1   2   3   4   5   6   7   8   9   10
Not at all angry   Extremely Angry

Being overly tired:

1   2   3   4   5   6   7   8   9   10
Not at all angry   Extremely Angry

1. Make a list of things that contribute to your anger and give those a ranking as well.

_____

_____

_____

_____

2. Describe a realistic plan on how you can avoid displacing things on others.

___

Personal challenge:
Be angry at whatever you are angry at – nothing more.

Different Ways of Relating to the World

Martin Buber was a philosopher who wrote about different ways people relate to each other and their world. From being self-centered, to treating other people as objects, to treating people as equals, what the philosopher taught can help all of us.

The different ways of relating are:

I-I
("Me to myself")

Us-them
("My side versus your side")

Us-Us
("I like whatever you like, so let's not have any problems")

I-It
("I'm important, but you're just an object")

I-Thou
("I am important, and you are equally important")

Different Ways of
Relating to the World Exercise

This exercise is geared toward helping you understand how you relate to others in the world.

1. The **I-I** type of relating to the world is a self-centered one. When we live from the I-I, we tend to not see anything other than ourselves and our own needs. An example of this is the classic joke line, "Enough about me, let's talk about you… what do you think of me?" But taken seriously, being self-centered hurts relationships.

    In what ways does your being self-centered impact your relationships?

    _____
    _____
    _____
    _____
    _____

2. The **Us vs Them** type of relating to the world is where we see things in black and white. An example of this is political parties. If you really like one side, you are likely to not like the other side. This is often hurtful because when we only see one side of an issue, we close our minds to other possibilities.

    How does seeing things in terms of "my side" versus "your side" impact your relationships?

    _____
    _____

3. The **Us-Us** way of relating to the world is one where we say and do things that we really don't mean just to get people to like us. An example of this is giving into peer pressure. It can be harmful because when we give into doing things that we don't want to do, it takes away from who we are.

   How does doing things just to be liked hurt either yourself or your relationships?

   _____
   _____
   _____
   _____
   _____
   _____

4. The **I-It** relationship is one where we treat people as objects. An example of this can occur at a coffee shop when you walk in, place your order, and never look at the person who is taking your order. To you, in that moment, that person is simply an object designed to fulfill your needs. This type of relating to others can be harmful for many reasons, the worst of which is that when we treat people as objects, we allow ourselves to be meaner than if we see them as equals.

   In what ways do you treat others as objects instead of people?

   _____
   _____

5. The **I-Thou** relationship is one when we treat others as genuine equals. An example of this can occur anytime we take the time to make eye contact and listen compassionately to someone else. This is when we take a genuine interest in the other person.

In what ways can you be in the I-thou with loved ones this week?

___

"I am a part of all that I have met." – Lord Alfred Tennyson

Personal Challenge: Recognize that we are all interconnected in some way.

Community Leader Exercise

"We can all complain about what is wrong, but who is willing to come up with reasonable solutions to our problems?"

Let's be honest, it is so easy to complain about the way things are! Leaders can never seem to get things right. From the outside looking in, it can seem awfully easy to do things differently and make entirely different decisions from the ones that those "ridiculous" leaders are making. All too often, people get together to complain about what is wrong, but it is very rare that people actually offer real alternative solutions.

Thinking beyond ourselves and our own problems is important for our own development. Thinking in terms of the "big picture" allows us to focus on others.

A Man Named Faust

There is a legend of a man named Faust who made a wager with the Devil. Basically, the bet came down to this.

If the Devil could get Faust to be satisfied with any one thing to the point where he would wish for that moment to last forever, then the Devil would get his soul.

Well, the Devil certainly tried. Faust asked for and got everything from riches to even the most beautiful woman in the history of the world, but nothing, no material thing or instant of gratification ever seemed to be enough to make Faust want that moment to last forever.

Finally, toward the end of his life, Faust had contributed to a community where people could farm, create, and sustain themselves. As he looked on at this incredible place, he longed for the moment to last. The Devil, seeing Faust satisfied, ultimately won the wager and was prepared to take Faust's soul.

Now in the famous dramatic version of the story by Johann Goethe, God saved Faust at the last minute on the technicality that the one thing that truly satisfied Faust was his being unselfish. He gained true satisfaction from contributing to other people's freedom and happiness.

That's a lesson we all might gain from: focusing on helping others leaves much less room for us to have dissatisfaction with our own lives.

Community Leader Exercise

You are elected a community leader. The community has given you the responsibility for creating policies to lessen domestic violence in your community. They have also charged you with teaching it.

1. What policies or laws would you create to lessen violence in your community?

___

2. How would you address people who think your ideas are garbage or stupid?

___

3. How will you deal with people who re-offend?

4. How will you define and describe what domestic violence is?

5. What strategies will you use to teach people how to control their anger?

6. What specific behaviors and techniques will you teach people who struggle with domestic violence?

_____
_____
_____
_____
_____
_____

7. What is your message that you want to get out to the community about domestic violence?

_____
_____
_____
_____
_____

"Freedom and life are earned by those alone who conquer them each day anew."-Goethe

> "If nothing changes, nothing changes."

> **Personal Challenge:**
> **Do something to make a positive impact on your community.**

Cognitive Dissonance

There is a difference sometimes between what we do and what kind of people we are. When what we do does not match up with what we believe about ourselves, it is called **cognitive dissonance**. Specifically, cognitive dissonance is the mental state we are in when we have either conflicting beliefs or when we *do* things that we recognize contradict what we *believe* about ourselves. In short, cognitive dissonance is the uncomfortable feeling that we have when our beliefs and our actions don't match up. For example, we all like to see ourselves as honest people, but all people lie; when we lie, it doesn't feel good, so we justify or come up with reasons why we *had* to lie.

Meet Ryan

Ryan's story is a very real example of what it is like for someone experiencing cognitive dissonance. Ryan told people, "I'm not a woman-beater!" Many times in his life, he would say "Anyone who ever hits a woman deserves to go to jail." He was outspoken about how "men should never hit women no matter what."

Imagine what might have been going through Ryan's mind in the moments after he was arrested for hitting his wife. He told officers that it "was not like him at all to do something like that," and that they would see that he "is a nice guy," and that "she forced him" to hit her by her actions.

Ryan could not fit himself into the category of "woman-beater" that he labeled others as, but he also could not take back what he already did. So, he was left only with changing his beliefs to fit his actions. He thought to himself, "I guess I can see now how sometimes you have to hit a woman." But the problem was, he didn't really believe that, so he was stuck. His beliefs and his behaviors did not match up.

The challenge that Ryan faced because of his actions was answering truthfully a set of life-altering questions. "What do I really believe about who is responsible for my actions? Do I define someone by a single action or event? Will I continue to rationalize my behavior and blame others, or will I find the balance in understanding my own behaviors, learning a new path, and moving forward?"

We may not know Ryan's full story, but what we can do is ask ourselves the same questions.

When we face cognitive dissonance, we can either change our beliefs, change our actions to match our beliefs, or altogether step out of the world of "either/ or" thinking. The reality is that we cannot always live up to ideals that we set for ourselves, and when we fail, it becomes time to reevaluate things. The problem that we all encounter is that when our thoughts and behaviors do not match up, we experience an uncomfortable feeling that can do physical damage to us in the form of stress.

Cognitive Dissonance Exercise

As was stated, to get around cognitive dissonance, we either change our beliefs or change our actions. Guess what? Our beliefs are easier to change, so we can rationalize why we do just about everything we do. Now let's figure this out for you.

1. Write down something that you've done that was not consistent with who you really are or what you really believe.

   _____
   _____
   _____
   _____
   _____
   _____
   _____

2. Write down what you said to yourself to justify why you did it and to make yourself feel better about it.

   _____
   _____
   _____
   _____
   _____
   _____
   _____
   _____

3. Once we justify something to ourselves, we spend a great deal of energy trying to look for things that confirm what we believe. How have you looked for things to help you confirm that you did the right thing, even though you don't really believe you did?

_____
_____
_____
_____
_____
_____

4. How can understanding this idea of cognitive dissonance help you?

_____
_____
_____
_____
_____
_____

> **Being honest about who we are leads to being proud of who we are.**

Personal Challenge:
Reevaluate your thoughts and actions.

Circular Causality

A man kicks a stone. If we know how big the man is, how big the stone is, and how much force the man kicks with, well, we can accurately predict how far the stone will go. But what if that same man kicks a dog? Can we predict what will happen? Maybe the dog will bite him. Maybe the dog will cower. The dog's experiences will largely determine the response, as well as how that response will impact the man's reaction.

When we deal with things that are not alive, there is much more predictability. When we deal with living beings, however, we can never be 100% certain of the reaction we will get. When we can predict that A will intersect with B and produce C, that is something called *linear causality*. Think of the example of the man kicking a stone. A (the man) intersects with B (kicking the stone) to produce C (how far the stone goes). Linear causality makes things very easy to understand. Unfortunately, when human beings are involved, linear thinking just doesn't apply.

Circular causality (think of a circle and how it "never begins and never ends") is the idea that many factors impact every situation. In the example of the man kicking the dog, we cannot say for certain what the dog will do. Furthermore, whatever the dog does gives information to the man to set up his future responses. In the first place, the man might say, "Well that dog was looking at me and threatening me, so I had to kick it," in which case the dog's "looks" impacted the man's experience (the dog's looks obviously didn't *make* the man kick him, but it could have played a role in impacting the man's behavior – we emphasize that the man always had a choice as to whether or not he would kick the dog), so we are left without a clear A + B = C that we would have in linear causality.

"Making" Versus "Impacting": Big Difference!

There is an enormous difference between someone *making* us do something and someone *impacting* us to do something. When we say that people *make* us do something, we are essentially saying that we had *no* choice in the matter. But we always have a choice.

People might not *make* each other do things, but they certainly *impact* each other.

Consider this example: Someone says, "Please pass the salt." No one does. In reaching for the salt, the person knocks over his water and says, "See what you made me do!" The person who did not pass the salt was not the cause, but merely a part of the circumstance.

People apply this faulty assumption against children in numerous circumstances, such as in driving and being distracted, leading to an accident or ticket. Children also get blamed for marital problems all the time, when in fact, they are not the cause at all.

There is a great difference between:

"She made me hit her." Versus "I felt hurt and embarrassed when she lied to me, so I chose to hit her." Knowing that difference makes all the difference.

Circular Causality Exercise

In a way, circular causality is the belief that everything ultimately impacts everything else. In terms of people, it means that everyone affects everyone else. That means regardless of whether we want to or not, we constantly impact others with our actions.

1. Give an example of a time when you blamed something on someone else.

_____

_____

_____

_____

2. Describe what part you played in contributing to the situation.

3. How does your mood affect the people around you?

4. In what ways do you pass along your anxiety, hence impacting others around you?

5. In what ways do you allow anxiety to be passed on to you from others?

6. In what ways can you stop yourself from passing along your anxiety to others?

7. In what ways can you prevent yourself from accepting other people's experiences?

8. Give one example of how you have been someone else's puppet.

___

9. Give one example of how you have avoided being someone else's puppet.

___

10. Give an example of a time that you may have said something to the effect of: "He/she made me do it."

___

11. Looking back on the experience you wrote about for number 8, how could you have reacted differently had you really understood that it was your choice to act that way in the moment?

_____

_____

_____

_____

_____

Personal challenge:
Be aware of the impact you have on others.

All Sides of a Story

There have been many times in life that we felt confident about the information we had, only to discover later that what we thought was wrong. It is certainly a blow to our ego to find out we were wrong after we loudly proclaimed how right we were. On the other hand, we have also experienced others declaring that they were right about a subject, only to later find out that they too, were wrong. Discovering that we were wrong about something after we asserted how right we were can bring up feelings of hurt and embarrassment, both of which lead to anger.

The Princesses

here once were 4 princesses who lived in a kingdom. One day, the gardener told them about a magical tree in the kingdom. He explained to them that it was an invisible tree that they could only see on their birthdays. One at a time, each princess got to see the tree. Each princess was told she share what she saw until all the princesses had their oldest girl's birthday was first, months later was girl's, followed in a few months by the next, and a later the youngest girl's birthday. Finally, the time the girls were permitted to discuss what they saw described something very different until eventually was a big fight. They fought so much that they talking for years. Then one day the gardener found princesses and told them the truth. Each girl saw in a different season… so what each girl saw was in fact, a part of the truth.

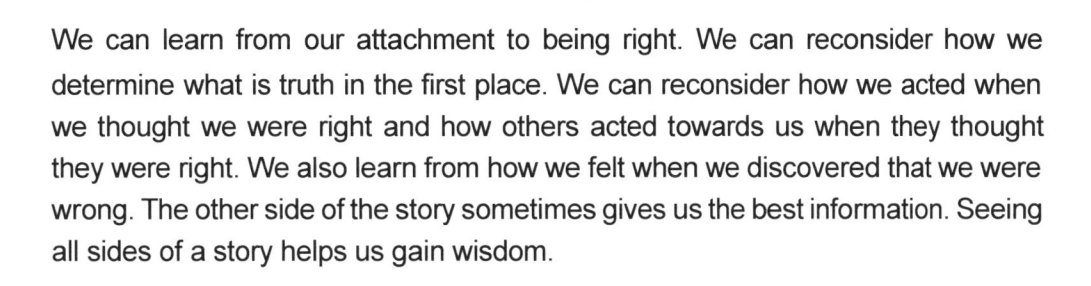

We can learn from our attachment to being right. We can reconsider how we determine what is truth in the first place. We can reconsider how we acted when we thought we were right and how others acted towards us when they thought they were right. We also learn from how we felt when we discovered that we were wrong. The other side of the story sometimes gives us the best information. Seeing all sides of a story helps us gain wisdom.

All Sides of the Story Exercise

1. Describe a time when you thought you were right about something, only to find out later that you were wrong.

   _____
   _____
   _____
   _____
   _____
   _____

2. Describe what feelings you had when you were certain that you were right.

   _____
   _____
   _____
   _____
   _____
   _____

3. Describe what thoughts and feelings you had when you found out you were wrong.

   _____
   _____
   _____
   _____
   _____
   _____

4. What lessons can you teach others from your experience?

5. How do you feel when other people assume they are absolutely right about something (and are closed off to the idea that they may be wrong or not have all the information)?

6. How would you rather someone approach you when he/she has information that you don't have?

7. How do you think you should approach others knowing that you may not always have the full story?

___

Personal challenge:
Be more open to other people's sides of the story.

Opposites

Finding balance may in fact be the eternal quest for human beings. All the great teachers throughout history have talked in some way about achieving balance in our lives. Anger tends to stem from a place of imbalance ("im" means "not," so imbalance means "not balanced"). One path to overcoming anger is to find balance in our lives.

An exercise that increases balance is to evaluate how opposites impact your life. By understanding the role that opposites have on you, you can live with more awareness. When we live in anger, we tend to narrow things down to usually about two options. When we live with more awareness, we can see more options in every given moment. With more options and choices, we have many more opportunities to live in balance.

Learning from Lions

If you have ever had a chance to observe (or watch a television show about) lions surviving through the harsh existence of African landscapes, you will likely have seen that regardless of how hard they work for a meal, they can lose it as quickly as they gain it.

It is interesting to observe that if they win the meal, they do not gloat and high five each other; and conversely, if they lose the meal, they do not have time or energy to spend on pining over the lost dinner. Lions do not go too high with their highs or too low with their lows. They (like all nature does) operate from a place of balance.

We could learn a lot from how lions live.

Opposites Exercise

Most likely the following pairs of opposites are a part of your life. You have probably experienced them in the past and are experiencing them now. Most likely you have memories of all of these pairs, some fond and some not.

How do the following opposites shape your life? Have you experienced both? Do you prefer one more than the other? What feeling do you have about these opposites? (Remember to focus on both sides of the equation):

Pleasure and **Pain**

_____
_____
_____
_____
_____
_____
_____

Gain and **Loss**

_____
_____
_____
_____
_____
_____

349
Praise and **Blame**

Pride and **Shame**

Fear and **Safety**

Success and **Failure**

_____
_____
_____
_____
_____
_____
_____

Whatever takes us up can also take us down. The degree to which we are affected by pleasure sets up the degree to which we are affected by pain. Finding balance occurs when we do not allow our highs to get us too high or our lows to get us too low.

**Personal challenge:
Find balance in your life right now.**

The Path to Changing Ourselves

Sometimes we need to take a very straightforward approach to changing. Robert Wubbolding is a psychologist who developed a great approach for helping people figure out how to help themselves. He called it WDEP.

WDEP stands for:

W = Wants i.e., figuring out what it is you actually want

D = Doing i.e., asking yourself what you are actually doing to try to get what you want

E = Evaluation i.e., figuring out whether what you are doing to get what you want is actually working or not

P = Planning i.e., if what you are doing is not working for you, then it is time to make a new plan for how you will get what you want

What we do impacts what we get

Sometimes we may say that we want a relationship that we are in to "get better." When we look at what we are actually doing to make that happen, however, we find that all we are *doing* is "wishing" it would be better instead of actually *doing* anything about it. Other times, we may notice that what we are doing is putting the responsibility for change onto the other person, rather than taking responsibility to work on changing ourselves.

Be mindful of your actions. Focus on what you can do differently in your relationships, and you will see change occur much faster than if you wait for others to make it better.

352 The Path to Changing Ourselves Exercise

For this exercise, try to identify exactly what it is that you want, and what exactly it is that you are doing to get what you want. Once you are clear about those, you can evaluate whether or not what you are doing is working or not. If what you are doing isn't working, then it is time to consider a new plan of action.

1. What do I want?

2. What am I doing to get what I want?

3. Is what I am doing working to help me get what I want? If not, what can I do differently?

4. What do I want to control most in my life?

5. What do I do when I cannot control things?

6. One thing that I want to learn about myself is:

7. One question I have about why people do what they do is…

___

8. When I really think about the question I came up with for number 7, I believe the answer is…

___

We always have a choice to start anew in this moment.

Personal challenge:
Be mindful of your actions in your relationships.

Assertiveness Versus Aggressiveness

At some point, the issues in everyday life can get to us all. Anytime we allow life's issues to build up enough, we are likely to explode. The fact is that the way many people handle their issues is by not dealing with them; but the reality is that if we do not learn to assert ourselves regarding the little things - - then the little things will eventually become big things.

A big difference exists between being assertive and being aggressive. There is a clear difference between saying what you want to say (assertiveness) and attempting to exert dominance over others (aggressiveness). To be assertive is to demonstrate self-control. To be dominant is to attempt to control others. We only attempt to control others when we cannot control ourselves, however, and one reason we lose self-control is we choose not to deal with things that are bothering us.

We have a tendency to push things down instead of dealing with them. We do this with good intention, thinking to ourselves, "Well, I'm trying not to explode." But without dealing with issues, we are only putting off the inevitable. Once people can learn to be assertive, the need to be aggressive shrinks away.

Remember that it is very natural for human beings to have a tendency to go from one extreme to another. Going from one extreme to another in terms of aggressiveness means this: if we try to "just ignore" something that is bothering us, and we do nothing about it until it builds up and we cannot take it anymore - then we are much more likely to erupt with anger. Saying, "I just won't say anything" then, is not helpful, because the human brain does not ignore things; it simply pushes things into the background until a time when it can deal with them.

Imagine standing on a boat holding a beach ball. If you put the beach ball in the water and try to keep it below the boat, you may be successful for short time. Remember, however, from the description of the ball and the boat in the introduction: Eventually, the ball will move under the boat and pop up on the other side – somewhere unexpected. And so it is with anger. We can push things down for a while, but if we do not deal with them, they will pop up later somewhere else and it's usually where we do not want them to come up.

Assertiveness Versus
Aggressiveness Exercise

Answer the following questions to see how you can learn from past instances of aggression:

1. Describe a time where you did something that was described by others as "aggressive."

   _____
   _____
   _____
   _____
   _____
   _____

2. What was it that you specifically did that made it appear "aggressive"?

   _____
   _____
   _____
   _____
   _____
   _____

3. What message did you want to convey in that moment?

   _____
   _____
   _____
   _____

4. Other than "just ignoring it," what else could you have done to have been heard?

_____

_____

_____

_____

_____

5. What can you do this week to say the things you want to say without becoming aggressive?

_____

_____

_____

_____

_____

Personal challenge:
Avoid extremes.

The Anger Management Workbook, The Program that Changes Lives

358

What are you taking from this exercise?

_____
_____
_____
_____
_____
_____
_____
_____
_____
_____
_____
_____
_____
_____
_____

Imagine Yourself as a Counselor

Sometimes a shift in angle gives us an entirely new look at the world. Counselors are charged with seeing the world from many different perspectives. Because of the job that they do, counselors have the opportunity to understand any given situation from multiple viewpoints.

When people are training to become professional counselors, they are often faced with these types of questions:

- Can you accept people for who they are rather than just see them for what they've done?

- Can you adequately understand each person's side to a story?

- Can you leave your own opinion out of things and instead help people find the best solutions for themselves?

- Can you be patient with others and understand that change takes time?

- Can you practice the things you are preaching?

- Can you be genuine?

When counselors can of these things, they simultaneously help others and find peace in their own lives.

When we are trapped in our own situations regarding anger, we tend to replay our side of things over and over again. This leads us to holding the same emotional state for longer periods of time. With enough time, even the most rigid perspectives seem to change. Knowing that time changes our perspectives leads us to a very valid question: What if we were able to speed up that time?

Though we cannot speed up time, what we can do is speed up the effects of time. In other words, with practice, we can gain different perspectives faster.

Imagine Yourself as a Counselor Exercise

1. If a victim of domestic violence came in to see me for support, here are the ways in which I would help him/her.

   _____
   _____
   _____
   _____
   _____
   _____

2. If a perpetrator of a domestic violence crime came to see me for support, here are the ways in which I would help him/her.

   _____
   _____
   _____
   _____
   _____
   _____

3. The key lessons I would want to teach people who are being victimized are...

4. The key lessons I would want to teach people who are continuing to act out of anger are:

5. The key lessons I would want to teach people who believe they don't have a problem (when they clearly do) are:

6. Why is it that people sometimes believe they don't have any problems when it is clear to the outside world that they obviously do?

_____

_____

_____

_____

_____

7. How can you help people who don't think that they have any problems?

_____

_____

_____

_____

_____

> *"Can you love the people and lead them without imposing your will?"* – Lao Tzu

Personal challenge:
Try to help others in a way that is best for them, not you.

How to Control Your Thoughts

Two children are standing on the edge of a beach when a big wave approaches; one child runs back to his family because he is scared, the other dives headfirst with excitement into the wave.

How can the same event cause people to feel and react completely differently?

A = Activating event (i.e., the event that triggers a response)
B = Belief (i.e, what I tell myself about the event)
C = Consequence (i.e., the feeling I'm left with)

For example:

First boy	**Second boy**
A: Wave comes in	A: Wave comes in
B: "This is terrible"	B: "This is great!"
C: Scared	C: Excited

The answer is that events do not cause us to feel a certain way. Instead, it is our view of those events that impacts how we feel about things. If events caused us to feel a certain way, then everyone would experience every event in the same way. Events can impact us, but the thoughts we tell ourselves have the ultimate say as to how we feel. We can to some extent, by controlling our self-talk, learn to control how we feel.

We all talk to ourselves, and what we tell ourselves determines not only our feelings, but how we choose to respond as well. Consider the difference between the following two types of self-talk that someone can utilize after getting fired from work.

Person A:

"I can't stand this!"
"Nothing ever goes my way!"
"I will never get hired again!"

Person B (Same situation):

"This is unfortunate."
"I don't like it, but I can handle it."
"This is not the end of the world."

Person A is much more likely to respond in extreme ways, either externally toward others, or internally with negative emotions. Person B is using language that doesn't necessarily make the situation a good situation, but does make the situation more manageable.

How to Control Your Thoughts
Exercise – Part 1

1. An event that I got angry over was…

___

2. My thoughts about the event were…

___

3. My feelings about the event were…

_____

_____

_____

_____

_____

_____

4. By acting out of anger, I did…

_____

_____

_____

_____

_____

_____

5. The beliefs I *could have had* about the event are…

_____

_____

_____

_____

_____

_____

6. The event could have been altered if, instead of acting out of anger as I did, I would have told myself _____, and then done: _____ .

How to Control Your Thoughts
Exercise – Part 2

Things that make me angry (fill in the blank below):

People should

_____

I can't stand when people

_____

I have to

_____

Other people have to

_____

I cannot handle when others

_____

People always

_____

People never

_____

People must treat me

_____

I need to

_____

In relationships, I need the other person to

_____

Change your self-talk, Change your anger

Changing our self-talk can change our levels of anger. The words that we tell ourselves have a physical impact on our bodies. For example, if we tell ourselves that we *"cannot take it anymore,"* then our brains will process that information very differently than if we tell ourselves, *"I wish that didn't happen, but I can handle it."*

When we use extreme language (words like "always," "never," "can't stand it," etc.), our brain sends signals via our fight or flight system to our adrenal glands to send adrenaline and cortisol throughout our bodies. With increased cortisol and adrenaline comes increased intensity in our reactions (i.e., amplifying our anger).

The alternative, telling ourselves something more manageable, such as, *"I wish that didn't happen, but I can handle it,"* prompts our brains to process information via the temporal-parietal junction emotional system and ultimately the frontal lobes. By using more manageable self-talk, we are able to literally process information differently; thereby giving ourselves an opportunity to provide a controlled response to events rather than react with knee-jerk anger.

What you tell yourself determines how angry you get. Just think, the world already provides enough experiences that infuriate you, so why use self-talk to augment that anger? Change your self-talk and you'll find that you change your anger.

We are what we think.

Personal challenge:
Be mindful of your self-talk.

Dreams

We sleep for almost half of our lives. When we sleep, we dream. All people dream; however, only those who wake up at the opportune time are able to recall their dreams. Dreams can have powerful meaning for us, or they can mean nothing at all. You might believe that dreams are meaningful, or you might believe that they do not mean anything. Regardless of where you stand on your belief about dreams, one thing is very true: by looking at your dreams you can learn more about yourself.

Be careful how you interpret a dream!

Dreams do not always mean one thing. Symbols can mean different things to different people, and there is always more than one way to interpret a dream. For example, sometimes when people have dreams about their loved ones cheating on them, they are having that dream because they are the ones who actually want to do the cheating. Other times, the dream could mean something completely different. *There is no hard and fast rule that certain dreams always mean certain things.*

We can learn a lot about ourselves from analyzing our own dreams. Amateur dream interpretation can be a great and fun hobby. The problem comes into play when people get stuck only interpreting a dream in one way or when they become attached to believing that their interpretation is absolutely correct. That is not the nature of dreams. Dreams are powerful, ambiguous, and can be seen many different ways. Dream guides can help you understand your dreams, but in the end, only you know best what your dream is trying to teach you.

Dreams Exercise

One way to interpret dreams is to look at every person and object in the dream as an aspect or a part of you. For this exercise, recall a recent or standout dream you had.

1. Describe a dream you have had.

   _____
   _____
   _____
   _____
   _____
   _____

2. Consider that every person in the dream was a representation of some part of you. What role did everyone who showed up in your dream play?

   _____
   _____
   _____
   _____
   _____
   _____

3. How can being aware of this or any dream help you with your anger?

   _____
   _____
   _____
   _____

4. If you really were every character and object in your dream, what does this dream say about you?

5. Imagine that your dream is a wise person trying to teach you something through the story of your dream. Ask yourself: What is my dream trying to teach me?

"Everything that irritates us about others can lead us to an understanding of ourselves." – Carl Jung

Personal challenge:
Confront the things you don't like about yourself.

Complexes

Complex = a group of related images centered on a specific theme.

Anytime people refer to others as having a "mother complex," they usually mean it in a negative way. The reality is, however, that all people have a mother complex; just as all people have a "father complex," and many other types of complexes as well. A "mother complex" means that you have a group of related images about your idea of what a mother should be. Sometimes complexes are negative, and sometimes complexes are positive. For instance, a mother complex can describe the negative images that we have or our mother. A mother complex can also be the group of positive images we have about our mother.

The point of uncovering complexes is to learn that from an early age, we began to develop our picture of how the world "should be." Finding the general image that we have about certain types of people is important. Once we uncover our complexes, we can also uncover the types of stereotypes that we have about people. Everyone stereotypes, but knowing our stereotypes and being aware of them helps us learn whether or not we treat people in terms of who they *actually* are, or whether we treat people in terms of who we *think* they are according to our complexes and the stereotype.

Harry's Story

Harry's mother cussed him out frequently. Growing up, he was rarely allowed to leave his house, but he was degraded for staying inside. He grew up with a mother who inundated him with a world of mixed-messages. Because Harry interacted with so few people outside the family, he began to develop a picture of all women as his mother was.

In school, Harry frequently was disrespectful toward female teachers and authority figures, because the only way he knew how to relate to women was through the image he had of his mother: as a person who was degrading, disrespectful, and angry. Harry's "mother complex" led him to years of treating others the way his mother treated him.

One day, Harry met a female therapist who taught him an entirely different way to relate to her, and ultimately to other women as well. Harry learned about the stereotypes that he created of women based on what he learned from his mother. He questioned whether or not he needed to keep seeing all women that way, and he came to the realization that he didn't.

He identified a negative complex, and then he did the work to change it. Harry ended up in a very happy relationship with his wife: a woman who treats his own children very differently than how his mother treated him....

Complexes Exercise

1. Write 3 images you have about women.

    A.

    B.

    C.

2. Write 3 images you have about men.

    A.

    B.

    C.

3. Write down where you think your images of women and men came from?

4. Write down one idea about how you can realistically begin to change your images regarding women.

5. Write down one idea about how you can realistically begin to change your images regarding men.

6. How do the words you use to describe women contribute to the complex that you have regarding women?

___

7. How do the words that you use to describe men contribute to the complex that you have regarding men?

___

8. What things would you not want said to your son or daughter?

___

9. Why should women attempt to change their view of men?

_____
_____
_____
_____
_____
_____
_____
_____

10. Why should men attempt to change their view of women?

_____
_____
_____
_____
_____
_____
_____
_____

11. What responsibility do people have to treat each other with respect?

_____
_____
_____
_____
_____
_____

12. What have you learned about yourself from how you answered the questions in this exercise?

_____
_____
_____
_____
_____
_____

> If we are open, we can learn about ourselves every moment.

> **Personal challenge:**
> Treat everyone you encounter with kindness.

The Roots of Being a Man

Though we are certainly in control what we do, the world around has undoubtedly shaped us.
the adults in our lives taught us children was indelible, meaning whether we like it or not, their teachings stuck to us. What we might not realize is that when we don't stop to question what we were taught, we often find ourselves living out other people's belief systems that do not resonate with us.

Quit Crying and Be a Man!

Outside the door to the kindergarten, little 5 year-old Marcus fell down. He walked over to his dad in tears, putting his arms up for his father to pick him up. His father took one look around at the other men who were standing there, then looked down at his little son and said, "Quit crying! You're embarrassing yourself! Be a man!" Little Marcus looked confused, he tried to wipe away his tears, though it was obvious he needed comfort in that moment. He didn't get the comfort he sought, however, and he sheepishly walked away from his father – with perhaps a very new idea about what it means to be a "man."

The Roots of Being a Man Exercise – Part 1

Discovering the messages that were given to us is a empowering step in figuring out what kind of people we want to be as adults. For this exercise, do your best to try to recall the earliest messages that you learned.

1. What message did you grow up hearing about what it means to be a man?

   _____
   _____
   _____
   _____
   _____

2. Do you believe what you learned as a child about being a man still holds true today?

   _____
   _____
   _____
   _____
   _____

3. How have your views on being a man changed since you were a child?

   _____
   _____
   _____
   _____

4. In your honest view, how does a real man handle being what he perceives to be "disrespected?"

5. How does a real man respond to a woman who attempts to be violent with him?

6. How should a real man discipline his children?

7. How should a real man deal with his emotions?

_____
_____
_____
_____
_____
_____

8. As you look at your answers to this section, what do you notice about how what you learned regarding being a man has shaped the kind of man you are?

_____
_____
_____
_____
_____
_____

The Roots of Being a Man Exercise – Part 2

My Experience with Women:

1. Women always

_____
_____

2. Women never

_____

_____

3. Women definitely cannot

_____

_____

4. When women are together, they

_____

_____

5. One thing about women that I cannot stand is

_____

_____

6. Women should

_____

_____

7. Women should never

_____

_____

8. Women are not capable of

_____

_____

9. What I would like to see different about women is…

_____

_____

10. What I really appreciate about women is….

_____

_____

11. This week I intend to demonstrate a little more respect to a woman I know by…

_____

_____

_____

_____

_____

_____

_____

_____

_____

To be understood is comforting; to understand is wisdom.

Personal Challenge:
Recognize how the past has shaped who you are.

The Roots of Being a Woman

Though we are certainly in control of what we do, the world around us has undoubtedly shaped us. What the adults in our lives taught us as children was indelible, meaning whether we like it or not, their teachings stuck to us. What we might not realize is that when we don't stop to question what we were taught, we often find ourselves living out other people's beliefs systems and they can even be belief systems that do not resonate with us.

Just Do What He Says, Dear

Little Sarah was excited about "Pirate Day" in her kindergarten class. When she got to school, she told one of the boys in class she was excited to be a pirate, and the boy laughed at her. "Only boys are pirates," he said, "The girls are supposed to be princesses." Sarah was devastated. She asked the teacher, and he said, "Yes, the girls are princesses, the boys come as pirates."

When Sarah got home, she told her mother the story. She had hoped her mother would tell her that they were wrong at school. She had hoped her mother would talk to the teacher and make it right. Instead, her mother, not wanting to make waves, said to her, "Just do what he says, dear." Girls are princesses. Only boys are pirates.

From that day forward, Sarah spent less time thinking about what she wanted, and much more time thinking about what she was supposed to be. It wasn't until Sarah became an adult and had a daughter of her own that she realized: A girl can be anything she wants to be.

The Roots of Being a Woman
Exercise – Part 1

Discovering the messages that were given to us is a powerful step in figuring out what kind of people we want to be as adults. For this exercise, do your best to try to recall the earliest messages that you learned.

1. What message did you grow up hearing about what it means to be a woman?

   _____
   _____
   _____
   _____
   _____

2. Do you believe what you learned as a child about being a woman still holds true today?

   _____
   _____
   _____
   _____
   _____

3. How have your views on being a woman changed since you were a child?

   _____
   _____

4. In your honest view, how does a strong woman handle being what she perceives to be "disrespected?"

5. How does a strong woman respond to a man who attempts to be violent with her?

6. How should a strong woman discipline her children?

7. How should a strong woman deal with her emotions?

_____

_____

_____

_____

_____

_____

The Roots of Being a Woman
Exercise – Part 2

My Experience with Men:

1. Men always

_____

_____

2. Men never

_____

_____

3. Men definitely cannot

_____

_____

4. When men are together, they

_____

5. One thing about men that I cannot stand is

_____

_____

6. Men should

_____

_____

7. Men should never

_____

_____

8. Men are not capable of

_____

_____

9. What I would like to see different about men is…

_____

_____

_____

_____

10. What I really appreciate about men is….

_____

_____

_____

_____

388 This week I intend to demonstrate a little more respect to a man I know by…

___

To be understood is comforting; to understand is wisdom.

Personal Challenge:
Recognize how your experiences shape who you are.

Enmeshment Versus Differentiation

The more two people are dependent on each other, the more *enmeshed* they are. Enmeshed means people are intertwined or "stuck" together. The goal for all people is to become differentiated, to be their own person and not tangled up in someone else. To be *differentiated* means to be completely independent and self-sufficient, both mentally and emotionally. We have all had relationships where we were much more enmeshed than we should have been.

It makes sense that as children, we are enmeshed with our parents. We need our parents, after all, for our basic survival. All people, then, start out life enmeshed with their parents. As we grow up, we begin to see the world in our own way, from our own perspectives. Many times, parents and family members attempt to "pull" us back into the worldview we had when they were teaching us about the world and we believed everything they said. Most adolescents, in an attempt to break free from the enmeshment of their parents, go to the extreme of doing or becoming the opposite of what their parents do. As long as others drive our behavior, however, we are still entangled with them. Therefore, doing the opposite of what our parents do just to be different from them means that we are still very much enmeshed with them.

To become differentiated is to genuinely become your own person. Differentiated people do not need others to think the way that they think or believe the things that they believe. Differentiated people are content with themselves regardless of what those around them believe. Differentiated people can still very much love to be around others, but they do not attempt to control others in any way.

390 Enmeshment Versus Differentiation Exercise

1. Describe a relationship in which you were or are enmeshed.

_____
_____
_____
_____
_____
_____

Being too close: Enmeshment as the Chameleon or the Bully

There are beneficial ways in which we are close with others, but unhealthful ways in which we are enmeshed with others. Two unhealthful enmeshment styles are the "chameleon" and the "bully." Both types need others to be emotionally close to them. "Chameleons" morph into the other person; bullies need others to conform to what they think and do.

Chameleons will change everything from their likes and dislikes to their core basic values to match what someone else wants. Chameleons will give up who they are or want to be just to protect themselves from having to be alone. Bullies will or use force by threatening the . Bullies will either threaten love away if the other person conform to what they want, or they will use guilt to force the other person into submitting to their beliefs or actions.

2. Write about how you've been either the chameleon or the bully, and how both ideas of chameleon and bully have impacted your relationships.

Enmeshed   Differentiated

1   2   3   4   5   6   7   8   9   10

On a scale of 1 to 10, rank how enmeshed you were / are in the relationship you described

3. What can you do to help YOURSELF become more differentiated this week?

_____
_____
_____
_____
_____
_____
_____
_____

> **We want to be our own person, not who others want us to be...**
> **Yet, we want others to be exactly who we want them to be....**

> **Personal challenge:**
> **Accept others for who they are.**

Games We Play

How often do we say one thing when we really mean something else? We are playing a game anytime we do this. We all play games. We have different reasons and justifications for why we play games. We are also as quick to deny that we play games as we are to point out how other people play them. And so the round of games goes….

Let the games begin…

Molly told her therapist that her ex accused her of playing games, *"But I don't play any games,"* she said. Then she went on, *"He told my dad that he can't pick up our son because he has to work on Thursday, but the court order says he gets him on Thursdays. I'm so sick of him! I'm just going pretend I didn't talk to my dad today and email him and say, 'What time are you picking him up Thursday?' – that way I'll have it documented that he isn't going to show up."*

The therapist replied, *"So you know that he is not going to get him, and you are going to purposely email him to ask what time he will be there – yet you're confused as to why he has accused you of playing games?"*

Before we are quick to judge Molly, however, it would be helpful for us to take some time to stop playing the games that we are playing in our own lives. We can always focus on what others are doing incorrectly and play the game of *"I'm innocent and don't do things wrong – look at her/him."* Why not take some time to focus solely on the one person we can truly control: ourselves?

Some of the games that we play help us to see the world the way we want to see it. For example, if we want to see someone as irresponsible, we do subtle or sometimes overt things to set him or her up to exhibit that irresponsibility. One game we play is *"I knew you were going to respond like that!"* We play this every time we intentionally act in ways that will bring out a specific behavior in others. We either think to ourselves or say out loud: *"I knew you were going to respond like that!"*

Safety tends to come through predictability. So, the more we can predict what is going to happen around us, the safer we tend to feel. Playing games helps us make sense of the world, because as long as people act the way we want them to, even if we don't like their behavior, we feel much safer than if things were unpredictable. Some examples of other games that we frequently play are:

- *"Yes, but…."*

    i.e., agreeing with a valid point, but then negating it by what you say after the "but"

- *"I can use silence to control you"*

    i.e., not answering someone, then being surprised when they get so angry

- *"I will use anger to control you"*

    i.e., screaming or intimidating someone so that your word is final

- *"I'll bring up your past, but want you to ignore mine"*

- *"I'll make you feel guilty"*

- *"I will smile so that you like me"*

- *"I will be nice to others so that they won't believe that I could be a real terror in my relationship"*

- *"I will use trusted information to threaten you"*

    i.e., threatening to tell others information that was shared with you in confidence

Games We Play Exercise

These are only a few of the many, many games that we play. For this exercise, you can consider some of these games, or describe completely different ones. There is no "set list" of games, so whatever you come up with or however you want to describe games that others play is OK. The important thing is to try to identify the types of games that you and others play.

1. What types of behavioral games do your children (or children that you know) play?

   _____

   _____

   _____

   _____

   _____

   _____

2. What types of games does their other parent or someone close to you play?

   _____

   _____

   _____

   _____

   _____

   _____

3. What kinds of games do you play?

   _____

   _____

4. What kinds of games would you like to see your family stop playing?

5. What kinds of games would you like to see your friends stop playing?

6. What kinds of games would you like to see stop at work?

7. How do you contribute to all of the games in your life?

All people play games: Those who understand the games they play can choose to be a part of them or change them. Those who don't understand the games they play are just pieces in the game. We play games for one main reason: We want something from someone. When we can figure out what it is that we want, we can learn to just directly ask for it, rather than hiding it behind a web of games. If you want to be close with someone, try asking that person what you can do to become closer. If you are insecure and worried about someone's leaving you, express that to the person instead of putting that person down, trying to impose guilt so the person will stay, or using demeaning or belittling language. The more you learn about your own games, the more you can learn to ask for whatever it is that you really want.

Personal challenge:
Avoid playing mental games with others.

What To Do With My Anger

What we do with our anger is often what we have learned to do with our anger by watching others. Taking time to find out what our first images of anger looked like can help us identify at least parts of why we react the way we do when we are angry. We tend to set guidelines for ourselves about how we will express anger and what is acceptable in terms of expressing anger.

What is acceptable?

Human beings have a tendency to push the limits of whatever boundaries encompass them. Both in positive and negative ways, throughout recorded history, people have gone beyond whatever limits were set. From toddlers reaching out with their tiny pointer fingers to touch the tablecloth that their mother tells them to not touch – to astronauts flying through space and landing on the moon, human beings seem to have a desire to go beyond the boundaries.

The moment we draw an outline around what we perceive to be acceptable behavior we are essentially creating boundaries for ourselves that, at some point in time, we are likely to test. When it comes to anger and violence, people set acceptable boundaries for themselves, encompassing what they perceive to be appropriate ways to express anger. The problem with the boundaries we create is that once we know the limits of what is acceptable, we are more and more likely to go straight to those limits the moment we are angry. The more we hover around the boundaries, the more likely we are to break them.

The point? What if we set the boundary for acting out of anger at zero? What if we decide, here and now, that we will not allow ourselves to act out of anger for any reason? Then, if we do go beyond that boundary, we will at least not be so quick to jump to the most extreme measures we have for expressing our anger.

Pull your boundaries in a little tighter for expressing anger.

When we practice a skill-set long enough, we are able to utilize that skill-set even in crisis situations. Consider, after all, the training of men and women in our military forces. They are trained time and again for years to remain calm in high conflict situations, because during wartime, it would not benefit soldiers to panic. After years of practicing and becoming efficient, soldiers can face bombs going off around them, but still maintain enough of a calm approach to make good decisions.

What To Do With My Anger Exercise

Fast fact

How we practice handling our anger is exactly the way in which we will get good at expressing it. If we want to express anger differently, we have to practice differently. Like anything in life, *what we practice doing is what we get better at performing.* If we practice having a bad temper, we will get really, really good at it, which, of course, we all know can lead to some very, very bad things.

What do you practice? How do you practice letting your anger out? Do you practice letting yourself do whatever you want to do, regardless of who is around you? Do you practice restraint in front of certain people such as authority figures, but allow yourself to get as angry as possible in front of family members? What you likely do with your anger is what you've allowed yourself to practice doing with your anger; and you may have practiced without ever realizing that you were practicing.

1. When my mother got angry, she…

_____

_____

_____

_____
_____
_____

2. When my father got angry, he…

_____
_____
_____
_____

3. When my siblings or friends got angry, they…

_____
_____
_____
_____

4. I have misdirected my anger toward others in the following ways:

_____
_____
_____
_____

5. My misdirected anger has been hurtful to others in the following ways:

_____
_____

6. I am afraid if I get really angry I will…

7. I cannot get angry because…

8. What is the difference between anger and violence?

401 ***Whether we like how it sounds on paper or not, all behaviors have benefits:*** **Albeit some benefits help others and other benefits hurt others.**

9. What are some rewards of expressing our anger through violence?

_____
_____
_____
_____
_____
_____
_____

10. What are some consequences of expressing our behavior through violence?

_____
_____
_____
_____
_____
_____
_____

11. People say we are 100% responsible for our behavior. When are we not responsible for our behavior?

_____
_____
_____
_____
_____
_____
_____

12. What is it that a person gains by being abusive?

13. What are the consequences of being abusive?

Personal challenge:
Reject violence in thought, word, and deed.

Evaluating Myself as a Dad (For Fathers)

Every day thousands of children are growing up in a home where domestic violence is a constant. The lasting negative effects of domestic violence on children do not necessarily have to do with the type of abuse (i.e. physical, verbal, emotional); the negative effects come from having to constantly live in a state of chaos and hyper vigilance. You may have grown up in a home where you constantly had to be watchful for violence. You may also believe, "Well, I had it tough and it didn't affect me." In reality, every experience impacts and shapes us.

Guarding the Amygdalae

As fathers, we often see it as our responsibility to protect our children. The amygdalae (center of the fight or flight response) are two almond-shaped structures in the brain that lie at the end of the hippocampus (center of memory). What that means is our alertness is closely tied to our memory. In other words, when we see violence or something that scares us, it sticks us; and the same is true for our children.

We may believe that "it's not big deal that we scream and yell at our children," or we may say, "I was yelled and I turned out fine." What we know now, in the 21st century, is that when children experience intense fear or violence, it directly impacts their amygdalae. When your children's amygdalae are affected, then it literally changes their brain chemistry.

As fathers, we are charged with guarding our children's amygdalae. In many ways it is our responsibility to not add to the violence and fear that our children experience when they see inappropriately expressed anger. We invite you to take the challenge to guard your children's amygdalae by doing all you can to teach your children with compassion, rather than intimidating your children with fear.

Evaluating Myself as a Dad Exercise

Please take a minute to think about what home life may be like for your children. If you do not have children, think about what kind of a home environment yours would be for a child.

1. If we interviewed your children for a documentary, what would they say about you right now?

   _____
   _____
   _____
   _____
   _____
   _____

2. Has what your children would say about you changed in the last five years? Why or why not? How has it changed?

   _____
   _____
   _____
   _____
   _____
   _____

3. What do you remember about your father when you were a child?

   _____
   _____
   _____

4. What would your children say about your yelling at them?

5. Do you believe yelling truly teaches your children the lesson that you want them to learn, or would you say that it generally teaches them to be afraid of you? Expand on your answer.

6. How do you think your children will remember you when you are gone?

7. How do you want your children to remember you when you are gone?

_____

_____

_____

_____

_____

_____

Personal challenge:
Be the best father you can be.

What It Means To Be a Man

Are men supposed to be tough? Are they supposed to be strong? Are they supposed to be able to fight? Are they supposed to be intelligent? Are they supposed to be intimidating? Are they supposed to be proud? Are they supposed to be funny? Are they supposed to be sensitive? Are they supposed to be providers?

For Discussion: What it means to be tough…

For many men, "toughness" is extremely important. But what makes a person tough? Showing anger? Talking tough? Intimidating others?

The definition of tough is "strong and durable" or "not easily broken." Nowhere in the definition of "tough" are things like "the ability to act strong and durable," or "the ability to intimidate those who are weaker." Despite this, many men are taught to believe that acting tough is a way to actually be tough.

Sometimes being strong means putting our own needs aside to be there for others. Sometimes being strong is standing up for ourselves or others. What being strong or tough seems to never be is "trash talking" or intimidating those who are physically weaker through anger. Being tough never involves needing to have other people with you as you outnumber a potential victim.

But what do you think? What does being tough mean to you?

408 What It Mean To Be a Man Exercise

What you believe about men in general shapes the kind of man you are. And what kind of man you believe you are supposed to be impacts how you relate to others. This exercise is intended to provide you with a little more clarity as to what your view of being a man is and how that view shapes you.

1. Where do your views on being a man come from?

   _____
   _____
   _____
   _____
   _____

2. In your view, what characteristics constitute being a man?

   _____
   _____
   _____
   _____
   _____

3. What characteristics about being a man are good traits?

   _____
   _____
   _____
   _____
   _____

4. What male characteristics make a man emotionally unhealthy?

_____
_____
_____
_____
_____
_____
_____

5. What male characteristics make you emotionally unhealthy?

_____
_____
_____
_____
_____
_____
_____

6. What role does "intimidation" and "fear" play in the development of being a man?

_____
_____
_____
_____
_____
_____
_____

In every moment we have an opportunity to define ourselves in any way that we choose. How we define ourselves and how we act can reverberate through generations. Some of the toughest men in the history of the world have left their mark on the world by sacrificing their own needs for the needs of others. Tough men do not need to pick on others because they know who they truly are, and they have no need to prove it. Want an example of toughness? Think of soldiers who threw themselves on grenades, sacrificing their lives for their fellow soldiers. You don't have to throw yourself on a grenade, but you can protect those around you, especially the most innocent and vulnerable.

> **Personal challenge:**
> **Be the kind of man that your community would be proud to know.**

Evaluating Myself as a Mom (For Mothers)

Every day thousands of children are growing up in a home where domestic violence is constant. The lasting negative effects of domestic violence on children do not necessarily have to do with the type of abuse (i.e. physical, verbal, emotional); the negative effects come from having to constantly live in a state of chaos and hyper vigilance. You may have grown up in a home where you had to live in a constant state of chaos, or your children may be growing up in a home like that now.

Teaching assertiveness to our daughters

Many young girls are given the indirect message that they can either be a "doormat" or a "bitch"; few young girls are taught that it is always okay for them to stand up for themselves and to be assertive. Because girls rarely get the opportunity to learn assertiveness, they tend to hold things down until they cannot take it anymore, and then they explode with anger or lash out at others. It is crucial, then, that we teach our daughters how to be assertive.

The goal in teaching assertiveness is to have girls learn that they have a right to express how they feel in every given moment, without having to bottle it up inside until it is too late. Assertiveness is about understanding that we all have a right to our own space. If we want something, we have the right to ask for it, and if we do not want something, we have the right to say no and have it not happen.

To teach assertiveness to our daughters, we have to remember that they will learn much more from what they see than what they hear. In other words, mothers are strongly invited to live out the assertiveness that they want their daughters to learn.

412 Evaluating Myself as a Mom Exercise

Please take a minute to think about what home life may be like for your children. If you do not have children, think about what kind of a home environment yours would be for a child.

1. If we interviewed your children what would they say about you right now?

   _____
   _____
   _____
   _____
   _____
   _____

2. Has what your children would say about you changed in the last five years? Why or why not? If so, how?

   _____
   _____
   _____
   _____
   _____
   _____
   _____
   _____

3. What do you remember about your mother?

_____
_____
_____
_____
_____
_____
_____

4. What would your children say about you yelling at them?

_____
_____
_____
_____
_____
_____
_____

5. Do you believe yelling truly teaches your children the lesson that you want them to learn, or would you say that it generally teaches them to be afraid of you? Expand on your answer?

_____
_____
_____
_____
_____
_____
_____

6. How do you think your children will remember you when you're gone?

_____
_____
_____
_____
_____
_____

7. How do you want your children to remember you when you're gone?

_____
_____
_____
_____
_____
_____

Personal challenge:
Be the best mother you can be.

What It Means to Be a Woman

Being a woman means many things. When it comes to anger, women are bombarded with mixed messages: *Stand up for yourself – but always be a lady. Don't put up with stuff from men - but don't be too mean. You can either be a doormat or a "bitch": there is no room for middle ground.* These messages provide conflicting views on what it means to be a woman.

What you believe about women in general shapes the kind of woman you are. And what kind of woman you believe you are supposed to be impacts how you relate to others.

1850-2013

In 1850, the following advice was written to women in a book entitled: *How to be a Lady: A Book for Girls, Containing Useful Hints on the Formation of Character.*

"To be a lady, one must behave always with propriety; and be civil, courteous, and kind, to all. Above all, behave with strict regard to propriety."

Propriety means to conform to the established standards of good or proper manners. Even though propriety might change with the times, are women really taught anything differently even 163 years after that book was published? What does it mean for you to be a woman? How *should* women be? More importantly, what does it mean for you to be a woman?

What It Means to Be a Woman Exercise

This exercise is intended to provide you with a little more clarity as to what your view of being a woman is and how that view shapes you.

1. Where do your views on being a woman come from?

   _____
   _____
   _____
   _____
   _____
   _____

2. In your view, what characteristics constitute being a woman?

   _____
   _____
   _____
   _____
   _____
   _____

3. What characteristics about being a woman are good traits?

   _____
   _____
   _____
   _____

4. What characteristics about being a woman are not healthy?

_____
_____
_____
_____
_____
_____

5. What unhealthy characteristics do you have?

_____
_____
_____
_____
_____
_____
_____

Personal challenge:
Face the negative traits you have and do your best to change them.

External Control Psychology

External Control Psychology occurs when people place blame for their life on outside events. When people say things like, "The system is messed up!" or "Society's messed up!" these are examples of external control psychology. Another expression, "I can't be happy because I can't get the job I want!" is an example of someone placing their happiness on a job, rather than within themselves. All people on some level at some points in their lives look to blame the outside world for some things.

Lesson in a video game

When people play a video game, they frequently spend more time learning the rules of the game and figuring out how to win than playing the actual game itself. They do this they can beat the game. Even younger adolescents are rarely heard complaining about "how big the monsters are" in the game, and instead, are busy trying to figure out how to beat the monsters within the confines of the rules of the video game.

In any given society or institution there are also rules. Oftentimes in life, we spend a great deal of time talking and complaining about how "the rules are unfair" versus concentrating more efforts on learning the rules and figuring out how to succeed within the confines of those rules.

External control psychology is understandable. It is easier for us to complain about the world and how the world is "messed up and unfair" than it is for us to take responsibility for the part that we play in the world.

External Control Psychology Exercise

There is a tendency for people who learn about external control psychology to say, "Yes, I play a part, BUT…" and then they go on to make an excuse for why they "can't" do whatever it is they would like. For this exercise, try to avoid the "Yes, but" game, and answer as honestly as you can.

1. Write down at least two examples of times when you use external control psychology, or when you look to blame other people for why your life is the way it is, rather than taking responsibility for it.

    a.

    _____
    _____
    _____
    _____
    _____
    _____

    b.

    _____
    _____
    _____
    _____
    _____
    _____

2. Imagine how it might look if you were to take COMPLETE responsibility for your life being where it is today. How might things start to change for you?

_____
_____
_____
_____
_____
_____

3. What can you do this week to assume complete responsibility for everything you do? That would mean you would avoid saying things like, "she made me..." (do something or get angry) or "he made me..." (respond the way I did or get angry).

_____
_____
_____
_____
_____
_____

> "As long as I can blame someone else for my life, I never have to change."

Personal challenge:
Take responsibility for every single thing you do today.

Internal Control Psychology

The opposite of external control is internal control. Internal control psychology occurs when we take complete responsibility for our lives. When we realize that our thoughts control our feelings, that we have control over our thoughts (with practice), and that we can choose whatever behaviors we want, we begin to gain control over our lives.

Controlling our decisions

Braxton came into his anger management group furious one day. He told everyone how he "knew" a guy at work had robbed him of $400. He said he wanted to kill him, and it didn't matter that he just spent 8 years of his life locked up, because as he said, *"nobody punks me!"*

The group leader asked Braxton if he liked prison. Braxton was already angry, and he thought the group leader was messing with him, so that seemed to just anger him more and more. Finally, the group leader said, *"Are there times when you were sitting there in your cell and you were thinking, 'man I wish I could get out of here?'"* and Braxton angrily replied, *"Of course there were!"* So the group leader asked another question: *"What would you have done to get out?"*

And Braxton said, *"I'd have done anything."*

So the group leader finally asked, *"Would you have paid $400 to get out?"*

That comment was enough to make Braxton stop and think. He chose not to assume that the person robbed him, and he chose instead to go home and sleep off his anger. When he woke up the next day, he was thankful he didn't kill the other guy for "disrespecting" him. In fact, he told us the next week that in that moment, he would have gladly paid $400 for his freedom.

Ironically, he found the money in his wallet underneath a pile of clothes in his room – but that wasn't the point. He realized that his freedom was worth a lot more than $400.

How much is your freedom worth?

Internal Control Psychology Exercise

In the following exercise, think about a specific relationship you have or goals for yourself.

1. What do I want today in my life?

___

2. What am I actively doing to get what I want?

___

3. How is what I am doing to get what I want working for me?

___

4. A good plan I could start working on immediately to get what I want is…

_____

_____

_____

_____

_____

_____

5. The things that I can foresee getting in the way of me following through with my plan are…

_____

_____

_____

_____

_____

_____

6. What I will do to get around the obstacles I listed in number 5 is…

_____

_____

_____

_____

_____

_____

> A free person is one who knows where control truly resides.

Personal challenge:
Know that you have control of yourself in every interaction.

From External to Internal Control

To move from external control to internal control is a journey of self-discovery. Whereas it seems much easier to blame the outside world for what goes wrong in our lives, at the end of the day, we alone stand trial for our behaviors. Most people go their entire lives without realizing how much control they actually had all along.

The world is a tough place to be sometimes. We can find ourselves asking advice from people so that, if we follow it and it doesn't work out, we can have someone to blame for why we chose what we chose. It can be overwhelming to think about taking control of our lives. A famous book called *Escape from Freedom* was based on the idea that people would rather be told what to do than face the pressure that they are ultimately responsible for everything they do.

Once we learn to accept responsibility, however, we learn to become empowered. We find less of a need for others' approval, and accept our own decisions more. When we accept responsibly for what we do, we also think more before we act. When we accept responsibility, we move from being externally controlled to our own internal control.

It's everybody's fault but mine!

We can blame everyone around us for why we are where we are in life. There will never be an end or shortage of people and institutions to blame. The problem with blaming everyone else in life is that it gives everyone else control over us. Everyone outside of us (external control) gets to determine what goes on in our lives.... That is, until we discover that whereas others can influence us, we alone are in control of everything we think and what we do in life.

If it truly is everybody else's fault but yours, then you're in for a long, long road, because nothing you can do will make a difference. But if you can learn that you are always in control of what you think and do (internal control), then you will begin to make the changes that matter most in your life.

Change can start now.

From External to Internal Control Exercise

1. Describe a situation where someone made you do something.

   _____
   _____
   _____
   _____
   _____
   _____

2. Is it possible that you could have done something different from what you did? If so, what could you have done differently?

   _____
   _____
   _____
   _____
   _____
   _____

3. What do you need to start taking responsibility for in your life right now?

   _____
   _____
   _____
   _____
   _____
   _____

4. What can you do this week to start taking responsibility for what you wrote in number 3?

___

5. What will stop you from taking responsibility this week (e.g., work, family, friends, habits, addictions, priorities)?

___

6. How can you get around the obstacles that you wrote for number 5?

___

Power and Control

Everyone wants to have a sense of control in life. The most difficult type of control to achieve is self-control. When people are weak, they attempt to control others. When people are strong, they control themselves. Most people like to say that they have pretty good self-control but in the next breath, most people will also talk about how they "give in to their weaknesses." Power and control are natural things to strive for. They can even be beneficial for us as long as the power and control that we are seeking is power and control over ourselves.

Being controlled by others

Jeremy never wanted to be considered someone else's puppet. He never wanted to admit that he often gave away his control. The fact was, anyone who called Jeremy something nasty or disrespectful could have complete power over him.

In an instant, Jeremy could go from having a nice day and minding his own business, to beating someone down for saying the wrong thing. He thought he was in control, until he came to the powerful and very difficult realization that other people constantly controlled him.

Jeremy had become a puppet to "toughness" and "respect." Those two concepts owned him – but despite that – he still could not get everyone to respect him – so he began searching for control over his loved ones. He did whatever it took to be controlling of his girlfriend. He told her what to wear, where she could go, who she "should" and "shouldn't" be friends with, and why she "shouldn't" talk to her family anymore. He did all of this until one day when he learned about power and control and he realized what he was doing.

In the end, he stopped allowing others to control him. In turn, he lessened his control of his girlfriend, who loved him and supported him. Before he knew it, Jeremy began to take control of himself and his life.

Power and Control Exercise

1. Rank yourself on how much self-control you believe you have.

   1   2   3   4   5   6   7   8   9   10
   None   A lot

2. Rank yourself on how much self-control your partner, or someone close to you, would say that you have.

   1   2   3   4   5   6   7   8   9   10
   None   A lot

3. Rank yourself on how much self-control you want to have.

   1   2   3   4   5   6   7   8   9   10
   None   A lot

4. List at least two ways you can gain more self-control this week. First Way

   _____
   _____
   _____
   _____
   _____

   Second Way

   _____
   _____

5. What might stop you from following through with trying to gain more self-control this week?

6. What can you do to not let that get in your way?

Personal challenge:
Find the power that resides within you.

Mr. X: Where the Anger Goes

Sometimes it's easier to see the mistakes that others are making than it is to see our own mistakes. As outsiders to situations, we seem to have much more insight than when we are in the middle of it all.

It's true many people will say that whereas they can easily give advice to others, it is infinitely more difficult for them to take their own advice. We believe, however, that the more a person teaches a concept, the more likely it is for him or her to begin to live out that message. With that in mind, this exercise is geared toward using your knowledge to help solve the situation that Mr. X has gotten into.

Keep in mind that professional counselors and psychologists have learned how to listen to people's stories with a "careful ear." Having a "careful ear" means that they are trained to cautiously hear the things that people tell them. What professionals understand is that there are always at least three sides to every story: the person's side who tells it, the side of the other person/people involved, and an outsiders' viewpoint. Keep the idea of having a "careful ear" in mind as you read the following situation involving Mr. X and his family.

For this exercise, look at Mr. X's family situation and see if you can write down some insight that might be helpful for him.

Mr. X comes home from work upset about his day. The moment he walks in the door his wife understands what mood he is in. She does not want to get in an argument or have him yell at her, so she begins yelling at the children for the smallest things. Mr. X gets even more enraged that "all his wife does is yell." He doesn't know how to deal with it, so he yells as well. The children bear the brunt of their parent's not communicating and not trying to deal with their relationship or their stress. The children in turn have nowhere else to put their anxiety, so they start acting out, which in turn, fuels the parents' anger more.

Mr. X: Where the Anger Goes
Exercise – Part 1

1. Where along the way could Mr. X's situation been stopped?

2. What can Mr. X do to make things different? What can he control?

3. Name ways in which your mood affects the people around you.

4. In what ways do you take things out on other people?

___

Mr. X: Where the Anger Goes
Exercise - PART II

___

Nobody likes anxiety. Just like Mr. X's wife, we would rather do just about anything than experience anxiety. In fact, like her, we even have a tendency to pass along our anxiety to others so we do not have to experience it.

1. In what ways do you pass along your anxiety?

___

2. In what ways is anxiety passed along to you from others?

___

3. What can you SPECIFICALLY do to stop passing your anxiety along to others?

The Story of Alex

Day after day, Alex found himself struggling with his work. He didn't feel like he could do anything right. He was constantly anxious. As his work became more stressful, so too, did his family life. His family was first to notice that he was short tempered with all of them. At first, he didn't see it. He just assumed that they were not being as supportive as they could have been.

At work, even Alex's coworkers noticed the change in him. He came to therapy. When they therapist made him aware of the anxiety he appeared to be experiencing, he resisted the idea. He thought it made him "weak" to admit he struggled with anxiety. The more he learned about it, however, the more he realized the therapist, his family, and his coworkers were right.

Alex used courage to face what he was doing that was hurtful to others, and because of his courage, he made tremendous changes in his life. His big changes all began with a little act: One day, he came home from work and was about to yell at his wife for something very little, when, all of a sudden, he realized what he was doing. Instead of yelling, he asked her to come sit down and talk. He told her how stressed he was, how scary things were for him at work.

Alex found his wife to be an incredible support. He realized in the deepest part of him, that had he come home that day and yelled, nothing would have changed. Because he chose to express his anxiety, however, his wife was supportive, and the two of them discovered a new way to communicate.

Alex changed his life by learning how to express what his emotions were. Understanding that he struggled with anxiety did not make him weak in any way. Understanding what was going on inside him gave him the key to have courage in the face of his fear of changing. Alex's family is still happily together today.

> **Personal challenge:**
> **Directly address your emotions rather than taking them out on your loved ones.**

Pushing "Buttons"

"She pushes my buttons!" "He knows my buttons and purposefully pushes them!"

Everyone has "buttons" or sensitive issues that can be triggered very easily. We all have issues that can "set us off" more quickly than how we respond to other things. We are not proud of these "buttons" but we are aware we have them. We are all also aware that others have these "buttons" as well. What's so intriguing, is that we don't like it when others press our "buttons" but we continue to press other's "buttons." Why do we have such a tendency to affect others negatively? Why do we try to control others in this way? Why do we permit such control of ourselves?

Please control me!

Anytime we allow ourselves to have "buttons," we are asking others to please control us. Ultimately, we determine which "buttons" we will choose to keep and which ones we choose to turn off.

In the movie *Back to the Future*, the main character would allow others to control him simply by calling him a "chicken." He could be having a normal day, but the moment someone called him a chicken, he would turn and confront or challenge that person. His button was being called "chicken." Instead of confronting or challenging the people who called him a chicken, he could have equally also said to them, "Hey, please control me!" because that is essentially what was happening.

Whether we want to admit it or not, when we allow ourselves to have "buttons," we are providing people with opportunities to control us.

Pushing "Buttons" Exercise

1. List three of your "buttons" and describe how others push them.

   a.

   b.

   c.

2. List 3 of your partner's "buttons" or most recent partner's "buttons" and describe how you push them.

a.

b.

c.

3. Rank yourself on how often you push your partner's "buttons."

   1   2   3   4   5   6   7   8   9   10
   Never   All the time

4. Rank how often your partner or others push your "buttons."

   1   2   3   4   5   6   7   8   9   10
   Never   All the time

5. Why do you think you have the "buttons" that you have? What kinds of things happened to you throughout your life that led to your having these "buttons"?

   _____
   _____
   _____
   _____
   _____
   _____

6. Why do you think that you sometimes choose to push your partner's "buttons"?

   _____
   _____
   _____
   _____
   _____
   _____

7. List one way you can prevent yourself from pushing "buttons" this week.

_____
_____
_____
_____
_____
_____
_____

Personal challenge:
Get rid of the "buttons" in your life.

Violence in My Own Life

Some of the following questions are very personal, but keep in mind the more we choose to crystallize ideas by writing them down, the more we own up to them. The more we own something, the more responsibility we take. The more responsibility we take, the more we are ready to change.

It can be difficult to look at the violence that we have experienced, but without looking at it and truly understanding the past, we are doomed to repeat it. It makes sense that if we learned violence that we are simply doing what we learned, that is, until we learn something new.

Compassion for ourselves

Children often witness tremendous violence that sticks with them for their entire lives. They grow up learning what they see, regardless of what adults around them might tell them. So often, parents believe they are telling their children the right things, only to turn around and act out of anger in front of them. Many times, parents minimize the anger that their children see. In other words, parents might not think that the anger/yelling that goes on around their children impacts them, but it does. What parents fail to understand is this: From the eyes of a child, even yelling is scary.

The part of the brain that is responsible for the fight or flight response is impacted every time children live in fear. The more they live in fear, the more they will develop fear-based reactions such as acting out, lower attention span, and mistrust for their world. The more children see anger-based relationships, the more likely they are to engage in those kinds of relationships as they get older.

If you grew up witnessing violence, understand that, regardless of whatever was told to you, you were not the cause of violence as a child. Children cannot cause adults to be angry and act out of anger. Children can merely act. How adults react, respond, or choose to teach their children is up to them, but children can never make adults fight, even if the adults overtly blame the children for their problems. If you've witnessed violence growing up, consider going back in time in your mind and having a talk with your younger self. The compassion you show yourself as you talk to the child in you can reverberate all the way back to the present moment to help you make an astounding change in your life right now.

Violence in My Own Life Exercise

1. What types of violence did you witness as a child?

   _____
   _____
   _____
   _____
   _____
   _____
   _____

2. What affects did watching violence have on you?

   _____
   _____
   _____
   _____
   _____
   _____
   _____

3. Write down at least one example of a time when a current anger-management technique would have helped you in a past incidence of violence.

   _____
   _____
   _____
   _____
   _____

4. What type of violence have you exhibited in front of children? This includes intense arguments.

_____

5. What impact might that show of violence have on their lives?

_____

6. Imagine that who you are today has an opportunity to talk to who you were at 5, 10, and 15 years-old. What would you say to yourself about the violence you witnessed?

_____

7. What would you tell your younger self about the violence you would go on to do?

_____
_____
_____
_____
_____
_____
_____

8. Imagine now that you are twenty years older from what you are today. If in twenty years, you could come back to this moment and talk to who you are today, what do you think you would tell yourself?

_____
_____
_____
_____
_____
_____
_____

Perspective changes everything.

Personal challenge:
Change your perspective, change your life.

Incident Report

We have a tendency to minimize what we do to others, whereas we have a tendency to maximize what others do to us. When an event that saw anger arise occurs, we have a tendency to minimize our own role while we maximize what the other person has done to us.

Example #1 (minimizing)

She stopped answering my calls. I wouldn't have made the calls but she told me countless times to show her that I wouldn't give up on her easily. I got upset and went to her house to talk to her. She said I was screaming but I wasn't, though I might have raised my voice a little after she did. She was in my face and kept putting her hand in my face trying to slap me I think. All I did was move her hand away and, of course, she tripped because she's always been clumsy. There ended up being a little mark on her wrist. So I got taken away by the cops, who of course, took her side.

Example #2 (an unemotional telling of the event)

11/1/11

At 2 a.m., PERSON 1 (male) attempted to make phone contact with PERSON 2 (female). After no phone contact was made, PERSON 1 showed up at PERSON 2's house and demonstrated frustration with PERSON 2 by using a loud voice and expressing negative sentiments to PERSON 2. PERSON 2 asked PERSON 1 to leave 4 times. PERSON 1 did not leave when asked, and insisted that they "finish this." PERSON 2 raised a hand to PERSON 1 motioning for him to leave. PERSON 1 grabbed the wrist of PERSON 2 and redirected her with enough pressure to force her to the ground. A neighbor (PERSON 3) stepped in between PERSON 1 and PERSON 2, and remained there until the police came.

Psychology behind it

The reason it's not easy to take emotion out of an event that we are experiencing is that our entire brain is experiencing it. Asking people to take the emotion away is in some way like asking them to not experience what they are experiencing. So what can we do?

Learning to experience things and simultaneously step outside of ourselves is a key to not allowing individual experiences to define us.

Incident Report Exercise

Think about an event in your life or a recent situation at which you got angry. Think about how your actions were ineffective. Write down an incident report about the event **without** using any emotional language. Be matter of fact in the way you describe the incident. Do your best to **objectively** describe as many details of the incident as possible.

Here are some guiding questions for your report:

1. What was the date and time that this happened?

2. Who was there?

3. What happened? Try not to use adjectives. Simply describe the behaviors that could be seen by others. Your challenge is to attempt to describe the situation from the eyes of a third party.

1. When you state the incident as facts, how does it change the situation?

   _____
   _____
   _____
   _____
   _____
   _____
   _____

2. How do you alter the incident report when you add the emotional details of the event?

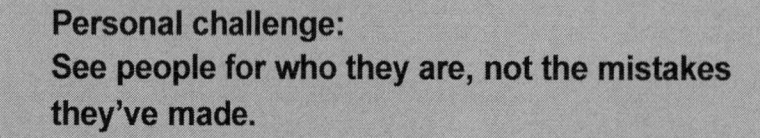

   _____
   _____
   _____
   _____
   _____
   _____
   _____

> It is not a single incident that defines us; nor can a single incident define anyone else.

> **Personal challenge:**
> See people for who they are, not the mistakes they've made.

Ruler of the Land

Ah! To be king or queen of all the land! complaints about society and we all have on how we can make it better. It's not have a vision of what it would be like the ruler of a land. The glory of being a would probably be great, so too, would the responsibilities. When we desire to have people think and act the way we want them to, we are essentially hoping to be rulers of their minds.

As long as we are in a society, we can get frustrated with the rules and the way things are. We can be disappointed with what others come up with for laws and we can feel strongly that if we were in charge, things would be different. Sometimes when we are on the other side of the fence, things can be different. Maybe we cannot control others or what they think, but what we can do, is imagine making the rules. We can imagine being ruler of the land.

Do as I say!

One thing we've noticed about working with thousands of adolescents through the years is that if they are asked to be in charge of an activity where they have to create the rules, they tend to get very defensive and upset if others break their rules. On the other hand, those very same adolescents tend to get upset when others give them consequences for the times when they themselves break rules.

People have a tendency to be strict and unforgiving with others; yet they seek compassion and understanding for themselves. Wise is the monarch who can lead the people with compassion and understanding while still maintaining the rules.

Ruler of the Land Exercise

Imagine you were given the task of starting your own society. You are charged with making all the rules and enforcing them.

1. What type of rules you would set up for your society?

   _____
   _____
   _____
   _____
   _____
   _____
   _____
   _____

2. What would happen when people break the rules? How would you enforce the rules?

   _____
   _____
   _____
   _____
   _____
   _____
   _____
   _____

The world the way I ordered it....

3. Write down the latest incident that made you angry with another person. Describe what the other person *did* to make you angry.

_____

_____

_____

_____

_____

_____

_____

4. What **should** the other person have done instead to **not** make you angry?

_____

_____

_____

_____

_____

_____

5. How are your rules in the society you created different from rules that exist in reality?

_____

_____

_____

_____

_____

6. What is the difference in how you enforce rules currently and how you learned them in the past?

_____

_____

_____

_____

_____

_____

_____

7. What makes your rules "fair" and others' rules "unfair?"

_____

_____

_____

_____

_____

_____

_____

Personal challenge: Rule your own life with wisdom and compassion

Stalking and Harassment

Stalking and harassment are real concepts. Oftentimes, what we believe is "passion" or "intensity" is considered by others to be too intrusive. Sometimes what we perceive as "intensity" is perceived as "stalking" by others. We may think, "Well, I just wanted her/him to know how much I care," but from that person's perspective, we are doing too much.

Stalking is a form of tracking or pursuit that is unwanted by the person being tracked or pursued. Harassment is the instance of repeatedly disturbing another person. Both stalking and harassment are serious offenses. Just as you have the right to not be stalked and harassed by others, so too, do all people have the right to not be stalked and harassed. This exercise is designed to help you learn the difference between "intensity" and "stalking and harassment."

"I just wanted to talk to her…"

It makes sense that we might think that what we are doing is okay, but seen through the eyes of others, our behaviors can take on a whole new meaning.

When we talk about other people's actions, we describe their behaviors. When we talk about our own actions, we have a tendency to describe our intentions. There is a big difference between the two. All too often, intentions can be innocent; but the behaviors that stem from those intentions can be hurtful.

For example, we may say, "But I just wanted to talk to her about…" and that of course sounds innocent enough. It's not until we consider that she repeatedly asked us not to come near her; but despite her asking that, we still repeatedly called and attempted to talk to her. By using the phrase, "But I just wanted to talk…" we minimize our behaviors and avoid facing the reality that we might be harassing someone.

Stalking and Harassment Exercise

We have all experienced being "intense" and "passionate" about someone else. For this exercise, think of someone you have been most "passionate" or "intense" about in a relationship (not children).

1. Write down up to three thoughts that go through your mind when you are feeling "intense" or "passionate."

   _____
   _____
   _____
   _____
   _____

2. Write down up to three behaviors that you do when you are at your most intense and/or most passionate.

   _____
   _____
   _____
   _____
   _____

3. What are realistic steps you can take to act differently or calm yourself down when you are feeling really intense or passionate about someone else?

   _____
   _____
   _____
   _____
   _____

453

4. What effect does stalking have on people?

_____

_____

_____

_____

_____

_____

5. Why do we choose to make others feel guilty?

_____

_____

_____

_____

_____

_____

6. What are ways we can threaten others?

_____

_____

_____

_____

7. What are ways we can stalk others?

_____

_____

_____

8. Do people deserve to be punished for not reciprocating our love?

Crossing the line

9. When is the line between *being in love* and *stalking* crossed?

10. When does passion for a loved one become too much?

11. Write down a person's first name who, if you really think about it, you were definitely too intense around.

___

12. Describe a specific situation when you went overboard with how you acted around this person.

___
___
___
___
___
___

13. Write down how you might handle the situation differently if it happened tomorrow.

___
___
___
___
___
___
___

> **People tend to use "soft" language to describe their own actions, but "harsh" language to describe others' behaviors.**

> **Personal challenge:**
> Try using accurate (rather than "soft" or "harsh") language to describe the things you do.

Eulogy

Many people consider what death is all about. There are times that we acknowledge that one day we will die. There are times that we may question what follows life or what happens after death. There are many questions about a greater being, a heaven or hell, an afterlife and reincarnation. These types of questions and issues are frequently discussed, but what about who we were before that day comes? So many people are afraid to talk about what they brought to this world, what mistakes they made and what changes they need to make. Many state that this doesn't matter. They say, "I'll be gone, who cares." The problem is, you're still here, making either a positive or negative difference, and that difference impacts others.

Near-Death is Not Death

Many people have told astounding tales of near-death experiences. Perhaps more amazing than the tales themselves, however, are the choices that people made after having such experiences. For some, having the opportunity to have a "second chance" is the very break they needed to become what they always wanted to become.

Whether or not you have had or ever will have a near-death experience, you can still ask yourself, "What would you do differently if you were given a second chance at life from this moment forward?" Even if you have experienced a near-death experience, you can rest assured this truth: Near-death is not death – so as long as we are alive, we have an opportunity to choose a different path.

457 Eulogy Exercise

In the space below, write your eulogy as though today is your last day on earth. How would you describe yourself as a person? How would you describe what you have done and accomplished? How would you describe how you have treated others?

_____
_____
_____
_____
_____
_____
_____
_____
_____
_____
_____
_____
_____
_____
_____
_____
_____
_____
_____
_____

Go to the next page only after you have completed this page.

Now, imagine that you have ten years from today to live and it is again time to write your eulogy. Write your eulogy in the space below as though you have lived for ten more years from today. For this exercise, imagine that you had an opportunity to work on all the things you hope to work on for the next ten years. Considering that it is now ten years from today:

• How would you describe how you changed over the last ten years?

_____
_____
_____
_____
_____
_____
_____
_____

• How would you describe how you've treated people over the last ten years?

_____
_____
_____
_____
_____
_____
_____
_____

Spirituality

There is a difference between religion and spirituality. Religion is a systematic approach to implementing your spirituality. Spirituality implies a belief in something beyond such as a higher power, God, the Transcendent, etc., but doesn't necessarily come in any pre-set form. Faith is a psychological construct that implies a strong belief. All human beings have faith. Some have faith that there is a higher power, whereas others have faith that there isn't; but all human beings have faith.

Meditation

Recent scientific studies have demonstrated that meditation can have significant health benefits for people. Meditation can be seen as a spiritual exercise, or simply a way to calm our heart rate and slow down our thoughts. In either case, meditation is largely about *not-thinking*, and has been described as the "period between the thoughts" or the "space between breaths."

Meditation is a disciplined activity whereby a person attempts to achieve a state of thoughtless awareness. Whereas simply resting is a relaxing activity, meditation is different. Meditation can be done by sitting still, relaxing your body, allowing your attention to rest on the flow of your breath, and by attempting to silence your mind. By taking time to meditate every day, you can transform the way you see the world, improve your health and focus, and find inner calmness.

Spirituality Exercise

1. Briefly write down what your religious or spiritual beliefs are.

_____

_____

_____

_____

_____

_____

2. On a scale of one to ten, how religious/spiritual do you consider yourself?

1	2	3	4	5	6	7	8	9	10
Not Very				Somewhat				Very Much	

3. How do you rely on your faith on a daily basis (all people have faith – for example, in order to believe that there is no such thing as a higher power, people have to have faith that they really are correct about that)?

_____

_____

_____

_____

_____

_____

4. How do your actions reflect your beliefs? (In other words, do you turn yourself over completely to a higher power --- or do you believe you have to work at things to make them happen --- or do you believe it is a combination?)

_____
_____
_____
_____
_____
_____
_____

5. Many people have a difficult time living out their religious/spiritual beliefs. Where do you think you struggle the most in regard to living out your beliefs?

_____
_____
_____
_____
_____
_____
_____

6. How do you think your beliefs have become an obstacle to your self-expression?

_____
_____
_____
_____
_____
_____
_____

7. How have you used your belief system to attempt to control others?

_____

_____

_____

_____

_____

_____

_____

8. Does your belief system include the notion of "do no harm" to others or yourself?

_____

_____

_____

_____

_____

_____

_____

9. What do you think you need to do this week to get yourself a little more back on track regarding your spiritual/religious beliefs?

_____

_____

_____

_____

_____

_____

10. How can you rely on your faith to get you through difficult times?

_____
_____
_____
_____
_____
_____
_____
_____
_____

The greatest devotion occurs in doing the little things each day.

Personal challenge:
Do the little things that make a big difference.

Past Successes

With the past behind us, we can choose to dwell on it, forget about it, or learn from it. Sometimes we fail to recognize our own strength of character and that we have survived even the most difficult times in our lives. As many mistakes as we have made, there were many more that we avoided doing. Being able to pinpoint our past successes is a way for us to call to mind what it is that we do well in the face of anger.

Every mistake we've ever made can be turned into a lesson; but we have all experienced tough situations that weren't our mistakes or fault at all. Because those situations are in our past, however, the fact is that we *did* find a way to make it through. The reality is that we *have* done successful things to make it through the difficult times in our lives.

Even if what you are experiencing currently is more difficult than anything you have ever encountered, you can still rely on what *you have done well* in the past to help get you through this moment. For example, there have been experiences where you felt intense anger, but you found a way to maintain control. By calling to mind such times, you can improve the way you approach every new troubling situation you face. When you remember the strengths you've developed in the past, you can make it through even the roughest periods of your life.

Noticing Success

Sometimes we ask loved ones to make changes. If we ask them to change five things, and they change three of them, then we face a choice: We can notice and appreciate the three changes they have made, or we can comment on the two things that they did not yet do.

The more we comment on others' shortcomings, the more likely we are to meet resistance. The more we notice even the little successes of others, the more we reinforce the types of behaviors we want. In others and yourself, take some time to notice the good things that are occurring.

Past Successes Exercise

1. What have you done in the past that has helped you be successful in managing your anger?

   _____
   _____
   _____
   _____

2. What is some of the best wisdom you have gained throughout your life?

   _____
   _____
   _____
   _____

3. In what ways was did you gain wisdom?

   _____
   _____
   _____
   _____

4. How do you try to give wisdom to others?

   _____
   _____
   _____
   _____

5. Do you ever try to force wisdom on others?

_____

_____

_____

_____

_____

_____

_____

6. What did the most successful and psychologically healthy relationship you ever had look like?

_____

_____

_____

_____

_____

_____

_____

7. Describe the time in your life when you felt most healthy. What was it that you were doing to contribute to that?

_____

_____

_____

_____

_____

_____

_____

8. Describe a time in the past where you felt the least stress in your life, even though you had responsibilities. How did you manage that stress effectively?

_____
_____
_____
_____
_____
_____
_____

> **We cannot change the past, but if we are mindful, we can learn from it.**

> **Personal challenge:**
> **Remember the good things you've done.**

Redemption

One way to look at the idea of redemption is to see it as the idea that we can be saved, make big life changes, and move forward. Whether we realize it or not, the past is gone. There is nothing we can do to recover even one second of the past. We can live our lives in reverse looking to change what cannot be changed, or we can focus on the present and the things that are actually within our power to control.

Past Pain, Present Lesson

Danny was sitting in his prison cell when he received notice about how he was going to lose the only property he ever owned. He thought about his non-stop drinking through the years, about hitting his wife, and he thought about the certain divorce he was about to go through. He thought about all the things he'd done through the years to push his children away, and why they would never come visit him. In that moment, he felt like he had hit rock bottom.

He was asked by a counselor to recall past successes. Inside, he wanted to hit the counselor for even suggesting the idea. He thought, "What have I ever been through that could ever compare to this?" But the counselor asked him to think about the worst time in his life before this. Danny did. He told the counselor about how he felt when his long time girlfriend left him. He talked about how much he loved her and how, when she left, he thought about ending his life. He talked about how, at the time, he truly believed that there could never be another person for him.

Danny found the strength to keep living through that situation with his ex-girlfriend by relying on others and by changing the way he viewed the break-up; and after some time, the pain began to disappear (as it always does). Eventually he met his wife. It's true that things weren't going well for him right now, but it's also true that he spent 20 good years with his wife before things took a turn for the worse. The reality is that he got through that initial break up by relying on others and changing what we call his "self-talk."

We all have hidden strengths; we just need to find them.

Redemption Exercise – Part 1

For this exercise, imagine that you had a chance to start over again from today forward. In other words, imagine that you have a chance to wipe away all your past mistakes and start a new life.

1. What kind of person would you be?

_____
_____
_____
_____
_____
_____
_____

2. How would you act?

_____
_____
_____
_____
_____
_____
_____

3. Where would you go?

_____
_____
_____
_____
_____

4. What would you do?

___

5. How would you treat people?

___

6. How would you be different from you are right now?

___

Redemption Exercise – Part 2

The fact is that you can start over from this moment forward. You can finish this exercise, get up, and become the person you want to be. The choice is yours. Do you want to remain the same person? Do you want to continue to feel the way you do now every day you wake up? Do you want to think about yourself and your life the same way you did earlier today, everyday? Again, listen, it's your choice!

1. What will you do differently today with your life?

   _____
   _____
   _____
   _____
   _____
   _____

2. What will get in the way to stop you from making the changes you want to make?

   _____
   _____
   _____
   _____
   _____
   _____

3. How can you get around those barriers?

   _____
   _____
   _____
   _____

Redemption Song

In Bob Marley's *Redemption Song*, there is a line that reads:

"Emancipate yourselves from mental slavery; none but ourselves can free our minds."

Regardless of whether we reside in an external prison or a prison we created in our own minds, the truth is that no one but us can set our minds free. By learning to view the world differently, we can change the way we approach life. When we take control of our minds by putting kindness and understanding above everything else, we can redeem ourselves with every action we take from this moment forward.

"Every moment we are alive is an opportunity to start over."

Personal challenge:
From this moment forward, find redemption in how you treat others.

Reach Out to Help

Mark is a 23 year-old young man who has a few more years in prison before he gets out. He was sentenced for seven years for open firing on his ex-girlfriend's house during a party. Though no one was injured, Mark knows he will never see his ex-girlfriend again. He was enraged with jealousy and high on drugs at the time of the event.

Mark is a good person, and struggling with an addiction, jealousy, anger, and loss are all understandable; but *his actions were unacceptable*. There were people in his life who enabled him to be the way he was, but there were also people reaching out to him constantly trying to help him. At the end of the day, however, regardless of who attempts to help or hurt, we are all ultimately responsible for our actions.

Mark has fears of repeating old patterns when he gets out of prison. The reality is he will likely return to the same house he lived in when he left. The temptations to return to his old ways when he gets out will likely surround him. Mark does not want to revert to the way he was; he does not want to hurt anyone or himself, and he certainly does not want to live in prison.

Mark, like the rest of us, has one chance to go around. He is a bright young man and wants to live differently when he gets out, but he is very lost. He is struggling with addiction, jealousy, anger, and how to mourn the loss of a loved one. In short, he needs to be surrounded with wisdom right now. The following exercise will help you organize how you reach out to help others, and how you accept the help that is offered to you.

Reach Out to Help Exercise – Part 1

What kind of advice or words of wisdom do you have for Mark? Take your time and give him your best. Below, write a letter to Mark.

_____

_____

_____

_____

_____

_____

_____

_____

_____

_____

_____

_____

_____

_____

_____

_____

_____

_____

_____

_____

_____

_____

_____

475 Reach Out To Help Exercise – Part 2

After writing the letter to Mark, consider the following.

1. What kind of advice did you give Mark?

   _____
   _____
   _____
   _____
   _____
   _____

2. Do you follow the advice that you gave?

   _____
   _____
   _____
   _____
   _____
   _____

3. Did you try to use the one-size-fits-all solution (in other words, "If it worked for me, it must work for him")? If so, what does that say about you?

   _____
   _____
   _____
   _____
   _____
   _____

4. Why do you think it is easier to impart wisdom than to live it out?

5. Was it easier for you to say to Mark that he "just made a mistake" because you didn't know what he did? If so, how might your letter have been different depending on what he did?

6. Is your forgiveness conditional? If so, what are the conditions of your forgiveness?

7. Is it easier for you to forgive others than yourself?

_____
_____
_____
_____
_____

8. What would it take for you to forgive yourself so that you could wipe the slate clean and give yourself a chance to start over from this moment forward?

_____
_____
_____
_____
_____
_____
_____

Self-forgiveness and redemption are symbiotic: forgive yourself and redeem yourself.

Personal challenge: Forgive yourself.

Friends

Friends

A frog and a mouse decided to be friends. They were best friends and always wanted to be together, so they decided to tie themselves together so they could always be near each other. This worked out for awhile because the frog could go on land with little problem. But eventually, when the frog dove in water the mouse couldn't breathe and drowned. When the mouse's body floated up to the top of the water a hawk swooped down to eat him. The frog panicked trying to get untied, but couldn't untie himself in time, so the hawk ate him too.

We are like the frog and the mouse every time we tie ourselves to someone or something. It is wise for us to be mindful of who and what we tie ourselves to, however, because sometimes what we tie ourselves to can be our ruin. Consider for example, when we have tied ourselves to a particular group, and then a member of that group acts in ways that contradict what we believe is right; yet we still feel compelled to defend that person simply because he or she was a part of "our group." That is why they say: *it takes a strong man to stand up to others, but an even stronger man to stand up to his friends.*

Friends Exercise - Part 1

It seems kind of ridiculous that the frog and the mouse would tie themselves together; that is, until we think about how we often tie ourselves to people who are dragging us down.

1. As you reflect on your experiences, can you identify more with the mouse or the frog? Why?

Friends Exercise - Part 2

True version of the frog and the mouse

Bryan knew that as long he hung around a certain group of people that he was going to use heroin. He said that he "knew" that; still he continued to hang around them. His friends supplied him with the drug; he supplied them with money. Who pulled whom down first is hard to say, but what is easy to say is this: as long as Bryan tied himself to that group of people, he was going to continue to act the way he did.

Bryan didn't make it. Neither did two of his friends. All three of them overdosed on heroin.

With whom do you associate? To whom do you tie yourself?

1. If you see yourself as the one dragging others down, write down specifically whom you believe you are dragging down.

   _____
   _____
   _____
   _____
   _____

2. Identify how you can specifically stop yourself from dragging that person or those people down.

   _____
   _____
   _____

3. If you see yourself as the one who is tied to others, write down specific people who are dragging you down.

4. Identify first how ready you are to "untie" yourself from that person and/or those people.

5. Identify exactly what it would take for you to get away from that person and/ or those people.

The Answer's "No"

In a rather large high school, some friends dared Jeremiah to write a bomb threat to help them get out of school for the day. Jeremiah knew it was wrong, and he didn't want to do it, but he was a 15 year-old boy, and he wanted their approval more than he wanted to do the right thing: so he did it. He was soon caught and it didn't take long to find out that his "friends" gave him up to the principal so that they would not get in trouble.

Jeremiah was placed on probation and sent to an alternative high school. Jeremiah suffered the consequences, but he was a likeable young man and fast made friends at his new school. One day, some of his new friends were planning to do something harmful to another student they didn't like. In more of a demand than question, they "asked" Jeremiah to join them. He was faced with a similar situation that got him there - - but this time he learned from his past.

Jeremiah said, "No." His so-called "friends" made fun of him, taunted him, and promised to do the same to him when they were done with the other kid if he didn't join them. He looked at them square in their eyes, and simply but firmly said, "No." When he walked away, he knew he had done the right thing: He didn't allow others to drag him down, and he was true to himself.

The result? The kids did what they said they were going to do, but they all got caught and sent to a more restricted juvenile detention center. Jeremiah was soon sent back to his regular school – where he graduated with honors two years later.

Who you choose to hang around can profoundly influence your future.

Personal challenge:
Have a positive impact on negative people.

Hero

Heroes are more than super-characters. They are more than people in special costumes or capes. They are even more than people with great catch phrases like Superman's "faster than a speeding bullet, stronger than a locomotive, and able to leap tall buildings in a single bound."

Growing up we all had heroes: people we looked up to. Heroes are people whom we admire and want to be like. Think back to who your hero was, or better yet, think about whom you admire right now. Who would you want to be more like?

Once we figure out who our heroes are, then we can figure out what *qualities* about them we admire. We may not just get the "power of flight" by wishing for it, but we can develop other qualities that our heroes have. We can be more kind and work toward a greater good. We can constantly look to help others, and heck, if want, we can even have a great catch phrase!

Hero Exercise - Part 1

For this exercise we want you to think about your hero. Think about what it is that makes that person so special for you. What catches your interest about this person? Maybe, with a little effort, you will find that you can be a whole lot more like your hero.

1. Who is or was your hero, or what kind of person do you admire?

   _____
   _____
   _____
   _____
   _____
   _____

2. What is it about that person that you admire?

   _____
   _____
   _____
   _____
   _____

3. What **can** you do to become more like that person?

   _____
   _____
   _____
   _____
   _____

4. What will you do this week to become more like the person you want to be?

_____
_____
_____
_____
_____

Hero Exercise – Part 2

For this part of the exercise, think of the people that you usually spend time with. This could be at home, work, during recreation, or just hanging out.

1. Write down the names of some people who you interact with most frequently.

   a.

   b.

   c.

   d.

   e.

2. Go back to each person's name and write down how they typically act around you.

Hero Exercise – Part 3

For this part of the exercise, assume everyone in your life is enlightened except for you. That means that in every interaction you have, people are trying to teach you something.

1. What do you think the people you named in **Part 2** are trying to teach you?

   _____
   _____
   _____
   _____
   _____
   _____

2. What can you learn or have you learned from those people?

   _____
   _____
   _____
   _____
   _____
   _____

> **All the superpowers in the world cannot equal the power of love and kindness. The truly strong are loving and kind.**

> **Personal challenge:**
> **Rely on your inner strength.**

The Case of Ms. X

People who are less mature look to blame others for why they do what they do. People who are more mature take responsibility for themselves and their actions and look to their own role in the negative interactions they have. For example, consider the case of Ms. X.

Ms. X is a single mother with two children and a drinking problem. One night her children begin to fight. Ms. X feels she "cannot take" the noise and stress anymore and yells at her children who are 10 and 13 to "shut up." The children reply by saying, "You shut up!" Ms. X grabs both of her children by the arms and throws each into their rooms and yells, "Stay the hell in there for the rest of the night, you brats!" The next day at school a teacher sees marks on the children's arms. Child Protective Services (CPS) is called to investigate. The children tell the caseworker from CPS this has happened more than once.

Everyone Has an Angle

Remember to consider every angle of a story. By being able to view situations from multiple angles, we have a much better chance to come to balanced conclusions. It's true that we are all limited by our own experiences; however, the more we are able to step back and see the whole picture, the more likely we are to get a better sense of the truth.

Consider as many perspectives as you can in every experience you encounter. The wider you can make your view of every situation, the less of an opportunity there is for anger to determine how you see things. Everyone has an angle to an interaction, and the more you find out about every angle, the more effective you can be at reaching a rational conclusion.

The Case of Ms. X Exercise – Part 1

1. If you were the worker from Child Protective Services assigned to the case, what would you say to Ms. X?

   _____
   _____
   _____
   _____
   _____
   _____

2. If you were Ms. X's lawyer, what would you say to defend Ms. X?

   _____
   _____
   _____
   _____
   _____
   _____

3. If you were the District Attorney, what would you say to the judge about Ms. X?

   _____
   _____
   _____
   _____
   _____
   _____

4. If you were the facilitator of the anger management class that Ms. X is in, what would you say to Ms. X?

___

The Case of Ms. X – Part 2

Ms. X had her children temporarily placed in foster care due to the incident and subsequent findings in the investigation. Ms. X has been ordered to continue her anger management, and to take parenting classes. Ms. X feels extremely stressed by all she has to do to get her children back. Ms. X goes to a bar to handle her stress by drinking excessively, to "blow off stress" in her words. Ms. X sees her boyfriend at the bar talking to a woman. Ms. X approaches the woman and asks what she is doing. The woman tells Ms. X she should be asking her boyfriend that instead, and she tells her to "get the hell out" of her face. The woman then turns to Ms. X's boyfriend and kisses him. The boyfriend smiles and tells Ms. X to get lost. Ms. X reaches out and grabs the woman's hair and a fight begins. The bartender calls the police and Ms. X is arrested.

1. If you were the judge assigned to the case, what would you say to Ms. X?

2. If you were Ms. X's lawyer, what would you say to defend Ms. X?

3. If you were the District Attorney, what would you say to the judge about Ms. X?

4. If you were Ms. X's CPS worker, what would you recommend to the judge?

5. If you were the facilitator of the anger management class that Ms. X is in, what would you say to Ms. X?

___

6. What is it like for you to evaluate Ms. X from so many different perspectives?

___

7. How do you see Ms. X differently after evaluating her from different perspectives?

___

Why Perspective Matters

When we evaluate ourselves, we see our intentions. When we evaluate others, we see their behaviors. Understanding behavior never excuses it, but the more we understand about why we do what we do and why others do what they do, the more peace we experience internally. Understanding why people do what they do helps us to meet them where they are and figure out solutions that can actually work for them. Regardless if they understand them or not, everyone has reasons for why they do what they do. Knowing the reason creates a sense of compassion in us that is difficult to achieve without understanding. Perspective matters. The more you expand your perspective, the more likely you will be

to experience inner peace.

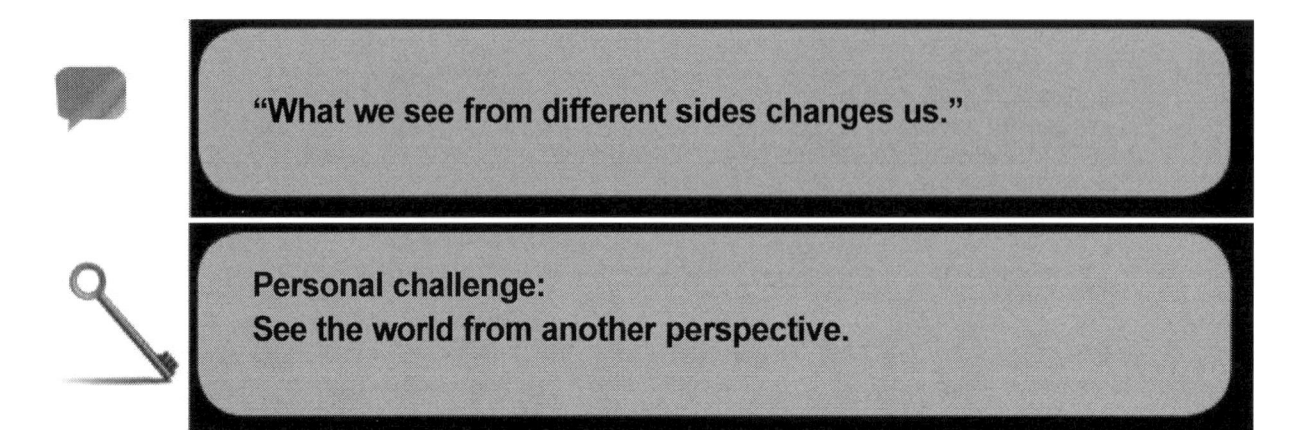

"What we see from different sides changes us."

Personal challenge:
See the world from another perspective.

Manipulation and Lying

Manipulation and lying are two hot-button issues. As soon as the words, "manipulation" and "lying" come up, people tend to get defensive and angry. Understanding manipulation and lying can be empowering. As we seek such empowerment, we should remember a couple things.

First, all people manipulate. At the most basic form of manipulation, we manipulate the temperature of a room by turning the thermostat to what we want to control our surroundings. At its more intense forms, we manipulate others to control them in hopes of controlling our own worlds. We have a tendency to see our own manipulation as "necessary," whereas we see others' manipulation as "intentional." In other words, when we manipulate others, we feel like we "had to," but when others manipulate us, we believe that they are somehow malicious or "bad."

Second, we all lie. We lie because we are afraid to face the consequences of our actions. A "little white lie" can be as minute as altering the facts about your family conflicts to make yourself look better. Bigger lies occur when we hide truths from our families and friends. When people do not want to get caught lying, they try very hard to convince others they are telling the truth (e.g., *"I didn't do it! I swear!"*). Before they do that, however, they have to justify to themselves why they are lying (e.g., *"The system's not fair, I had to lie just to get by"*). The lies we tell ourselves end up as lies to others.

Not many people like to consider themselves manipulative. Not many people like to consider themselves liars. Only when we face our actions head-on can we really change. Only when we own up to how we manipulate others and when we lie to others, can we possibly begin to change it.

Manipulation and Lying Exercise

1. In the space below, list some times when you lied, got caught, and tried to manipulate your way out of it.

   _____
   _____
   _____
   _____
   _____
   _____
   _____

2. Describe how you felt through the whole process.

   _____
   _____
   _____
   _____
   _____

3. There is a tendency for people to believe they are justified when they bend the truth; like they deserve to say things went the way they are telling it. Describe how you feel when you are not honest with others.

   _____
   _____
   _____
   _____
   _____

4. What are some things that you typically lie about?

5. What harm can come from lying about those things?

6. How can you tell when someone else is lying?

7. How have you been able to get through to others to have them own up to their lies?

8. How can others tell when you are lying?

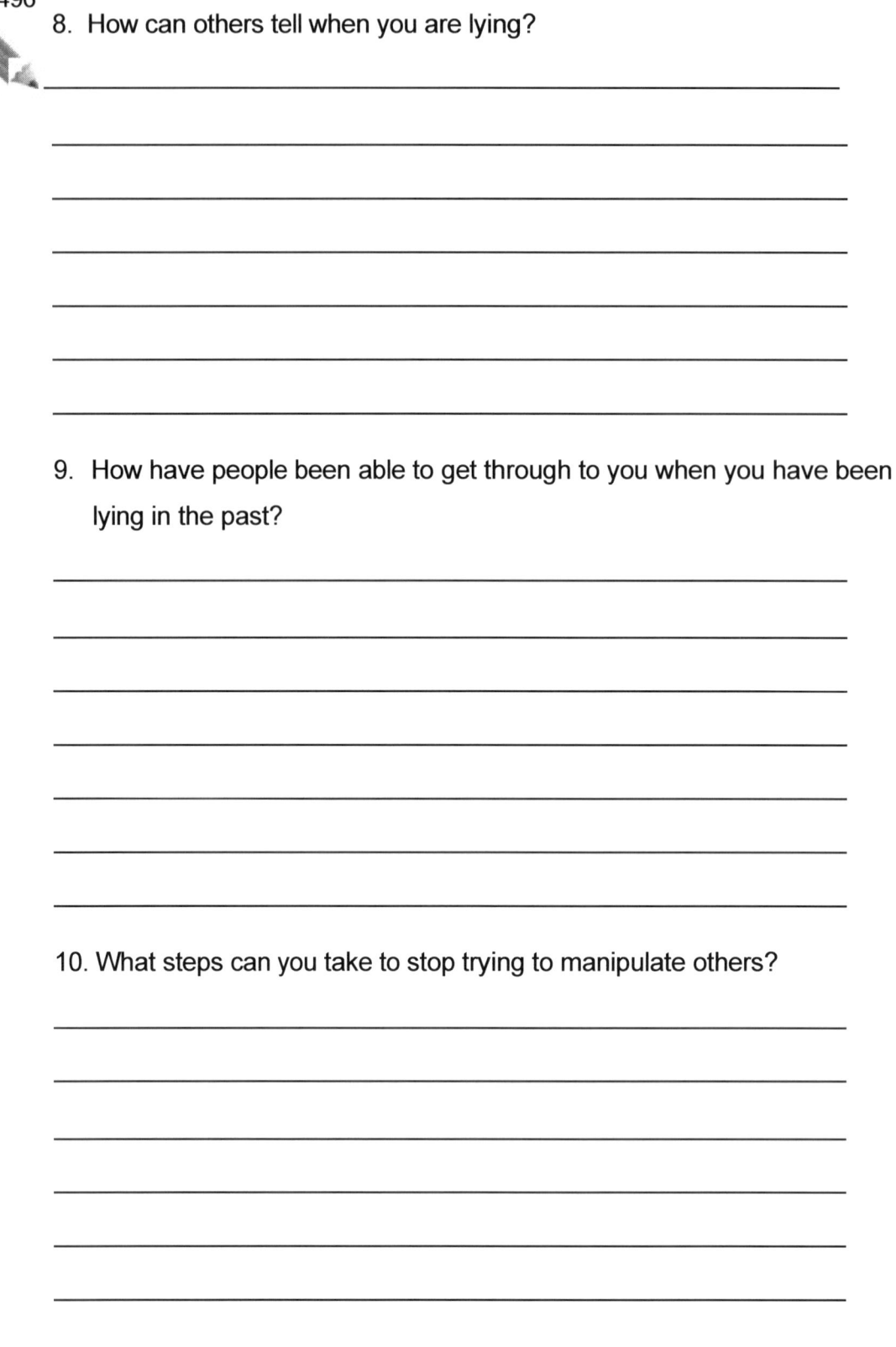

9. How have people been able to get through to you when you have been lying in the past?

10. What steps can you take to stop trying to manipulate others?

11. If you have written that you never lie or attempt to manipulate, you are only fooling yourself. Sometimes we lie because we cannot face seeing ourselves the way we think we would be seen if we owned up to our behaviors. Write about things you have lied to yourself about in the past (or things you can see that you are lying to yourself about right now).

___

12. How can looking honestly at your life make a difference for you?

___

Liar, Liar, Pants on Fire!

When someone lies to us, we tend to call that person a "liar." When we lie to others, we tend to justify why we lied. Consider the following conversation between 10 year-old Jamal and his 12 year-old brother Tyree:

Jamal: "Here's my video game. It was in your room! You said it wasn't! You're a liar!"
Tyree: "I am not a liar! I didn't lie. I just forgot it was there."
Jamal: "No you didn't! You lied, that means you're a liar!"
When their mother stepped in to break up the fight, she was able to get them to calm down and then taught them a lesson about lying. "You two have to learn to be honest. No one likes liars."

As the two children headed off to school, Tyree turned to his mom and asked, "Hey you forgot to tell Mrs. Winter if you were coming to the meeting after school."

Casually, his mother replied, "Oh, I forgot all about that. Just tell her that your grandfather is in town and I can't make it."
Tyree replied excitedly, "Grandpa's coming today?"
"No!" his mother replied, "You're so gullible. He's not coming. I just don't want her to think that I forgot the meeting. Do not tell her I forgot! Just tell her he's coming today."

"Okay mom." And Tyree, not consciously thinking about it, just headed off to school.

Parents want to teach their children not to lie, but all too often, they do not lead by example. How many times, after all, do children simply practice what they are taught? Furthermore, how many times do parents scream at or punish their children when they finally do tell the truth? Thereby creating reasons for children to continue to lie.

People lie for lots of reasons. If someone is not being honest with you, ask yourself if you are creating a safe place for this person. If the person knows he or she is going to get yelled at, put down, or otherwise demeaned, there is a good chance you are creating an atmosphere that will set others up for lying. That doesn't mean that you are responsible for others lying to you, but it does mean that you can work harder to create a safer place for others to tell you the truth.

Fundamental Attribution Error

Mary fails a test – she blames the teacher for making a bad test.

Sally passes the test – she thinks to herself, "I am so smart."

Ryan yells at Katie. He tells her, "You made me yell at you."

Rebecca tells her husband, "I'm the reason our friends got married and are so happy now."

Did you ever notice that when we mess up, we tend to blame something else for our mistakes? Whereas, when we do something well, we tend to take the credit for what we did?

Whenever things happen, we attribute causes to them. If we like the outcome, we usually take credit for it. If we don't like the outcome, we blame someone else. In many ways this is very convenient. When we blame outside forces for our mess-ups, it is called the fundamental attribution error. When we take credit for whatever we did well, it is called a self-serving bias.

Society made me do it!

Have you ever found yourself blaming "the system" or "society" or even someone else for the things that you do? If you have, then you've experienced fundamental attribution error. As long as you think that society "makes" you do things, you will essentially be a "puppet to society."

Once you recognize the fundamental attribution error, you no longer have to be controlled by it. Instead you can realize that you always have free will. You always have a choice. Whereas it can be easier to blame society, it is much more freeing to realize that we always have a choice. We not only impact our outcomes but also are accountable for them.

500 Fundamental Attribution Error Exercise

1. Describe a time when someone hurt you, but blamed you for why they hurt you.

2. What did that feel like for you?

3. Describe a time when you did something hurtful to someone else, but blamed them for why you did what you did?

4. What did you gain by blaming someone else for your actions?

___

5. Why do you think it might be important to understand the fundamental attribution error?

___

As long as others are to blame for why we do what we do, we have no control in our lives.

**Personal challenge:
Free yourself from misconceptions.**

Anxiety and Anger

Anxiety is such an uncomfortable feeling that human beings would rather be angry than anxious. At least when we are angry, we are able to exert energy that allows us to get some relief, even if we later regret what we did. Anxiety, on the other hand, can often feel crippling. Anxiety can at times make us feel immobile, like we can't do anything. Think about how many times you showed anger because what you really wanted to do was get rid of that anxious feeling inside. If we can learn to recognize anxiety, then we can find successful ways to deal with it that do not involve using anger.

Be Mindful of Mindfulness

Mindfulness is a mental state that can be achieved by focusing one's awareness on the present moment and calmly acknowledging and accepting one's feelings, thoughts, and sensations. In regard to anxiety, mindfulness can occur when we are able to recognize and accept the awful feeling we are experiencing.

Accepting the feeling of anxiety does not mean never dealing with it or "giving up." To the contrary, accepting the feeling of anxiety means not fighting against it. The reality is that when we fight anxiety, we make it worse. By mindfully not resisting the feeling, we are much more likely to move through the state of anxiety more quickly.

Anxiety and Anger Exercise

1. In what ways have you shown anger to others to mask the anxiety you were feeling?

   _____
   _____
   _____
   _____
   _____
   _____

2. How can you recognize anxiety in yourself (in other words, where do you experience anxiety in your body)?

   _____
   _____
   _____
   _____
   _____
   _____

3. How can you express to someone that you are experiencing anxiety rather than erupting with anger?

   _____
   _____
   _____
   _____
   _____
   _____

4. Where can you turn to talk to someone so that you can deal with anxiety that you feel without subconsciously turning it into anger just to feel better?

___
___
___
___
___

The Yelling Couple

Matt was anxious about meeting deadlines at work. Diane was anxious about not doing things right at the office. When the two of them came home at the end of the day, the stress and anxiety would have been built up so much during the day, that each was ready for an argument at the smallest slight.

The moment one of them would even look at the other wrong, they would begin a screaming match. When they first came to counseling, they each believed the other needed "anger management." They each believed that the other person was causing him or her to be so angry. The therapist noticed each of their facial expressions as they individually described their work, and commented on how each appeared to be struggling with anxiety in some form. Neither had ever considered anxiety to be a root of anger, but once they did, something remarkable began to happen.

Through counseling, Matt and Diane learned to express the anxiety that they felt as anxiety, rather than unconsciously expressing it as anger. It took effort for each of them to learn how to respond to each other rather than react and to express themselves accurately, but in time, they learned how to do both. The yelling couple eventually became the couple who rarely raised their voices.

The energy of our conversation changes when we make the effort to listen to others first rather than push for them to see our side of things. Imagine how different your own interactions would be if you learned how to say, "I'm struggling with anxiety right now," instead of lashing out. If we fail to see how anxiety impacts us, we will likely continue to take our anger out on others in an unconscious attempt to feel better.

Temptations

Many years ago a very thirsty traveler stumbled upon a stream. After the traveler finished drinking, he shouted at the water: "I am finished drinking now, you may stop," but of course the water kept flowing. So, the man shouted even louder, "I already told you that I've finished drinking, I said to stop flowing!" Just then a passer-by laughed at the man and said, "What a great fool you are! The water will not stop flowing just because you ask it to!" And he laughed at the foolish traveler and sent him on his way.

As ridiculous as it is to tell a stream to stop flowing just because you have had your fill of drink, so too, is it equally ridiculous to expect that temptations will just go away. Practice and preparation is needed to defeat the temptations in our lives. We must challenge ourselves to practice the skills we need to face the temptations that surround us.

We may think of the person who wants water to just stop flowing as foolish until we realize that we are doing the same thing every time we think temptations are just going to stop because we don't want them anymore. All of us have temptations. They are a part of life. So, too, is the choice to prepare ourselves to battle temptations.

The Warthog's Tusks

A fox came upon a warthog that was sharpening his tusks against a stone. The fox said, "Why are you sharpening your tusks? You are not in a battle right now." To which the warthog replied, "My dear fox, if I waited until I was in battle to sharpen my tusks, it would then be far too late."

Do not wait to prepare to handle difficult situations. If you think, *"I was only angry in that one relationship or that one situation. I don't have a problem with anger."* then you will likely not take the time to prepare to handle your anger when it arises again.

Temptations Exercise

1. What tempts you to express your anger the most?

2. If you were to handle what tempts your anger the most, what would be the next thing in line to make you angry? (Realize that if you think that nothing else could tempt you to make you angry, you are just like the foolish traveler in the story)

3. What is your plan to deal with anger as it continues to come up for you?

4. What temptations in life get in your way the most?

_____

_____

_____

_____

_____

5. What is your thought process *before* you give in to your temptations?

_____

_____

_____

_____

_____

6. What is your thought process *after* you have given in to your temptations?

_____

_____

_____

_____

_____

7. How do you feel after you give in to your temptations?

_____

_____

_____

_____

_____

8. What can you do to deal more effectively with temptations in your life?

_____

_____

_____

_____

_____

_____

"We cannot stop temptations and problems, but we can prepare for them."

Personal challenge:
Control your fate by understanding your temptations.

Actual Self / Ideal Self

There is a difference between who we are and who we think we should be. The greater the difference between the two, the worse we feel about ourselves. The closer our actual self (who we are) is to our ideal self (who we think we should be), the better we feel about ourselves. It all comes down to being comfortable with who we are. Fulfilling our expectations is one way that we can feel more comfortable with ourselves.

So, should we just lower our expectations for ourselves and be happy?

No. The reason we cannot just "lower our expectations" for ourselves is that we are not likely to believe that we genuinely have lower expectations for ourselves. What can we *really* do then? We can align our expectations with reality. We can learn how to accept ourselves for who we are, and still set good, achievable goals for our future. The more we bring our actual self and ideal self closer together, the better chance we have to focus on exactly what we need to do from this moment forward to show the world the kind of person we truly are. Let's see how.

Actual Self / Ideal Self Exercise

. Where should you be in life right now?

_____

_____

_____

_____

2. What kind of person should you be by this point in your life?

_____

_____

_____

_____

_____

3. If 10 represents being exactly where you should be in your life right now, where would you rank yourself on a scale of 1-10?

   1   2   3   4   5   6   7   8   9   10 Not
                                     Exactly where I *should* be
   very close

. Again, with 10 representing being the exact kind of person you believed you should be by this point in your life, rank how close you are to that on a scale of 1-10.

   1   2   3   4   5   6   7   8   9   10
   Not very close   Exactly where I *should* be

5. We all have expectations of ourselves. What do you expect out of yourself that you seem to struggle with being able to do?

___

6. What is the hardest part of the struggle you wrote down for number 5?

___

7. If you are not exactly where you believe you should be in life right now, how big of a gap is there between where you are and where you expect yourself to be?

___

8. What steps can you take to lessen the gaps between the two?

   _____

   _____

   _____

   _____

   _____

   _____

9. List those characteristics of your life where your ideal self and your real self match or almost match:

   _____

   _____

   _____

   _____

   _____

   _____

If you *should* be something and you're not, you have *an issue*.

If you *want* to be something and you're not, you have *a goal*.

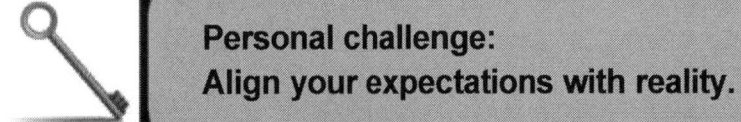

Personal challenge:
Align your expectations with reality.

Making Meaning

People seem to fall into two categories when it comes to the meaning of life. Some people believe that our lives have meaning from the start. They believe that from the very beginning there is a purpose and a path for any given individual. This purpose and path are designed specifically for that individual to experience. Others believe that we make our meaning as we go. They believe that the choices we make contribute to creating our meaning. Either way you see it, the type of meaning that we accept has a powerful control on us.

Angels in disguise

If you believe life happens for a reason, then how can you get angry in traffic when someone cuts you off or drives too slowly? Couldn't those moments be happening, after all, to protect you from going too fast or from being in a certain spot at a certain time?

If you believe that things happen for a reason, then try allowing yourself to be mindful that thought throughout your entire What you then see as "jerks" and "idiots" may in fact turn out to be angels in disguise.

Making Meaning Exercise

Sometimes it's helpful to figure out why things are happening the way they are for us. Whether we believe that we are creating our meaning or the meaning is coming from somewhere else, it still brings us comfort to know what meaning exists for us. In this exercise, challenge yourself to understand the meaning that is in your life.

1. Why do you think that some of the negative things in your life happened to you?

   _____
   _____
   _____
   _____
   _____

2. What would you say that you have done in your life to contribute to some of the negative things that have happened to you?

   _____
   _____
   _____
   _____
   _____

3. Do you believe that you have free will? Why or why not?

   _____
   _____
   _____
   _____
   _____

4. If life does happen for a reason and everyone, absolutely everyone, in your life was put there to teach you something, what are you learning from people?

___

5. Can a person learn positive things from negative situations?

___

6. Can a person learn negative things from positive situations?

___

7. What positive things have you learned from negative situations?

___

8. What negative things have you learned from positive situations?

___

9. How would your life be different if you looked at everyone you encountered this week as a person with a lesson for you?

___

Personal challenge:
Look for the lesson in every circumstance.

Black and White

There is a difference between black and white thinking and gray thinking. Black and white thinking says things are either this or that, not both! This thinking is much easier to do than gray thinking. When we think in terms of black and white, we are free to say that "we are right" and "you are wrong." These types of statements provide us with a sense of power. They allow us to feel we have control over people and situations. It can feel great to be in the driver's seat. The problem is, we might not be right. We may be wrong.

When we think in terms of "gray," however, we are open to the idea that both people in any given situation have a side to the story. Gray thinking allows us to see that experiences are based on perspective, and everyone has a perspective. So, as the old saying goes: *"There's your truth, then there's my truth, and then there's the actual truth somewhere in between."*

No One Is Ever Wrong!

If we follow faulty logic, we may come to the conclusion that, "If there is no black and white, then there can never be anyone who is wrong." To say that, "no one is ever wrong," however, is not gray thinking at all; it's black and white thinking.

Speaking in extremes can get us into trouble. Extreme thoughts lead to extreme emotions. The more we are intent on being right, the more we set ourselves up for a one-up/one-down type relationship. The trouble with one-up/one-down relationships is that inevitably what comes up must come back down.

Taking time to see the gray will provide you an opportunity to respond rather than react to situations. Be mindful of stepping out of the world of black and white and into the world of gray. You might just find a lot less anger in the gray.

Black and White Exercise

1. Describe some "black and white" thinking that you have.

2. Describe a situation that makes you angry. Describe it in terms of black and white.

3. Describe the same situation as you wrote about in number 2, but this time write about it in terms of gray thinking.

4. Describe the most recent argument you had with someone.

_____

_____

_____

_____

_____

5. What made you "right" in that situation?

_____

_____

_____

_____

_____

_____

6. What was the other person's side of the situation?

_____

_____

_____

_____

_____

7. Describe an argument that you had where you were right about something, but you probably came across in a difficult way for the other person to handle?

_____

_____

_____

_____

8. Describe something in which you used to think in terms of black-and-white but now you see it as gray.

___

9. What changed for you in how you saw the situation?

___

10. Look back at your answer for number 1 now. How can seeing those things you wrote down in terms of gray be helpful for you?

___

Children through adulthood

Children do not have fully developed brains. They are concrete thinkers and therefore tend to see the world in terms of black and white. Many storybooks for children are even filled with "good" and "bad" people, which may contribute to their either/or mentality. As their brains develop, they begin to see that human interactions rarely unfold neatly into black and white, but it is not until adulthood that people appear to become capable of thinking in terms of gray more often than not.

Adolescents largely hold onto black and white thinking when they are correct about something, but shades of gray emerge as they find themselves in trouble. For example, the shift from black and white to gray thinking can be seen in adolescents who, when right, proclaim, "I told you so!" and when they are wrong, say, "Well, I didn't mean to…." In the first instance, only the observable actions/words matter to them. In the second instance, they hope to have someone see their intentions in addition to their actions.

As adults, we have the physical brain development that enables us to evolve into gray thinkers. The problem emerges when people get locked into old patterns of behavior and do not allow themselves to grow psychologically. A simple exercise in attempting to see the world from other people's perspectives can increase how much gray you learn see in the world.

Personal challenge: Find the gray in your life.

Oncoming Traffic Does Not Stop

At certain bends in adjoining roads, there is a traffic sign that reads: "Oncoming traffic does not stop." When drivers see this sign, they are being warned to be mindful that cars approaching them may turn in front of them, even if those oncoming cars do not signal a turn.

In life, sometimes people do not give us a signal they are going to change their mind about something or do something unexpected. Sometimes we are hit with an experience that we didn't see coming, yet we are expected to be able to handle that situation. We are, essentially, expected to be prepared that oncoming traffic may not stop in our everyday personal lives.

Responding versus Reacting

There is a big difference between reacting to things and responding to things. To react implies a knee-jerk, stimulus-response action that is largely determined by the first action. To respond implies acting with intention. By definition, when we react to something, we do so without thinking. From our perspective, when we respond, we do so with purpose. We encourage people to take the time to learn how to respond to diverse situations rather than continuing to react in the same patterns that have not worked in the past.

523 Oncoming Traffic Does Not Stop Exercise

1. Give an example of a situation when you became angry because someone said or did something that you did not expect him or her to do.

   _____
   _____
   _____
   _____
   _____
   _____
   _____

2. How did you express your anger in that situation?

   _____
   _____
   _____
   _____
   _____

3. Now that you have had that experience, how might you respond to a similar-type of experience in the future?

   _____
   _____
   _____
   _____
   _____

524 4. What can you do to mentally prepare yourself for difficult situations?

_____
_____
_____
_____
_____

We cannot always prepare for every situation, but we can always be prepared for the unexpected.

Personal challenge:
Ready yourself for the unexpected.

The Shadow

There is a term in psychology called the *shadow*. The **shadow** is the part of us that we are unwilling to recognize – so we see it in others. For example, consider the person who hates liars so badly, but does not recognize his own lying. Or, for another example, consider the materialistic person who says that she hates when others are materialistic. In both cases, people failed to recognize that what they hate about others is the very thing that they cannot stand about themselves. More significantly, what we do not like about others is what we cannot *accept* about ourselves.

The shadow is difficult to see. Upon hearing about the shadow, most people report that they do not have a shadow. The reason that they report not having a shadow is that the shadow is unconscious, in other words, we are not aware of it. Upon further reflection, however, people are able not only to recognize their shadow, but also to come to terms with it, making them healthier.

Into the Darkness

By learning about your shadow, you can choose to face it and learn from it, or continue to stuff it down and ignore it. Either way, the choice is yours. The journey we take into the darker parts of who we are, is not always easy. We rarely like what we find but the journey is worth it.

If we recognize, for instance, that we lie to people from time to time, then we will realize that, technically, people can call us liars. We have, after all, told lies. Few people would be comfortable being called a "liar," however. The reason we are uncomfortable with the term is that we understand that there was a reason that we were untruthful; and we also realize that no one action can define us. So when we lie, we somehow understand it more, and we do not easily accept being called a liar.

Despite our refusing to be defined by our past actions (like the times we have lied), when others lie, we are quick to define them as "liars." We are quick to label their entire being as a "liar," when we would not accept being defined as such for our own lies. By going into the darkness of ourselves and recognizing that as human beings, we have a tendency to lie when we do not feel safe or do not want to face specific consequences, then we have a better chance of accepting the reality that all people lie at some point. When we accept that, we are less likely to define others as "liars."

Imagine how much less steam an argument would have if you say something along the lines of, "I'm hurt that you lied to me," rather than screaming out, "You're a liar!" The small difference between those two statements can have enormous results.

The Shadow Exercise

1. Think of a person whom you do not like. What are the qualities about that person that bother you the most?

___
___
___
___
___
___
___
___
___
___

2. Pretend that you are offered a million dollars to come up with an answer to this question. In other words, try really hard to answer it. How might you have those same qualities that you do not like in others?

___

3. If you can recognize that you do in fact have these qualities, how can that help you?

___

> Owning our own shadows helps us to have a better sense of control of our lives. If we do not recognize it, the shadow will control us.

> Personal challenge:
> Own every aspect of who you are.

What are you taking from this exercise?

Addiction

Addictions can grip us. Addictions are powerful. All kinds of addictions exist. Think about addiction as a thought or set of thoughts that somehow get into a pair of glasses. You put those glasses on then struggle getting them off. You are therefore left with seeing your addiction in everything.

Whether we are addicted to drugs, alcohol, working hard, pleasing others, or even addicted to feeling like we have to be right about things, addiction can be all we see. Looking at your addiction from more than one angle can expand your worldview and open your mind to the possibilities that exist outside of the current thoughts you are having.

Fighting addiction is never easy. In fact, if a habit can be broken easily, then by definition, it wasn't an addiction. True addiction is gripping and takes a great deal of effort to conquer. Regardless of how bad addiction gets, however, it can *never* be used as an excuse to hurt others.

This exercise is geared toward helping you understand the hidden force behind addiction: the *thoughts we have*. By identifying and understanding the thoughts that we have, we can begin to rip out addiction from its roots and change our habits one by one.

"I know what I need to do, but I don't want to do it."

People often say that they know what to do, but they are not ready to do it yet. Sometimes recognizing the consequences is enough to help us decide whether or not we want to start doing what we know is helpful for us.

The journey of a thousand miles truly does begin with one step.

The Anger Management Workbook, The Program that Changes Lives

530 Addiction Exercise

Breaking addictions takes more than one action or one step. Addictions cannot be broken until we at least take one action, or take one step in the right direction. For this exercise, you will be asked to pinpoint the thoughts and actions that lead to your continuing in addiction.

1. The thoughts that I tell myself when I am feeding my addiction are…

   _____
   _____
   _____
   _____
   _____

2. The thoughts I tell myself when I am outside of my addiction and doing well are…

   _____
   _____
   _____
   _____
   _____

3. One way that I try to hide my addiction is…

   _____
   _____
   _____
   _____

4. I deny my addiction by saying things like…

5. I break free from addiction when I am practicing these life habits.

6. This week, I will do these things to separate myself from the addiction.

What are you taking from this exercise?

_____

_____

_____

_____

_____

_____

_____

_____

_____

_____

_____

_____

_____

_____

_____

"I will become the things that I tell myself I will become."

Personal challenge: See the results. Choose a path to get there.

Great Pyramid of Emotional Pain

Here is how big our hurt is:

HURT

Here is how big our hurt is after we cover it up by acting out of anger:

We seem to be inclined to cover our pain with anger. For example, when someone says or does something that hurts our ego or our pride, we have a tendency to lash out at or about that person. When we act out of anger, we tend to say and do things we regret, thereby causing ourselves more hurt. We can chip away at the anger bit by bit (which is definitely better than nothing), or we can deal directly with the source: our original block of hurt. By talking about our hurt and by acknowledging the emotions that go along with our ego not always getting what it wants, we can deal directly with the pain we feel without adding the extra block of anger.

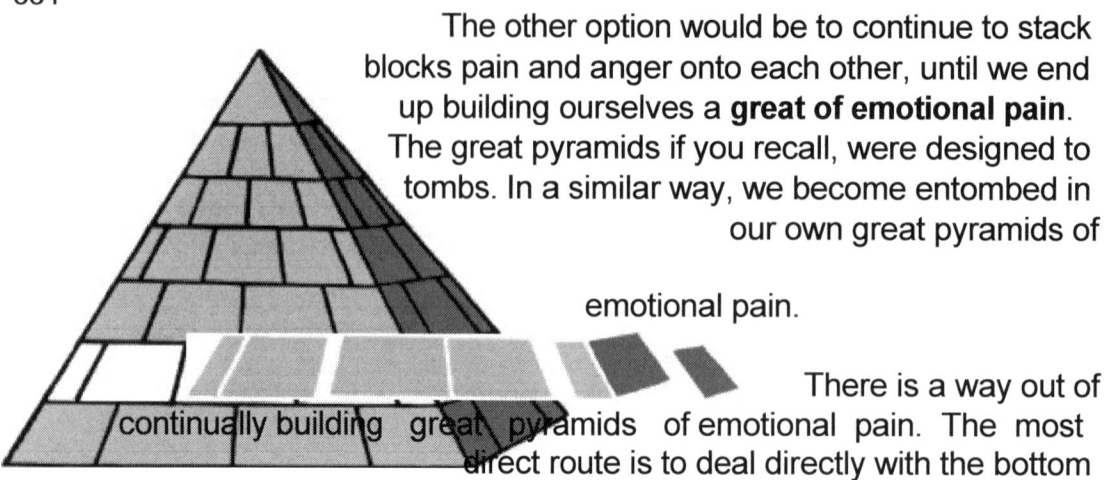

The other option would be to continue to stack blocks pain and anger onto each other, until we end up building ourselves a **great of emotional pain**. The great pyramids if you recall, were designed to tombs. In a similar way, we become entombed in our own great pyramids of emotional pain.

There is a way out of continually building great pyramids of emotional pain. The most direct route is to deal directly with the bottom blocks of hurt. In other words, when we address the hurt that we are feeling, we are less likely to have anger pile on top of it. Find and deal with your original blocks of hurt and watch unnecessary anger dissipate from your life.

The Great Pyramid of
Emotional Pain Exercise

For this exercise, identify the original pain that is the foundation of your anger.

1. Describe the hurt or emotional pain you feel.

___
___
___
___
___
___

2. Describe the anger that you have covered that hurt with.

___

3. In what ways did it seem helpful to cover your hurt with anger?

___

4. In what ways can you now deal directly with the hurt that you are experiencing?

___

Single-Mindedness Exercise

A man made his way through intersection the moment he eyes on the golden prize. He through the crowds and tried walk past twenty guards just to get to the piece of gold he sought. He was of course easily detained, and when he was brought before the judge he was asked, "Why did you try to steal the gold when twenty guards were surrounding it?" and the man said, "I did not see the guards. I only saw the gold."

We are like this man when we become single-minded Sometimes we get our minds on certain things and those things consume us. Anger has a way of making us single-minded. When we are angry, we set our sights on relieving that anger, and way too often, we sacrifice what we love just to relieve the tension of being angry.

When we are single-minded we can destroy ourselves as well as others. When we are single-minded, we usually act out of desperation and regret what we have done. Nonetheless, single-mindedness happens.

Single-Mindedness Exercise

1. Describe a situation where someone was single-minded against you.

   _____
   _____
   _____
   _____
   _____
   _____

2. Describe something that got into your mind and you had tremendous difficulty getting out of your mind. In other words, describe an instance of your own single-mindedness.

   _____
   _____
   _____
   _____
   _____
   _____

3. How did your single-mindedness affect you?

   _____
   _____
   _____
   _____
   _____
   _____

4. How did your single-mindedness affect others?

_____

_____

_____

_____

_____

5. How can you rise above single-mindedness to become what you want to become?

_____

_____

_____

_____

_____

Personal challenge: Step back and see more.

Epilogue

Ancora Imparo

Change is a process and it takes time. Years of clinical experience have taught us that people get as much personal growth out of self-exploration as they put into it. The more we look at our own lives, the more we learn about ourselves. Learning never ends. We can always learn things in a way that provides us a richer, deeper understanding.

Now that you have completed this workbook, take some time to reflect on how you are different as a person than you were when you started it. In the beginning, we posed these questions to you:

- What state of mind am I in and how does that impact my actions?
- What is the difference between what I expect the world to be and what the world is? (i.e., cartoon world versus the real world)
- What can I do to not stuff the ball under the boat?
- How can I avoid being the puppet?
- What can I do to stop myself from drifting further along my continuum of violence?

We invite you to answer these questions again. If you can, compare the way you answer these questions now with how you answered them when you started. What differences do you see? What have you done to grow as an individual through all these exercises?

More questions that you can ask yourself to gauge your growth are:

- Do I now recognize when I am making one of the Five Errors of Communication?
- Do I seek self-control, or do I still try to control others?
- Am I internally taking responsibility for my choices and actions?
- Do I bounce from one extreme to the other, or am I living a balanced life?
- Am I aware of the stories I tell myself?

- Do I understand that my memory is not perfect, or do I still cling to thinking that my memory is perfect?
- Am I aware of what ego state I am in and what impact that has on others?
- Have I worked through shame over past events, or do I still live in a place of shame?
- Can I recognize that what I don't like about others is often a characteristic of my own personality or behavior?
- Do I understand where my own anger comes from and what I can do about it?
- Am I focused on the "foot-in-the-water" principle and waiting for others to change, or am I intent on working on myself regardless of what anyone else around me does?
- Can I create and follow a plan of action to change?

There is no perfect person. There is no perfect way to handle tough situations. There is no "final" training – because living in this world is an ongoing process, and learning perpetually occurs. Continue to focus on the only person in the world you can control without imposing your will on another person: yourself. As you change, you will begin to see changes in others. You are welcome to return at any time to any exercise; that is the reason, after all, that we chose to make this available in a workbook format.

A Final Quote
"Beware of the man of one book."

We chose this quote to end The Anger Management Workbook because we believe that it encompasses all we tried to teach within these pages. A little learning is dangerous. The less we know about things, the more we fill in the gap with messages from our cartoon worlds. People have different perspectives and experiences. Different books have different things to offer us. Even the greatest of spiritual texts does not detail how to build a car. The point? We can learn constantly from different books, and we can learn constantly from different people's viewpoints. Learn constantly. Learn about life from multiple perspectives, and open yourself up to seeing the big picture. Seeing and being continually mindful of the big picture will change your perspective on anger and literally transform your life.

A Final Story

"Stand up"

Years ago, we attended a workshop where the speaker invited people to stand up if they saw them selves as people who want to impact the world around them. Some people in the crowd stood. The speaker looked around the room at the people standing and at the people sitting and said, "Some of you wanted to stand up, but chose not to and wish you had. Take a moment and stand up if you wished you would have stood up the first time." More people stood up. He asked them to remain standing.

The speaker looked again to the crowd and said, "Thank you. That takes amazing courage to do. I see that still more of you who are sitting are thinking, 'I wish I stood up' that time also, well, here is your chance. If you would have liked to stand up even that second time, please stand up now." Again, more people stood. Then the speaker said, "In life, we don't always follow our instincts to do the right thing. But here is a lesson: many times in life, we do get
another chance to do what we messed up the first time (or even the first couple times). We will be given new opportunities to stand up all our lives. Please take the opportunity to stand up whenever it's right to do so, because this is your life."

No matter how many times you have fallen, we strongly invite you to "stand up" now. If you did not put the effort into the exercises that you could have, it is not too late to go back and do them again. You have another chance to "stand up," because regardless of where you are in life, as long as you are alive, it is never too late

BIBLIOGRAPHY

Aligihieri, D. (1957). *The divine comedy.* New York: Random House.

Allen, J. (1992). *As a man thinketh.* New York: Barnes & Noble, Inc.

Aquinas, T. (1956). *Treatise on law.* Washington, DC: Regnery Publishing, Inc.

Ashliman, D. L. (2003). *Aesop's fables.* New York: Barnes & Noble Books.

Bach, R., (1977). *Illusions: The adventures of a reluctant messiah.* New York: Dell Publishing.

Bateson, G.D., Jackson, D., Haley, J. & Weakland, J. (1956). Toward of theory of schizophrenia. *Behavioral Science* 1: 251-254.

Beck, A.T. (1976). *Cognitive therapy and the emotional disorders.* New York: Meridian.

Bennett, W. (1993). *The book of virtues: A treasury of great moral stories.* New York, NY: Simon & Schuster Inc.

Bennett, W. (1995). *The moral compass: Stories for a life's journey.* New York, NY: Simon & Schuster Inc.

Berne, E. (1967). *Games people play.* New York: Grove Press.

Bettelheim, B. (1989). *The uses of enchantment: The meaning and importance of fairy tales.* New York: Random House.

Bierlein, J.F. (1994). *Parallel myths.* New York: Ballantine Wellspring.

Boas, G. (Trans.). (1993). *The hieroglyphics of Horapollo.* Princeton, NJ: Princeton University Press.

Brown, R., (1958). *The little flowers of Saint Francis.* New York: Doubleday.

Buber, M. (1970). *I and thou.* New York: Touchstone.

Bulfinch, T. (1959). *Mythology.* New York: Dell Publishing.

Campbell, J. (Ed) (1971). *The portable Jung.* (R.F.C. Hull, Trans). NY: Penguin Books.

Campbell, J. (1991). *Creative mythology.* New York: Penguin Books.

Campbell, J., (1999). *Transformations of myth through time.* New York: Harper & Row.

Campbell, J. (2001). *Thou art that* (E. Kennedy, Ed.). Novato, CA: New World Library.

Campbell, J., & Moyers, B. (1988). *The power of myth.* Garden City, NY: Doubleday.

Camus, A. (1989). *The stranger.* New York: Random House. (Original work published 1942).

Camus, A. (1991). *The myth of Sisyphus and other essays* (J. O'Brien, Trans.). New York: Vintage Books.

Castaneda, C. (1968). *The teachings of Don Juan: a Yaqui way of knowledge.* New York: Pocket Books.

Castaneda, C., (1987). *The power of silence: Further lessons of Don Juan.* New York: Simon and Schuster.

Cawley, A.C. (Ed.). (1999). *Everyman and medieval plays.* London: Orion Publishing Group.

Chaucer, G. (2006). *The Canterbury tales.* (P. Tuttle, Trans.). New York: Barnes & Noble Classics.

Chesterton, G. K., (1989). *Saint Francis of Assisi.* New York: Bantam Doubleday Dell Publishing Group.

Chopra, D. (1995). *The way of the wizard: Twenty spiritual lessons for creating the life you want.* New York, NY: Crown Publishers, Inc.

Cialdini, R. B. (1998). *Influence: The psychology of persuasion.* New York: Collins. Cochran, J.L., & Cochran.

Cochran, J.L., & Cochran, N.H. (2006). *The heart of counseling: A guide to Developing Therapeutic Relationships.* Belmont, CA: Thomson/Wadsworth.

Conte, C. (2015) *Zen Parent,*

Zen Child. Createspace Publishing: Charlestown, SC.

Conte, C. (2014) *Teaching Stories*. CreateSpace Publishing: Charlestown, SC.

Conte, C. (2013) *Life Lessons* CreateSpace Publishing: Charlestown, SC.

Conte, C. (2012) *Getting Control of Yourself: Angermanagement Tools and Techniques*. Videos available through www.pyschotherapy.net

Conte, C. (2012) *the art of verbal aikido: The path of least resistance to successful communication*. (available as an audiobook only)

Conte, C. (2009) *Advanced Techniques for counseling and psychotherapy*. New York: Springer Publishing.

Cook, T. (1991). The great alternatives of social thought. Savage, MD: Rowman & Littlefield Publishers, Inc.

Cornford, F.M. (Trans.). (1961). The republic of Plato. New York: Oxford University Press.

Cozolino, L. J. (2002). The neuroscience of psychotherapy: Building and rebuilding the human brain. New York: W.W. Norton & Company.

Csikszentmihalyi, M. (1990). Flow: The psychology of optimal experience. New York: Harper & Row.

Descartes, R. (1993). Meditations on first philosophy. (Third ed., Vol. V). Indianapolis, IN: Hackett Publishing Company.

Dickinson, E., (2002). Poems. Edison, NJ; Castle Books.

Eliot, T.S. (1934). The waste land and other poems. New York: Harcourt, Brace and Company.

Ellis, A. (1994). Reason and emotion in psychotherapy: A comprehensive method of treating human disturbances (Revised and Updated). New York: Carol Publishing Group

Ellis, A. (1998). How to control your anxiety before it controls you. Secaucus, NJ: Carol Publishing Group.

Ellis, A., & Harper, R. (1997). A guide to rational living (Third Edition). Hollywood, CA: Melvin Powers Wilshire Book Company.

Ellis, A., & Tafrate, R. (1997). How to control your anger before it controls you. Secaucus, NJ: Carol Publishing Group.

Epstein, M. (2001). Going on being. New York: Broadway Books.

Evan-Wentz, W.Y. (2000). The Tibetan book of the great liberation: The method of realizing Nirvana through knowing the mind. London: Oxford University Press.

Fitzgerald, E. (Trans.). (2005). Rubaiyat of Omar Khayyam. (1st, 2nd & 5th eds.). New York: Cosimo.

Forward, S. (1990). Toxic parents: Overcoming their hurtful legacy and reclaiming your life. New York: Bantam.

Frankl, V. (1963). Man's search for meaning. Boston: Beacon.

Frazier, J. G., (1961). The new golden bough. Anchor Books.

Fromm, E. (1976). To have or to be. New York: Harper & Row.

Fromm, E. (1992). The dogma of Christ. New York: Henry Holt and Company.

Frost, Jr., S.E. (1955). Basic teachings of the great philosophers. New York: Barnes & Noble, Inc.

Geldard, R., (2000). Remembering Heraclitus. Lindisfarne Books.

Gilbert, D., (2005). Stumbling on happiness. New York. Vintage Books.

Glasser, W. (1998). Choice theory: A new psychology of personal freedom. New York: HarperCollins.

Glasser, W. (2000). Reality therapy in action. New York: HarperCollins.

Glasser, W. (2001). Fibromyalgia: Hope from a

completely new perspective. Chatsworth, CA: William Glasser, Inc.

Goethe, J.W. von. (1961). Faust. (W. Kaufmann, Trans.). New York: Doubleday.

Goleman, D., & Speeth, K.R. (Eds). (1982). The essential psychotherapies. New York: Meridian

Graves, R., (1960). Greek gods and heroes. New York. Bantam Doubleday Dell Books for Young Readers.

Graves, R., (1979). The golden ass. New York: Farrar, Straus, and Giroux.

Guterman, J. (2006). Mastering the art of solution-focused counseling. Alexandria, VA: American Counseling Association.

Haley, J. (1993). Uncommon therapy: The psychiatric techniques of Milton H. Erickson. New York: W.W. Norton & Company.

Hare, R.D. (1999). Without conscience: The disturbing world of the psychopaths among us. New York: The Guilford Press.

Hawkins, D. R., (2002). Power vs. force. Carlsbad, CA: Hay House, INC.

Herrigel, E. (1953). Zen in the art of archery. New York: Random House.

Hesse, H., (1956). The journey to the east. New York: Farrar, Straus, and Giroux.

Hoffman, L. (1981). Foundations of family therapy: A conceptual framework for systems change. New York: Basic Books.

Housman, A.E. (1966). A Stropshire lad. New York: Avon Books.

Huxley, A. (1946). Brave new world. New York: Harper Collins

Huxley, A. (1962). Island. New York: Harper & Row.

Izzo, E. (2007). The Bridge to who I am: Rapid advance psychotherapy. Lincoln, NE: iUniverse.

Jacobs, E. (1992). Creative counseling techniques. Lutz, FL: Psychological Assessment Resources.

Jacobs, E. (1994). Impact therapy. Lutz, FL: Psychological Assessment Resources.

Jacobs, W.W. (2005). The monkey's paw and other tales of mystery and the macabre. Academy Chicago Publishers.

Johnson, S. (2005). Mind wide open: Your brain and the neuroscience of everyday life. New York: Scribner.

Jung, C.G., (1944). Psychology and alchemy. London: Routledge.

Jung, C.G. (1958). The undiscovered self (R.F.C. Hull, Trans). New York: Mentor.

Jung, C.G. (1961). Memories, dreams, reflections. New York: Random House.

Jung, C.G. (Ed), von Franz, M.L., Henderson, Joseph L., Jacobi,

Jolande, Jaffe. (1968) Man and his symbols. USA: Dell Publishing.
Jung, C.G. (1970). Psychiatric studies. New York: Princeton University Press

Jung, C.G. (1981). Psychology and the occult (R.F.C. Hull, Trans.). Princeton, NJ: Princeton University Press.

Jung, C.G. (1990). Psychology and the east (R.F.C. Hull, Trans.). Princeton, NJ: Princeton University Press.

Jung, C.G. (1992). Four archetypes: Mother / rebirth / spirit / trickster (R.F.C. Hull, Trans.). Princeton, NJ: Princeton University Press

Jung, C.G., & Kerenyi, C. (1993). Essays on a science of mythology: The myth of the divine child and the mysteries of Eleusis (R.F.C. Hull, Trans.). Princeton, NJ: Princeton University Press.

Jung, C.J. (1999). The psychology of Kundalini yoga: notes of the seminar given in 1932 by C.G. Jung (S. Shamdasani, Ed). Princeton, NJ: Princeton University Press.

Karasu, T. (1992). Wisdom in the practice of psychotherapy. New York: BasicBooks.

Kaufmann, W. (Ed.). (1989). Existentialism from Dostoyevsky to Sartre (F. Kaufmann & W. Kaufman, Trans.). New York: Meridian.

Kell, B. & Mueller, W.J. (1966). Impact and change: A study of counseling relationships. New York: Appleton-Century-Crofts

Kierkegaard, S. (1992). Either/ or: A fragment of life (A. Hanay, Trans., V. Eremita, ed.). New York: Penguin Books.

Kluckhohn, C. (1961). Mirror for man. New York: McGraw- Hill.

Kopp, S.B. (1976). If you meet the Buddha on the road, kill him!: The pilgrimage of psychotherapy patients. New York: Bantam Books.

Kopp, S., (1991). All god's children are lost, but only a few can play the piano. New York: Prentice Hall Press

Lagerkvist, P. (1975). The marriage feast. New York: Hill and Wang.

Lebell, S. (1995). The art of living: The classic manual on virtue, happiness, and effectiveness. New York: HarperCollins.

Levin, D., (2005). The Zen book. Carlsbad, CA: Hay House, INC.

Lowen, A. (1958). The language of the body. New York: Macmillan.

Lucado, M. (1990). The Applause of Heaven. Nashville, TN: Word Publishing.

Maitreya, A.(Trans). (1995). The Dhammapada. Berkeley, CA: Parallax Press.

Marinoff, L. (1999). Plato not prozac: Applying philosophy to everyday problems. New York: HarperCollins.

Maritain, J. (1962). A preface to metaphysics. New York: New American Library.

Maslow, A.H. (1943). A theory of human motivation. Psychological Review 50(4) 370-96.

Maslow, A. H. (1976). Religions, values, and peak- experiences. New York: Penguin Books.

May, R. (1967). Existential psychology. New York: Random House.

May, R. (1991). The cry for myth. New York: Dell Publishing.

May, R. (1994). The courage to create. New York: W.W. Norton & Company.

Miller, W.R. & Rollnick, S. (2002). Motivational interviewing: Preparing people for change (2nd ed.). New York: Guilford Press.

Mitchell, S. (trans). (1988). Tao Te Ching (1st ed.). New York: HaperCollins.

Mitchell, S. (trans). (2000). Bhgavad Gita (1st ed.). New York: Harmony Books.

Mookerjee, A. (1986). Kundalini: the arousal of the inner energy. (3rd ed.). Rochester, VT: Destiny Books.

Mosak, H.H. (1985). Interrupting a depression: The push-button technique. Individual Psychology, 41, 210-214.

Murphy, T., & Oberlin, L. (2005). Overcoming passive- aggression: How to stop hidden anger from spoiling your relationships, career, and happiness. New York: Marlowe & Company.

Myer, R. A. (1992). Assessment for crisis intervention: A triage assessment model. Belmont,CA: Brooks/Cole.

Neumann, E. (1956). Amor and psyche: The psychic development of the feminine. New York: Bollingten Series, Princeton University Press.

Neumann, E. (1990). Depth psychology and a new ethic (E. Rolfe, Trans.). Boston: Shambhala.

Neumann, E. (1995). The origins and history of consciousness (R.F.C. Hull, Trans.). Princeton, NJ: Princeton University Press.

O'Flaherty, W.D. (Trans.). (1975). Hindu myths: A sourcebook translated from the Sanscrit. New York: Penguin Books.

Orwell, G. (1950). 1984. New York: Signet Classic.

Ovid. (2004). Metamorphoses. New York: Penguin.

Perls, F. (1973). The Gestalt approach & eye witness to therapy. Willmette, IL: Science and Behavior Books.

Postman, N. (1994). The disappearance of childhood. New York: Vintage Books.

Potter-Efron, R., & Potter-Efron, P. (2006). Letting go of anger: The eleven most common anger styles & what to do about them (Second Edition). Oakland, CA: New Harbinger Publications, Inc.

Power, E. (1990). If change is all there is, choice is all you've got! Brentwood, TN: E Power & Associates.

Prochaska, J.O., DiClemente, C.C., & Norcross, J. (1992). In search of how people change. American Psychologist. 47 (9), 1101-1114.

Ramanujan, A.K. (Ed). (1991). Folktales from India: a selection of oral tales from twenty-two languages. New York: Pantheon Books.

Rank, O. (1964). The myth of the birth of the hero and other writings. (P. Freund, Ed.). New York: Vintage Books.

Richie, D. (1991). Zen inklings: Some stories, fables, parables, and sermons. New York: Weatherhill.

Rogers, C.R. (1961). On becoming a person. Boston: Houghton Mifflin Company.

Rosen, S. (1991). My voice will go with you. New York: W.W. Norton & Company.

Ross, D., Ackrill, J., Urmsom, J., & Aristotle, F. (1980). The Nicomachean ethics (World's Classics). (1st ed). New York: Oxford University Press.

Ruitenbeek, H.M. (Ed.). (1962). Psychoanalysis and existential philosophy. New York: E.P. Dutton & Co., Inc.

Sandars, N.K. (Ed.). (1972). The epic of Gilgamesh. New York: Penguin Books.

Sartre, J.P. (1981). Existential psychoanalysis (H.E. Barnes, Trans.). Washington D.C.: Regnery Publishing, Inc.

Sartre, J. P. (2007). Existentialism in a humanism (C. Macomber, trans., J. Kulka, Ed.). New Haven, CT: Yale University Press.

Sharf, R. (2008). Theories of psychotherapy and counseling: Concepts and cases fourth edition. Belmont, CA: Thomson. Brooks/Cole.

Stamenov, M.I., & Gallese, V. (Eds.) (2002). Mirror neurons and the evolution of brain and language. Philadelphia: John Benjamins Publishing Company.

Talmon, M. (1990). Single session therapy: Maximizing the effect of the first (and often only) therapeutic encounter. San Francisco: Jossey-Bass Inc., Publishers.

Tanahashi, K. & Levitt, P., (2004). A flock of

fools. New York: Grove Press.

The Holy Bible. (1983). New American Bible. Wichita, KS: Catholic Bible Publishers.

Van Dyke, H. (1925). Half- told tales. New York: Charles Scribner's Sons.

Voltaire. (1978). Candide (J. Butt, Trans.). New York: Penguin Books.

Watson, L. (1979). Lifetide: The biology of the unconscious. New York: Bantam Books.

Watts. A., (1966). The book: On the taboo of knowing who you are. New York: Vintage Books.

Watts, A. (2000). What is Tao? Novato, CA: New World Library.

Watzlawick, P. (1988). Ultra-Solutions: How to fail most successfully. Ontario: Penguin Books.

Wentz-Evans, W.Y.(Ed.). (2000). The Tibetan book of the dead. New York: Oxford. University Press.
Weston, J.L. (1993). From ritual to romance. Princeton, NJ: Princeton University Press.

Wilber, K. (1985). No boundary: Eastern and western approaches to personal growth. Boston: Shambhala.

Wilber, K. (2000). Integral psychology: Consciousness, spirit, psychology, therapy. Boston: Shambhala

Wilhelm, R. (1962). The secret of the golden flower: A Chinese book of life. With foreword and commentary by C.G. Jung. San Diego: Harcourt Brace & Company.

Wilson, R. (2009). Don't panic: Taking control of anxiety attacks (Third Edition). New York: HarperCollins Publishers, Inc.

Winslade, J. & Monk, G. (2007). Practicing narrative mediation. San Franscisco: John Wiley & Sons.

Wittgenstein, L. (1973). Philosophical investigations. Upper Saddle River, NJ: Prentice Hall.

Wubbolding, R. E. (1991). Understanding reality therapy. New York: HarperCollins.

Wubbolding, R. (2000). Reality therapy for the 21st century. Bridgeport, NJ: Taylor & Francis.

Yalom, I. (2002). The gift of therapy: An open letter to a new generation of therapists and their patients. New York: HarperCollins Publishers, Inc.

Yalom, I. D., (2008). Staring at the sun. Overcoming the terror of death. San Francisco: Jossey-

Index

5 errors of communication 97, 100

A

Abandonment rage 87–95

ABC model 37–38

Abuse 19, 118, 144, 145, 146, 147, 148, 149, 150, 151, 152, 153, 154, 155, 156, 158, 313, 405, 411

Acceptance 6, 8, 13, 296

Accountability 5, 6, 12, 105, 217, 218, 221, 222

Action 32, 37, 38, 65, 68

Actual self 509, 510

Addiction 529, 530, 531

Adult 28, 29, 30, 33, 440, 521

Advice 290, 291, 292, 293, 312, 413, 430, 474

B

Blame 25, 60, 67, 102, 209, 272, 276, 279, 305, 419, 420, 424, 440, 500

Blinders 194, 196, 198

Buber, Martin 325

Bully 390, 391

C

Cartoon world 4, 19-21, 54, 298, 539

Certainty 182, 183, 184, 237

Chameleon 390, 391

Child 28-33, 113-119, 125, 140-, 148, 156-164, 173, 174, 214, 233, 234, 248, 249, 262, 272, 300, 320, 338, 372-411, 440-442, 452, 468

Choice 14, 19, 24, 25, 40, 74, 107, 110, 166, 204, 219, 220, 221, 223, 249, 255, 264, 288, 342, 347, 499, 505, 513, 525

Circular causality 337-340

Cognitive behavioral therapy 27

Cognitive dissonance 332 - 336

Compassion 3, 6, 8, 10, 11, 12, 15, 80, 81, 99, 144, 159, 257, 291, 328, 403, 404, 440, 447, 450, 492

Complexes 371, 372, 375

Conceit 183, 184, 185

Confirmation bias 170, 263, 298, 304, 305

Confucius 182, 183

Conscious education 3, 12, 13, 15

Contemplation 65, 68, 69, 74

Content 18, 34, 35, 264, 389

Continuum of violence 27, 35, 48, 49, 50, 51, 56, 75, 76, 77, 539

Control 3, 4, 18, 19, 22, 24, 27, 29, 31, 32, 38, 41, 44, 47, 51, 52, 53, 54. 59, 60, 62, 63, 68 75, 87, 95, 96, 97, 103, 106, 122, 126, 134, 139, 144, 145, 1146-157, 164, 172, 201, 217, 237, 350, 255, 280, 294, 304, 305, 314, 331, 353, 355-367, 377, 389, 392, 393, 418, 419, 421, 422, 423, 424, 427, 429, 431, 435, 447, 462, 468, 472, 499, 501, 508, 573, 578, 578, 527, 539, 540

Counselor 3-5, 10-15, 25-28 45, 111, 145-146, 195, 359, 360, 430, 468

Creativity 13, 14

Critical parent 28-33, 140 - 142, 170, 233, 234

Crystallize 8, 26, 440

Cycle of shame 92, 116, 251

Cycle of violence 132-138, 231, 232

D

Dad 148, 229, 271, 377, 392, 403

Defense mechanisms 295, 296, 299

Deflection 298

Denial 150, 297

Depression 5, 40, 41, 43, 87, 88, 313, 702

Diamond, John 41, 79

Differentiation 389

Direction of our energy 255, 256

Displacement 296, 320, 321

Doing 8, 22, 23, 30, 31, 32, 35, 38, 39, 49, 50, 66, 72, 74, 83, 87, 92, 103, 134, 146, 148, 153, 156, 160, 162, 164, 165, 166, 170, 176 204, 209, 221, 222, 238, 251, 265, 287, 288, 301, 312, 327, 351, 352, 398, 403, 422, 427, 434, 438, 529, 530

Domestic violence 331, 332, 360, 403, 411

Dreams 10, 368, 369

E

Ego 28-33, 141, 155, 173, 182, 233, 295, 513, 533, 540

Elimination of shame 13, 14

Emotional abuse 145, 146, 152, 153

Empathy 6

Enantiodromia 4, 21, 159, 160, 161

Enmeshment 389 - 390

Epictetus 37

Error of approach 98, 99, 100

Error of interpretation 98, 100

Error of judgment 98, 100

Error of language 98, 99, 101

Error of omnipotence 98, 99, 101

Eulogy 556 - 457, 458

Evaluation 55, 352

Excuses 32, 45, 151, 214, 262, 263, 264, 265, 266, 492

Explosion 132, 133, 138, 165, 231

Explosive layer 238, 240

External control psychology 418, 419

F

Fading affect bias 129

Family 24, 29, 99, 135, 146, 147, 154, 160, 231, 227, 271, 272, 273, 274, 275 276, 277, 278, 279, 320, 363, 371, 389, 395, 398, 426, 427, 430, 433, 434, 493

Family tree 228, 230, 229

Father 118, 149, 159, 249, 271, 313, 377, 399, 403, 404, 498

Faust 329, 330

Fear 8, 12, 23, 36, 42, 44, 46, 88, 90, 91, 145, 236, 237, 238, 267, 270, 399, 403, 439, 440, 473

Financial abuse 147, 148, 154, 155

Flight response 12, 88, 98

Forgiveness 8, 41, 79, 176, 182, 476, 477

Friends 478, 479, 480, 482, 493, 500

Frog and a mouse 478

Frontal lobes 42, 43, 367

Fun child 29, 140, 142, 174, 233

Fundamental attribution error 499, 500, 501

G

Games 213, 392, 393, 394, 395, 396, 397

Glasser, William 280

Great pyramid of emotional pain 534

Group leader 4, 5, 6, 7, 12, 13, 14, 15, 16, 18, 421

H

H.A.L.T. 60

Harassment 451, 452, 453, 454

Hawkins, David 14, 41, 79

Hero 483, 484, 485, 486

Honeymoon 132, 134, 139, 159, 165, 231

Hunger 42, 43, 44, 129, 323

Hurt 11-13, 19, 23-25, 116-122, 133, 138, 241, 248-251, 264, 280, 295, 296, 304, 326, 327, 338, 343, 399, 401, 433, 451, 473, 500, 506, 529, 533-536

Hurt child 28-33, 140, 142, 173, 233, 234

Hypothalamus 42, 61, 88

I

Ideal self 509-512,

I-I 325, 326

I-It 325, 327

Imitation 111-115

Impasse 237, 240

Implosive layer 238, 240

Impotent rage 87, 94

Incident report 197, 444-446

Inflexibility 182-185, 317

Intellectualization 298
Internal control psychology 421, 422

Intimidation 254, 409

introjection 15, 296, 299

I-thou 325, 328

J

Johari window 82, 84-86

Jung, Carl 45, 379

L

Life map 284, 285, 286, 288

Limbic system 42, 64

Linear causality 337

Low blood sugar 44

Lying 221, 250, 322, 493, 494, 495, 496, 497, 498, 525

M

Mailbag of excuses 263, 264

Maintenance 66, 69, 70

Manipulation 147, 154, 155, 493, 494, 495, 496, 497

Maximizing 103

Meaning 368, 376, 383, 396, 513, 514, 515

Memory 88, 199, 201, 202, 203, 540

Middle ground 242, 415

Mind-body congruence 43

Mindfulness 13, 14, 47, 502

Minimizing 103, 105, 150, 444

Mirror neurons 16, 125, 126

Mistakes 10, 11, 16, 24, 107, 181, 185, 204, 205, 206, 207, 208, 209, 212, 222, 224, 231, 242, 430, 446, 456, 464, 469, 500

Mom 181, 271, 300, 411, 498

Mother 118, 149, 159, 181, 190, 313, 371, 372, 385, 397, 398, 431, 487, 498

N

Non-attachment 15, 16

Nurturing parent 28, 33, 141, 175

O

Obstacles 124, 160, 163, 258, 284, 286, 288, 423, 426

Opposites 347, 348

P

Parents 19, 98, 99, 118, 160, 213, 272, 285, 389, 430, 440, 498

Peace 21, 25, 63, 120, 213, 214, 242, 253, 260, 359, 492

Perls, Fritz 236

Phobic layer 236, 237, 239

Phony layer 236, 239

Physical abuse 144, 145, 151

Planning 351, 482

Potter-Efron, R.T. 87

Power 7, 27, 52, 53, 60, 147, 148, 154, 156, 300, 427, 428, 459, 460, 461, 468, 483, 486, 517

Power and control 147, 148, 154, 156, 427, 428, 429

Precontemplation 65, 68, 69, 74

Premotor cortex 125

Preparation 65, 69, 505

Process 5, 7, 8, 12, 16, 17, 18, 26, 28, 34, 35, 53, 54, 66, 67, 82, 92, 97, 134, 239, 262, 288, 295, 308, 367, 494, 507, 539

Projection 297

Pushing buttons 435, 436, 437, 439

R

Reacting 248, 250, 312, 522

Real world 4, 19, 20, 21, 54, 295, 539

Recidivism 5

Redemption 468, 469, 470, 471, 472, 477

Relapse 66, 67, 83

Relationship habits 280, 281, 282

Relationships 12, 32, 43, 90, 97, 136, 138, 160, 170, 171, 172, 173, 174, 175, 176, 177, 280, 282, 283, 326, 351, 354, 366, 390, 391, 440, 441, 517

Repression 297

Responding 312, 522

Road block 286, 288, 289

Rules and roles 271, 273, 275, 277, 279

S

Scale of consciousness 41, 134

Scapegoat 272

Seething rage 87, 95, 96

Self-awareness 14, 24, 55, 82, 138, 186, 188, 190, 192, 193, 312

Self-serving bias 499

Self-talk 33, 37, 38, 39, 54, 66, 90, 91, 92, 95, 96, 122, 165, 363, 367, 368, 468

Sexual abuse 146, 147, 153

Shadow 10, 45, 46, 525, 526, 527

Shame 5, 6, 10, 13, 14, 40, 41, 79, 80, 87, 92, 93, 116, 118, 119, 120, 121, 134, 166, 168, 248, 249, 250, 251, 254, 253, 349, 540

Shame-backwards 40, 92

Shame-based rage 87, 92, 93

Shame-forward 40, 92

Shaming 5, 14, 40

Single-mindedness 536, 537, 538

Social learning 125, 126, 127

Solution 5, 95, 258, 259, 260, 475

Speculation 182, 184

Spiritual guidance 267, 268, 269

Splitting 4, 21

Stages of change 65, 67, 68, 69, 71, 72, 73

Stalking 451, 452, 453, 454

State-dependent learning 199

States of being 140

Stereotypes 308-313, 371, 372

Stories 43, 44, 121-124, 193, 213, 214, 241, 267, 308, 320, 430, 539

Stress 42, 118, 334, 430, 467, 487, 489, 504

Success 53, 106, 149, 350, 464

Sudden rage 85, 88, 89

T

Temptations 473, 505, 506, 507, 508, 509

Tennyson, Alfred Lord 329

Tension 132, 133, 138, 165, 176, 231, 536

Thoughts 8, 20, 21, 24, 26, 37, 38, 40, 44, 87, 92, 94, 95, 96, 98, 129, 131, 152, 182, 334, 336, 363, 364, 366, 421, 452, 459, 502, 517, 529, 530

Time-outs 95

Traffic 11, 20, 39, 121, 122, 165, 322, 513, 522, 523

Transactional analysis 27, 28, 139

Types of abuse 144, 149, 150, 151, 152, 153, 154, 158

Types of rage 87, 88, 89

U

Us-them 325

Us-us 325, 327

V

Verbal abuse 148, 149, 156

Verbal aikido 55, 56, 60, 63

Violence 10, 12, 23, 27, 35, 40, 45, 48, 49, 50, 51, 54, 75, 76, 132, 133, 134, 135, 136, 137, 138, 139, 144, 159, 213, 214, 215, 231, 232, 330, 331, 332, 360, 397, 400, 401, 403, 411, 440, 441, 442, 539

W

Wants 29, 46, 52, 147, 154, 236, 237, 240, 250, 295, 351, 383, 390, 427, 473, 505, 533

Wisdom 107-110, 138, 182, 184, 212, 216, 231, 267, 291, 393, 382, 388, 450, 465, 473, 474, 476

Wubbolding, Robert 144, 145, 351

Y

Yes-but game 25

Yield theory 9, 10, 11 12, 13, 16,

Printed in Great Britain
by Amazon